THE CHRISTIAN
AND THE COUCH

An Introduction to
Christian Logotherapy

by
Donald F. Tweedie, Jr.

BAKER BOOK HOUSE
Grand Rapids 6, Michigan
1963

Library of Congress Catalog Card Number: 63-15080

Copyright, 1963, by
BAKER BOOK HOUSE

PHOTOLITHOPRINTED BY CUSHING - MALLOY, INC.
ANN ARBOR, MICHIGAN, UNITED STATES OF AMERICA
1963

TO
GLADYS AND LOUISE
the two "other women" in my life
to whom I owe so much.

The conclusion of my *Logotherapy and the Christian Faith* left upon me the burden of a sequel. The yoke has been easy and the burden light, however, for such a task coincides with my personal and professional interests and enthusiasms. If it provides a context out of which a Christian Logotherapy develops, this will be a pleasing bonus to the already highly rewarding experience of considering in some detail the relevance of the person and work of Jesus Christ to the theory and practice of psychotherapy.

I should like to acknowledge, with thanks, the generous permission of the following publishers for quotations contained within this volume:

Augustana Press, Rock Island, Illinois; T. & T. Clark, Edinburgh, Scotland; Wm. B. Eerdmans Publishing Company, Grand Rapids, Michigan; Harper & Row, New York, New York; The Macmillan Company, New York, New York; Moody Press, Chicago, Illinois; Muhlenberg Press, Philadelphia, Pennsylvania; Prentice-Hall Inc., Englewood Cliffs, New Jersey; Charles Scribner's Sons, New York, New York; D. Van Nostrand Company, Inc., Princeton, New Jersey.

I would be remiss in my responsibility if I did not also give grateful acknowledgment to my parents-in-law, Mr. and Mrs. Ivan Smith, in whose garage garret I found the necessary solitude to clothe in writing those skeletal ideas which formed the structure of this book.

D.F.T.

Veterans Administration Hospital
Lexington, Kentucky
1963

TABLE OF CONTENTS

CHAPTER I

INTRODUCTION

The Two Worlds

The twentieth century may well be remembered as the century in which man broke away from his earthly environment, entered, and explored outer space. The present state of technological development makes the fantasy of the nineteenth century the reality of the twentieth. The inventor of the comic strip character, Buck Rogers, who penned an imaginative account of inter-planetary space travel and the social process in other worlds, supposedly pertaining to the twenty-fifth century, little realized that he was making prophetic utterances which will no doubt come true in the experience of some of his contemporary readers. It may be that man will never reach the moon, or at least find it and our other neighboring planets to be so inhospitable in terms of climate that the taking up of residence will be impractical, if not impossible; but even the most chronic doubter about the actuality of leaving the earth must temper his doubts with "maybe's." Even if it should turn out that the moon is really made of green cheese, it looks as if man at least will have a chance to taste it!

11

Even before man approached the edge of outer space in the twentieth century, he has plumbed deep into the regions of inner space. Just as the second half of this century will herald the boundless array of facts about the boundless universe, so has the first half of the twentieth century brought to life an enormous collection of facts and fancies concerning the inner world of man, the psyche. In the beginning Freud discovered the depth of the unconscious dimensions of personality and the complexity of the psychological process. His one-time colleague, and subsequent competitor for the honors of most completely describing the mind of man, Carl Jung, claimed that this inner space of man is much deeper and more complex than even Freud seemed to realize. Inner space is not a microcosm, a "little world," but is, in parallel with the physical universe, a vast world of individual psychic solar systems with countless galaxies of mental archetypes. Thus the twentieth century has brought forth to man a full realization of the frightening complexity of reality, whether he looks within or without.

The universe seems to reveal a magnificent orderliness and a vastness which is pure, clean, and beautiful. As recently as last evening the author was thrilled again with the grandeur of God's handiwork as he gazed at the glowing, romantic moon which sailed across a blue-black sky, accompanied by a host of friendly, twinkling stars. In the Buck Rogers account, the main problems of wandering in this wonderful world were those of keeping a proper compass setting and one's rockets charged. The negative conditions were pretty much confined to the ray gun of Killer Kane. However, scientists tell us that this apparently innocent outer world environment is permeated with deadly rays and dangerous meteoric missiles which may be the real obstacles to a Sunday afternoon drive to outer space. A similiar condition seems to be true of the inner world of the mind. A positive appreciation of its depth and complexity is counterbalanced by the diversity of defects in its structure and function. Just as the deadly radiation of a disintegrating physical particle in outer space promises to make it an implacable foe rather than a cordial friend, so the relentless waves of mental pain, or anxiety, transform the psyche into a murky depth, fraught with danger and despair.

THE AGE OF ANXIETY

We are living in an era which has often been characterized as the "Age of Psychology." A recent issue of a widely-read weekly newsmagazine[1] indicates that it also may be rapidly transforming into an "Age of Anxiety." If this be true, and there is more than the felt imminence of the multi-megaton bomb and the general scurry to the fall-out shelters to indicate that it is, it will tend to increase the already enormously heavy burden of mental and emotional disorders in our society. "Nothing is more striking than the medical evidence for the prevalence of anxiety. 'Happiness pills' are said to make up one-third of all prescriptions filled by today's druggists. One variety sold nearly a billion the first year, a two-day supply for every man, woman and child in the United States."[2]

The scope of the mental health problem can be realized when one considers that more than half of all of our hospital beds are assigned to persons with mental and emotional problems, about 750,000! In addition to this there are multitudes of persons who are outpatients in psychiatric and mental health clinics and many others who, though having serious personal problems, are unable either to muster the necessary courage, or, in some instances, the necessary cash to receive the help that they need. The mental health problem in the twentieth century is a major social problem, and one which may get worse before it gets bet-

---

[1] *Time,* March 31, 1961.

[2] Orville Walters, "Christian Faith in an Age of Anxiety," Radio Lecture, University of Illinois, September 6, 1958.

14

ter, if we can rely upon the report from the professionals, in the area of insufficiency of both money and personnel.

THE ASSAULT ON ANXIETY

There is presently a concerted effort on many scientific fronts to mobilize the necessary forces to eradicate, or at least subdue, this great enemy of mankind. To use a military metaphor, a recent Nobel prize winner in chemistry has volunteered for ordinance; and a great foundation, flushed with the heady wine of recent victory in curbing the forces of infantile paralysis, has seriously considered the handling of the logistics. Reserve officers from hospitals, clinics, and laboratories, are polishing up their brass and an intensive conscription is taking place in a door to door campaign that aims to overlook not a single possible recruit nor a single contributory coin. The enemy, mental illness, fills more than half of our hospital beds, saps the strength and ingenuity of the small corps trained to combat it, and is responsible for millions of dollars in defense and millions of heartaches in defeat.

1. Physical

Historically two approaches have been used to combat mental health problems—physical and psychological methods. The former is the point of much intense interest today and is the apparent basis for the upsurge of hope in the field of mental health. This hope is sparked by the development of new chemicals, originally designed to serve other ends, which make amazing changes in both physical and psychological behavior patterns. In mid-1954 the Science News Letter stated "a chemical to save men's minds as sulfa drugs and antibiotics save men's lives seems close."

Two drugs, chlorpromazine-hydrochloride and reserpine, have been to this point the key weapons in the chemical assault on mental disorder. The former is said to have "brought in a new

Zeitgeist, the new and dynamic climate of opinion in regard to mental health." In just a half dozen years these drugs have tended to make passé such methods as electric and insulin shock therapies, hydrotherapy, chemical therapy with sedatives, "psychosurgery," and even the simple, though time honored, physical restraints. These "tranquillizing" drugs exercise a symptomatic control over almost any kind of severe excitement. They have also radically changed institutional atmospheres, in which they are a steady diet, from bedlam to sanitorium. From the red brick buildings of state institutions to the ivory towers of private hospitals and university research, they have changed the whole concept of custodial care. Early reports were glowing with statements of "complete remissions" and some even hinted at an early demise of psychiatry as a profession. Popular magazines quoted "authoritative" statements whereby tranquillizers not only solved mental health problems, but also checked juvenile delinquency (one early adolescent is quoted as saying, "It gives me a conscience."), raised the I.Q. of the mentally retarded and the emotionally blocked, and promised a chemical basis to ensure personal peace and ataraxia in the pursuit of happiness.

Later reports speak more soberly. They allude to possible side effects, symptomatic deterioration in some patients, and toxic and depressive effects. These reports describe similar improvement of placebo patients, that is, those who only think they have taken a certain drug. There now is a tendency to speak of the supportive, rather than curative, role of this new drug therapy.

The "miracle drugs" of mental health do appear to be very helpful in the reduction of behavior disorders, the hallucinations and elusive experiences in both neurotic and psychotic personalities. On the other hand, they apparently do not affect the primary process which, according to the psychological literature, goes deep into the tangled jungle of the psyche. Robert Felix, Director of the National Institute of Mental Health, stated that "it does not strike at the root of the illness." Those drugs however, often help to lay the illness bare, as they assist in establishing or re-establishing communication with the suffering persons. However there is at the same time revealed the great dilemma of additional thousands of patients who are in need of some sort of psychological treatment while there is only a very small corps of trained personnel to treat them.[3] The pursuit for a complete chemical cure is still very much in process, however, and legion are those who agree with Dr. Gerard of the Mental Health Research Institute of the University of Michigan that "there can be no twisted thought without a twisted molecule."

2. Psychological

Others, while thankful for the supportive assistance of the chemist, attempt to resolve mental health problems through the psychological method. By this method they seek to unravel the tangled skein of twisted psychic processes which reside in the depths of the mysterious unconscious as they are revealed (and then only incognito) through dreams, anxieties, neurotic phobias, and bizarre psychotic experiences. Through analysis these therapists hope to relate the sick person's thoughts to reality and to enable him to understand, and in a measure to control, his dynamic psychological powers which have gone awry. This unraveling they say, is true psychotherapy and the only actual "cure for sick souls." The most influential of such movements has been the psychoanalytic movement of Sigmund Freud and his followers. The basic concepts of this movement are widely, if not well, known, for they permeate not only the technical journals but also popular magazines, comic strips, and polite teatime conversation.

---

[3] For a recent discussion of the problem the reader is referred to *Action for Mental Health*, Basic Books Incorporated, 1961, a very readable treatment which, according to a comment on the jacket by Albert Deutsch, "affords a rallying-point around which the concerned professions and the interested citizenry can mobilize in a fresh drive to narrow the yawning gap between mental health needs and resources."

The present group of psychotherapists do not seem to be in sufficient strength either in number or knowledge. Rather than stemming the tide of mental illness, they seem to be losing ground. This may be due to the increased incidence of illness (not so much due to a proportional increase but rather to the absolute burgeoning increase of population), the lack of trained psychotherapists, the "closed shop policy" of the medical society, the length of time required for analysis — or a variety of other reasons. What may be the chief obstacle, to contemporary psychotherapy, however, is that with all its demonstrated ability to analyze the human personality and to label the parts, there is no ability to synthesize these parts or bring them together. J. A. C. Murray, a British psychologist, puts it this way: "They dig, but cannot build; they destroy but cannot fulfill. Ask of them what it is to cement the pieces they have readjusted, and to fill the gap of dear illusions that they have abolished, and they will offer a little mild philanthropy, or an open-air life splintered with Art, and bandaged with Literature."[4] They accurately affirm that man's psychic process must maintain contact with reality, but they firmly deny that God is essential in reality, or that the religious nature and spiritual powers of man, if existent, are anything but detrimental to mental health.

PSYCHOTHERAPY AND CHRISTIANITY

Psychotherapy as a movement has been increasingly distressed and frustrated by the inadequacy of a procedure which merely analyzes the historical factors of childhood which predisposes one to a personality disorder, but which finds no means to synthesize these factors into a positive personal function. Thus in many areas of this special field which has been developed in order to alleviate mental and emotional disorder, there has been an increasing tendency to turn toward religious goals and adjustment.

---

[4] *An Introduction to Christian Psychotherapy*, T. & T. Clark, 1941, p. 12.

This does not mean that all psychotherapists are becoming religious counselors, but it is to say that religious adjustments are no longer looked upon as necessarily neurotic processes. Increasing the personal strength of the individual with a religious commitment is seen to be a positive rather than a negative factor. There are still psychoanalysts who would consider their activity an utter failure if their patients should have a religious conversion, but these professionals are becoming more and more rare. A significant amount of literature is being produced with reference to the relationship of psychology and religion. The Academy of Religion and Mental Health, which started just a few years ago, now numbers its membership in the thousands. Those affiliated with this organization are seeking to find some relationship between the techniques of mental and emotional adjustment and the religious life.

In the midst of this activity, the increasingly alert evangelical Christian is hard put to answer the questions that come to his mind concerning his own attitude toward the constantly expanding field of psychotherapy. In our society more and more people are overcoming the initial sense of shame and frustration resulting from their personal problems, and are seeking professional help and guidance. Of this number not a few are persons who have a Biblical orientation and are members of evangelical churches. We are given various statistical figures from about one in ten to one in thirteen as the proportion of those persons living in the United States who may expect at some time in their lives to be treated as patients in a mental hospital. Thus the Christian person is confronted with two possible relationships to this movement. He is a possible candidate for psychotherapeutic help, and also a possible candidate for the vocational opportunities that exist in this area of great social and spiritual need.

What shall be the Christian's attitude toward psychotherapy? As a special field of psychology, it is a direct outgrowth of the two major psychological movements that have characterized

American psychology in the twentieth century — psychoanalysis and behaviorism. This may be a threatening factor to the Christian because both of these movements, in their initial formulations, were not only hostile to objective religious values, but in their dogmatic philosophical presuppositions they completely excluded the possibility that there was a God who could reveal Himself through Scripture, or in any other way. The contemporary toning down of such hostility and even the reappraisal of their initial theories have not caused many of these psychologists really to consider the possibility of the Christian philosophy of life. They still regard a commitment to the Bible as a symptom of regression, an unhealthy defense which is too unrealistic to be able to effect an abiding sense of security in the modern world.

WHO IS A CHRISTIAN?

But, nonetheless, the Christian, either driven by the frustration and despair of his own soul, or prompted by the increasing sensitivity to the tremendous area of opportunity for witness in this vocational field, must make a decision with reference to psychotherapy. At this point there should be some clarification as to what the term Christian, which shall be so frequently used in this volume, means. This term has a very wide application in our society and sometimes may be very vague in terms of exact communication. In the minds of some it refers to all of those persons who are influenced by the rise of western culture based on the Greco-Roman civilization as it was influenced by the Christian church. For others it refers to those individuals who are not members of a Jewish synagogue. Some use the term to refer to anybody who has a rather pleasant personal impact upon his neighbors and society in general, and who is prompt in the payment of his debts. However, I should like to use the term to refer to those who give allegiance to the Bible as the authoritative Word of God and who have made a personal commitment of trust in the person and work of Jesus Christ. This may seem a rather narrow scope in which to confine such a widely used word as "Christian" but it has a good historical precedent inasmuch as this was the title conferred upon those in Antioch who had made just such a commitment to Christ.

The scope of this commitment for our purposes is well summarized in the doctrinal statement of the American Scientific Affiliation, which is a fellowship of Christians working in the various sciences: "1. The Holy Scriptures are the inspired Word of God, the only unerring guide of faith and conduct. 2. Jesus Christ is the Son of God and through His atonement is the one and only Mediator between God and man."[5] This statement will seem much too broad for some and much too narrow for others, but, in any case, it is succinct and closely approximates the viewpoint of the author.

It will not always be easy to determine whether a particular author should be numbered with the Christians in terms of the above statements, for usually a statement of creedal faith is not incorporated in the psychological literature, whether professional or popular. My intention, however, is not to organize an index of psychological literature free from theological heresy, but rather to investigate the relevance and relationship of a special area of psychology to a Biblically oriented faith.

The Christian and the Couch

The title, "The Christian and the Couch," grew out of some interesting observations obtained while discussing the general theme of the Christian's attitude toward psychology and psychotherapy. Technical questions, or simple questions using technical vocabulary, often drew blanks or occasioned hedging about "exactly what it meant"; but the question concerning the "couch" invariably drew a knowing smile and a ready, if not very well

---

[5] This is taken from an official ASA pamphlet published at 414 South Broad Street, Mankato, Minnesota.

thought out, opinion. If our society cannot be properly entitled a "Couch Culture," at any rate it cannot avoid the ominous shadow of Sigmund Freud. The couch has become a humorous symbol, perhaps to cover our anxieties about the question of mental health, which everyone seems to understand. In perusing a file of psychiatric joke cartoons I noticed that nearly half of them used as the foreground this universal piece of psychiatric furniture and all but two of the cartoons were at the expense of Freud.

Such a social situation would be expected to produce a considerable amount of literature discussing the problems, and such has been the case. It is impossible to keep abreast of the cloud of current books, articles, and pamphlets which attempt to relate the religious experience with the psychological process. An announcement of an annotated bibliography in religion and psychology, by W. W. Meissener of the Academy of Religion and Mental Health, lists thousands of articles and books on the subject. In spite of the flood of general literature, however, there has been a dearth of Biblically oriented discussion.

An inquiry recently sent to more than two dozen evangelicals who are professionally active in the field of the relationship between psychology and religion drew mostly negative replies. My request — "I wonder if you might be able to help me by suggesting bibliographical items related to the general area of psychology, psychotherapy, and religion from the conservative theological perspective?" — drew a scattered few answers of which the following examples are typical. "I am afraid I cannot be of much assistance to you in this matter. This is true in spite of the fact that I am deeply interested in this area and I attempt to read everything that has some relationship to it." It seems that nothing of this kind is available at present." "Very little has been written from the evangelical point of view."

Nonetheless, a small but growing body of literature pertaining to our topic is easily discovered. I discovered also that, although this literature stems from a more or less common theological perspective, it reveals a very wide variety of attitudes toward mental health and modern psychotherapy. Although these attitudes are as numerous and various as are the articles that embody them, perhaps we will be able to put them into a broad outline.

1. The "Anti" Group

The first group refers to those who are negative to any inroad of psychological science into the area of dealing with personal problems. They see it as an erosion of the Christian faith and a threat to the Christian church. Any rapprochement between psychotherapy and religious experience is an attempt to be "unequally yoked together" and, therefore, inherently sinful. Although I believe that there has been a decided trend away from such an attitude in the last half decade in the conservative Christian context, the following quotation is still pertinent to a large segment of the fundamentalist sector. "Yet thorough-going evangelicals are reluctant, by and large, to discuss a truce. Persuaded that psychiatry is possibly demonic in origin and outworking, they are keeping up a barrage of criticism and invective. Their reasons for doing so are understandable, even commendable. But how regrettable it is that evangelicalism, while holding fast to its God-revealed truths, has with equal tenacity refused to investigate the values of psychotherapy as an adjunct to the pastoral ministry — an adjunct, notice, not a substitute for the illumination and enablement of the Holy Spirit."[6]

This attitude is only partially accounted for by the fear of the intrusion of ungodly forces into spiritual realms. It is also due to the belief that psychopathology, at least in its functional and nonphysical aspects, is a symptom of spiritual defeat. At a recent research conference on Mental Health which I attended I was chal-

---

[6] Vernon Grounds, "Has Freud Anything for Christians?" *Eternity*, July 1956, p. 9.

lenged by a well-educated layman to justify my interests and
activity in clinical psychotherapy because "people with neurotic
problems are obviously backslidden." My wife was also called
into account by a Christian missionary for my vocational interests because it could hardly be a divine vocation if it engaged
in "a non-Christian approach to spiritual problems." This was
all the more interesting in the case of this hopefully well-meaning missionary for he had suffered for several months from a
series of neurotic symptoms which had to a large extent curtailed
his missionary activity. He believed that seeking the alleviation
of emotional problems through psychological counseling is a
deepening of the sinful state. This viewpoint is strikingly voiced
in the following statement: "Many carnal, worldly Christians
believe that they can be cured of their so-called nervousness by
modern psychological therapies. Patients may be helped by these
treatments and relieved of some symptoms, but this does not
deliver them from fear and guilt. I have never seen them lifted
out of their worldly state or drawn any closer to God by the
psychological reasoning of man."[7]

Some Christians consider this to be a consistent following of
the thesis that in the redemption of Jesus Christ there is provision made for all aspects of human well-being. This prompts
them to refuse not only psychotherapeutic help, but also any
form of medical help as a cure for personal disability. They consider that all attempts to regain health whether through psychological or medical means runs counter to the message of the
Scriptures. Thomas Wyatt succinctly summarizes the convictions
of this group: "It would be more logical for a Christian to deny
himself any and all the benefits he might receive from doctors
and medicine than to ignore the redemptive provisions God has
made for the sick and afflicted. ... Seeking help from any given
source implies that one has faith in that source, but to seek help

---

[7] Gilbert Little, *Nervous Christians*, Moody Press, p. 70.

24

both from God and from medicine indicates no faith in either"[8]

Others, however, readily go to the physician of the body but believe that there is no real analogy between diseases of the body and "dis-ease" of the mind. This conclusion they regard as inescapable, for "the Bible gives numerous examples of men in dire need who possessed faith in prayer and consecration but failed to be healed."[9] On the other hand these same persons believe that any departure from the physical automatically brings them into spiritual realm where either Satan rules or which is God's exclusive territory. These are not only lay people but also those who are trained in the medical disciplines. Says one of the professional spokesmen: "It is our firm conviction that the Christian has the full armamentarium to deal with fear, anxiety, and worry through faith in our Lord and Savior, Jesus Christ."[10] This negative attitude toward psychotherapy represents the perspective of a large number of Christian people who believe that such help is a violation of spiritual laws and the usurpation by sinful men of the power of God, as well as being for the sick person an ultimate sojourn into deep despair as he drifts farther away from true spiritual reconciliation. "The patient sought psychiatry, expecting relief from his distressing symptoms, but psychiatry could give him only temporary relief; it could not cure. For such patients there is only one cure. When they accept Jesus Christ as their Savior and believe in the finished work of Christ on the cross of Calvary, they have peace in their souls. When there is peace in the soul, there is no fear, no anxiety, no worry."[11]

---

[8] *Christian Herald,* January 1961, p. 14.

[9] A. Z. Hall, "Cross and Caduceus," *Christianity Today,* January 30, 1961, p. 6. Cf. also II Corinthians 12:7, I Timothy 5:23, II Timothy 4:20, and Philippians 2:25-27.

[10] Paul Adolph, *Health Shall Spring Forth,* Moody Press, p. 64, 65.

[11] Little, *Nervous Christians,* p. 7.

2. *The "Pro" Group*

As opposed to this group who believe that any concession to psychological science in the realm of mental health is entirely unnecessary for the committed Christian, if not a concession to demonic powers, there are those who believe that the unfortunate lot of many Christians is to fall prey to mental and emotional disorders. They believe that psychological means should be sought out in the alleviation of human suffering, just as food, clothing, shelter, and medicine. They contend that the Christian faith, though it is the "best possible form of mental hygiene"[12] and "no rules for mental health ever laid down can surpass those that are inherent in the original Christian teaching,"[13] is not a panacea for psychopathology. Orville Walters states it succinctly: "In spite of the fact that some Christians do suffer breakdowns, the inner resources of faith undoubtedly help many others, not only to avoid a crushing load of guilt, but to remain stable under adversity."[14]

It has been a great mistake to identify Christian experience with a state of bubbling happiness free from mental stress. This is certainly not the result of an exegetical conclusion from a study of the Scriptures. Ernest White sagely remarks that "the Pauline Epistles are full of teaching about the Christian conflict, and the apostle uses a variety of images to illustrate it. He speaks of the old man and the new man, of running a race, of striving toward the goal, of keeping the body under, of fighting a good fight."[15] H. G. Goodykoontz also puts it very nicely, "but as Christians we ought to be crystal clear on this point, the goal of life is not emotional tranquillity. For the Stoic, perhaps yes, but

---

[12] H. G. Goodykoontz, "Christianity and Mental Health," *Pastoral Psychology,* May 1960.

[13] B. H. McNeel, "The Relevance of Christianity to Life Adjustment," Gordon Divinity School lectures, 1956.

[14] "Faith: A Built-in Psychotherapy," *Christian Herald,* January 1959.

[15] *Christian Life and the Unconscious,* Harper and Brothers, 1955, p. 165.

not for the Christian. While we proclaim the gospel of comfort
to the broken-hearted, and rest to the weary, there is never in
Christianity a glorification of 'peace of mind' of 'relief from
tension' as ends in themselves. In the last analysis, the Christian
cannot escape 'living in tension' with a pagan world. We have
mental health, for we have right relationships, and the love and
peace and hope and joy in community those right relationships
bring. But the Christian who is committed is one who is led by
a 'divine discontent' to participate in the struggle for a better,
more brotherly world."[16] A Christian experience does not of
necessity bring about the sudden healing of a maladjusted personality. "It is very apparent from clinical experience with the
mentally distressed that an assertion of personal allegiance to
Christ is *of itself* no guarantee of mental well-being."[17] One
must be careful not to conclude that faith has no positive effect
upon mental health of an individual but rather that it is not
absolutely nor automatically efficacious in all cases. "Growth in
grace is slow and personality disorder may persist beyond forgiveness. Neurosis may be entangled with religious devotion. It is
certain that some psychopathology has its origin in faulty body
chemistry. Nevertheless, even Freud and others antagonistic to
religion have acknowledged the stabilizing and healing influence
of religion upon personality."[18]

This attitude also embodies the belief that psychology as a
science is no way is inherently antagonistic to the Christian faith
and the Biblical revelation. The Christian has nothing to fear
from a careful observation of the psychological truths expressed
in the Bible or the psychological factors involved in Christian
experience. This is well set forth in one of the earliest attempts

16 "Christianity and Mental Health," *Pastoral Psychology*, May 1960, p. 28.
17 Edward Heerema, "Christian Faith and Healthy Personality," mimeographed paper, no date, p. 8. This apparently is a part of a lecture series
given at the Reformed Episcopal Seminary.
18 O. Walters, "The Psychiatrist and the Christian Faith," *Christian
Century*, July 20, 1960.

to indicate the relationship of psychological factors to the Scriptural revelation: "The book of nature and the book of Scripture are precisely two books which from the beginning were intended to be compared with one another."[19] Unfortunately, however, such advice has not always been heeded by Christians during the century following Delitzsch. This has caused the Christian church oftentimes to repudiate scientific help which might have advanced the Kingdom, and to identify itself with an obscurantist position. But we are convinced with J. A. C. Murray that "There is no necessary divorce, as some think, between such psychological study or the therapeutic practice, and the work of the Christian in the cure of souls."[20]

There has, however, been a decided change in attitude among Christians in more recent years, and there is among them a wide-spread interest and activity in the field of psychology. "Unfortunately, however, Christian psychological research has till now lagged far behind, and this neglect has caused a tremendous assumption to gain ground, that the mind can be dealt with, and cured, without regard to spiritual issues, and even that God and Faith are projections and sublimations, higher in degree, but in essence the same, as other escape mechanisms of the ailing mind."[21]

Thus we see there are Christians who, rather than repudiating psychotherapy as a Christian need or a Christian vocation, encourage application and only lament the fact that Christians have for so long disregarded its Kingdom possibilities. Simply to lump them all together in a "pro-psychotherapy" classification would not do justice to the varied insights and numerous modifications that are expressed in this group concerning the topic at hand. A somewhat arbitrary, but hopefully instructive, means of reflecting the various attitudes would be to divide them into

---

[19] F. Delitzsch, *A System of Biblical Psychology,* T & T. Clark, 1867, p. 23.
[20] *Introduction to Christian Psychotherapy,* p. viii.
[21] *Ibid.,* p. 7.

the following three groups: (1) those who see the Christian faith and psychotherapy as being more or less neutral spheres, complementing but not interacting with one another; (2) those who criticize contemporary psychotherapy, especially psychoanalysis, for not taking the moral realm into consideration; and (3) those who believe that a psychotherapy is only acceptable if it is an expression of specific Christian principles.

THE NEUTRALISTS

Those who hold that the Christian faith is neutral to psychotherapy do so upon practical and/or theoretical grounds. They hold this view to be practical and expedient because one can utilize the body of psychotherapeutic data apart from the necessity of correlating it with the data of Scripture. It also has its practical aspects in professional life both from the point of view of clients and colleagues. For the client "it seems to be easier to turn to the physician with one's 'bad nerves' than to the pastor with one's spiritual anxiety."[22] It is an obvious fact, and perhaps a sad commentary upon the times in which we live, that people tend to take to the therapist the problems that they in former times would have taken to their pastor.

The Christian therapist may also consider it helpful to compartmentalize his Christian experience from his professional activity because of his professional associates. They look with benevolence upon a man who is moral in his private life and will perhaps amusedly tolerate his going to church or even teaching Sunday school, but are decidedly threatened by any carry over of this activity into his weekday work. They fear that what they deem to be a "priest in the robes of psychotherapy" will rob them of their scientific status. It is interesting to note that such persons are active in the encouragement of seminars on "psychiatry and religion" but not in order to merge the two. The implicit

---

22 Arvid Runestam, *Psychoanalysis and Christianity*, Augustana Press, 1958, p. 1.

aim is rather to separate them further, and to reinforce the
minister in his role as one who must not meddle with those who
deal in mental and emotional disorders. "The psychiatrist who is
asked to make such an evaluation [of religion as a joint resource
for ills] may point to his status as a scientist, in which role he
professes to deal solely with facts, to refrain from value judgments and to maintain ethical neutrality in his relationships with
patients. In contrast, the minister may be cited as a proponent of
a system of metaphysical constructs. By identifying himself in
this way, the psychiatrist is able to share the vast prestige of
science and to place the clergyman on the defensive in a new
variation of the science-religion conflict."[23]

This tendency to place psychotherapy in the realm of science
while relegating religious experience to the area of "belief" is
not without its dangers, since it is both unnecessary and false.
It is, nonetheless, common practice among Christian psychotherapists who, while earnestly affirming man's need for God,
stress that this is decidedly distinct from, and must not be confused with, man's need for psychotherapy. These needs, so
they concede, are not antagonistic, of course, but rather are
complementary. One might sum this up by saying that any
success achieved by psychiatry in straightening out a tangled
mind, in helping a man to think more clearly and honestly,
must inevitably help him also to open his mind and his heart to
God — "if he so chooses."[24] To see how thoroughly this is worked
one need only read Stafford-Clark's volume *Psychiatry Today*[25]
in which there is not a single reference to religious faith as bearing upon modern psychiatry. Such a dichotomy is also in the
thinking of Professor Wijngaarden of the Free University of
Amsterdam who in a recent conversation told me that in the

[23] Walters, "The Psychiatrist and the Christian Faith."
[24] D. Stafford-Clark, "The Nature of the Problem," In *Christian Essays
in Psychiatry* (D. Mairet, ed.), Philosophical Library, p. 23.
[25] Penguin Series, 1956.

last ten years he has moved from a view which held that psychotherapy must operate in terms of Christian presuppositions to a
position in which psychotherapy is a scientific discipline on the
one hand and the Christian faith a religious discipline on the
other.

Another "neutral" approach is that based upon the theory of
anthropological trichotomy. Norvell Peterson accepts this view
of man as body, soul, and spirit.[26] According to this view disease
may attack any of these areas and the therapy must be appropriate to the disease. If it is in the body, one calls a physician; if
in the soul, a psychiatrist; and if in the spirit, a chaplain. This
approach, if valid, certainly makes for an easy outline even if it
does involve the difficulty of a very specific differential diagnosis.
Murray protests, however, that such a three-fold division of
labors, though seeming efficient and productive, may in the end
be a dead end street: "Yet so far, in spite of solid achievement,
each of these has missed the mark because he has worked on but
a part of an indivisible whole, and has ignored that psychosomatic unity which is the very essence of human nature. Once
again, therefore, the way seems to be clearing for the advance of
a Christian psychotherapy which will envisage spirit as well as
body and mind, and will seek to enfold their earthly trinity in a
unity of saving help."[27]

CONTEMPORARY CRITICS

A second group consists of those who, while accepting psychotherapy as a proper tool of the Christian church, criticize contemporary theories of psychotherapy for their disregard of the
essential spiritual nature of man and the moral and ethical implications that are thereby involved. B. H. McNeel expresses
this viewpoint well when he says, "Many orthodox Christians,

[26] Peterson, N., M.D., "Psychiatry and Christianity," *Christianity Today*,
Nov. 9, 1959.
[27] *An Introduction to Christian Psychotherapy*, p. 151.

including some of the Reformed Faith, believe that Psychiatry
and Psychology are immoral and anti-Christian. This charge can
hardly be laid to the scientific observations made by psychiatrists or psychologists though it may be sustained by some of
the interpretations put forward. Religious people, however,
could make a more valid objection to psychiatric practice, namely, that it avoids moral and religious issues."[28]

This criticism has for the most part been lodged against
psychoanalysis and behaviorism. These two theories, which, in-
cidentally, engulf most of modern psychiatry and psychotherapy,
do not merely ignore the spiritual nature of man and his ethical
involvement, but rather exclude this important area of life. O.
M. Mowrer, while no friend of evangelical Christianity, sees
these two "schools" as the most potent dangers of psychotherapy,
the Scylla and Charybdis of contemporary psychology. His
criticism is interesting inasmuch as he, one of the leading American psychologists, has in the past personally embraced both
theories and held them to be both complementary and true.
"The behavioristic doctrine of total determinism manifestly does
not deliver us from the one-sided determinism of Luther and
Calvin any more effectively than does the brand of complete irresponsibility adduced by Freud. If the doctrine of Luther and
Calvin dispose the western world to 'Christian despair,' those of
Freud and Watson have, it seems, engulfed us in a despair that
is infinitely deeper and more absolute. Luther gave us the
Bondage of the Will, which was a frankly speculative and
theological work; but now, direct from the scientific laboratories,
came a more total bondage: S-R 'bondage.' "[29]

A variety of viewpoints find Freud either missing the mark,
incomplete, or consider him catastrophic with reference to the

---

[28] "The Reformed Faith and Mental Health," *Evangelical Quarterly*,
October 1952, Volume 24, No. 4, p. 216.
[29] "The Rediscovery of Responsibilty," *The New Group Therapy* (to be
published), ms. p. 10.

Christian faith. Says Philip Mairet, "Certainly, what was essential in his [Freud's] findings could have been elucidated by motives from his Hebrew scriptures; but he turned to the Gentiles instead; presented his doctrine as the solution of the riddle of Oedipus."[30] Another psychologist expresses himself as follows: "The psychologist who ignores the spiritual aspect of man's nature, or who assumes indifference or even hostility toward religion, thereby renders himself incapable of dealing with the total personality. He may be able to relieve or cure many mental symptoms, but he cannot hope to bring about a sound integration of personality."[31] Complete condemnation of Freud is stated by another: "The application of psychoanalysis to Christian life is disastrous."[32]

Others who affirm the use of psychotherapy as a potential Christian instrument are at the same time fearful that it will usurp the place of Christian experience in the life of a patient. The close parallel between psychoanalysis and certain aspects of the Christian faith are frequently detailed, and were put in a rather comprehensive manner several years ago by C. L. Barbour in *Sin and the New Psychology*.[33] G. H. Muedeking makes this point more recently as he sees psychoanalysis substituting for true religious faith in the lives of patients: "As always, a 'savior' appeared. Psychoanalysis offered a threefold message: cleanse the mind by speaking out these guilty secrets; relieve the guilt-bearing experiences of childhood and thereby discover their inappropriateness at the adult level; channel the energy of intolerable behavior toward acceptable goals. It takes little insight to see the close parallel in this method to the ways of guilt relief which the church had heretofore prescribed, with the analyst

[30] *Christian Essays in Psychiatry*, p. 49.
[31] E. White, "Spiritual Factors in Mental Disorders," *Journal of the Transactions of the Victoria Institute*, Volume 71, p. 108-9.
[32] S. E. Lindquist, "Sin and Psychoanalysis," *Journal of the American Scientific Affiliation*, Volume 12, No. 3, September 1960, p. 89.
[33] Abingdon Press, 1930.

replacing the pastor and priest. For thousands of distressed
hearts the invitation from psychoanalysis opened the future
again. Rather than getting to heaven safe in the arms of Jesus,
men went to heaven, or thought they could, on a psychoanalyst's
couch."³⁴

Thus there are many who find no antagonism to the Christian
faith in psychotherapy *per se,* but who detect in the underlying
theories of psychoanalysis and behaviorism a view of man which
is incompatible with the teachings of the Scriptures. Inasmuch
as one's view of anthropology will tend to control his psychotherapeutic theory and practice, we will give considerable attention to this subject later in the book.

Christian Therapy

The third group of persons interested in psychotherapy in
evangelical Christianity see no inherent incompatibility between
these two areas. That is, they see no *necessary* incompatibility.
However, their thesis is that the psychotherapy must not be
neutral to the Christian faith. They are not satisfied with a
"baptized" psychotherapeutic theory which is made compatible
to a spiritual dimension in man. They demand, rather, a psychotherapy grounded in Biblical presuppositions. It must be a
Christian psychotherapy. They insist that there is a distinction
between Christians who happen to be psychotherapists and
Christian psychotherapists.

The following quotations are representative of this point of
view. The first is from an interesting paper by T. J. Jansma, a
chaplain-counselor in a Christian sanatorium for mental and
emotional disorders, who gives an intriguing title to his paper,
"Kill the Conjunctions," and insists that the relationship between Christianity and Psychiatry must not be either Christianity *and* Psychiatry, or Christianity *or* Psychiatry, but rather, with

---

³⁴*Emotional Problems and the Bible,* Muhlenberg Press, 1956, p. 58.

the two concepts joined together without a barrier — Christian Psychiatry. Says he, "I am using the term 'Christian' in the sense of a large and comprehensive *Weltanschauung,* a philosophy of life and meaning based on a specific concept of God, man, and the universe. And I insist that Psychiatry cannot be a healing science (making man whole) without such concepts. ...we are engaged in Christian Psychiatry, not pagan-rooted Psychiatry. The person we treat is the image-bearer of God, his functional sickness is related to the sickness of us all: our fundamental alienation from God, our proneness to hate God and our fellow man, the disintegration of the personal self, and the tension of a fallen world of nature and men. We must be more bold, nay, more godly, and apply clinically what we profess creedally."[35]

"But psychotherapy, the process by which one person shares his skill and insight with another in the healing of personality ills, can go only part of the way in relieving the guilt of sin. Psychotherapy can expose the unconscious motives and can strip off the disguise of specious character defenses to help the troubled individual see himself and all his shortcomings. But analysis is a process of paring down, and there comes a time when personality must be restored and made whole. In whose image or pattern is the unsatisfactory and inadequate personality to be restored? How is the conquest over human weakness and besetting sin to be achieved? It is here that the insufficiency of psychotherapy alone to deal with anxiety and guilt of sin becomes apparent. It is just here that Christianity offers an answer, for that faith has healed the anxiety and guilt of sin for centuries before scientific psychotherapy was conceived."[36]

Let us hear a third voice sympathetic to this position. "There

---

[35] Address delivered at the 50th Anniversary Banquet of Bethesda Hospital, Denver, Colorado, August 24, 1960.

[36] Walters, "Christian Faith in an Age of Anxiety." Radio Lecture, University of Illinois, September 13, 1958.

is but one flame hot enough to weld, and having welded, to
supply heat and light and life, and only a Christian psychotherapist can apply it. Only one psychology has a future, and
that is the psychology which *has* a future. We are so constituted
that we must have a rationale of the universe and of life, and
no system can satisfy save that which can give meaning to the
past, and hope for the future; and of these two, the latter is the
more necessary. Once more, therefore, the conclusion is forced
upon us that the overstrain and disorganization of life today
have their cause and their cure alike, just here; and that all
roads lead to what, for the Christian, is the central truth. 'Thou
has made us for Thyself, and our hearts are restless till they find
their rest in Thee.' "[37]

As I review the above distinctions as to the various Christian
attitudes toward psychotherapy, I am not without some misgiv-
ing; for the apparently very clear distinctions are really quite arbitrary and do not in reality embody the categorical divisions
that are presented. However, they do give some insight into the
various attitudes and give some background for the discussion
that will take up a good part of the ensuing volume. They also
indicate that this problem which we have set before us is both
important and complex.

However, before we launch into the discussion of the nature
and basis of mental and emotional disorder, and the appropriate
therapies to apply, we must set ourselves to the task of a prior
problem which persists to the present day in spite of the fact
that it was set forth many centuries ago in the questioning cry
of the psalmist, "What is man that thou are mindful of him?"

---

[37] Murray, *Introduction to Christian Psychotherapy*, p. 13.

CHAPTER II

MAN

On the surface it would seem that little could be more unnecessary than to stop at this point and have an extended discussion of the topic: Man. Everybody knows what you mean by the term and almost everybody thinks that he has a better than average knowledge of at least a few of these creatures. Moreover we have not only a knowledge gained through observation but we also have some "inside" knowledge which further increases the questionability of raising such a trivial issue.

When one seeks to collate this inside information, however, he soon comes face to face with perplexing problems which easily persuade him to join in the inquiry as to what man is, or as it is more often phrased in recent times, who man is.

There are no classification tags that one finds in the midst of his stream-of-consciousness nor do other men walk about bearing specific outlines in which one can categorize their multitudinous varieties of behavior patterns. Therefore it seems that any serious attempt to understand the nature of man will be based upon a prior assumption not gained from observing man. The observations may well tend to support or repudiate the particular view that the observer has, but at any rate it will have been gained apart from his observation. There is nothing particularly disparaging about this state of affairs so long as the observer does not attempt to smuggle in a view of man, claiming that he has none, or else try to establish that he has gotten his viewpoint exclusively from his observations.

That it is important to attempt to understand the nature of man for the purpose of our study will be easily seen in view of its being a prerequisite to any theory of mental and emotional disorder, or to any therapy intended to overcome such.

ANTHROPOLOGICAL PERSPECTIVES

Historically there have been many points of view concerning the nature of man, or as they are often called, theories of anthropology. I have previously tried to point out the four basic categories that seem to have been popularly used[1] and still feel that these more or less accurately reveal the basic philosophical assumptions underlying the different views of man.

The following extended quotation from my book *Logotherapy and the Christian Faith*[2] presents these assumptions in a clear and concise context.

> In spite of the innumerable variations in anthropological presuppositions, it is possible to designate a few central theories that tend to summarize man's thinking about man. Some of them sound rather recent in the history of thought, but upon investigation turn out to be ancient theories, having appeared in the earliest literary efforts, and now and then reappearing, garbed in contemporary verbiage more befitting the scientific era. The ancient Greek thinkers brought them first to light, and they have since waxed and waned in popularity, but never have expired.

> *1. The Mechanical Man*
> The first is what may be called the physicalistic view of man. A human being is regarded as a chance concatenation of physical particles in a universe containing only "atoms and the

---

[1] "A Prolegomenon to Educational Psychology," The Gordon Review, I, ii, May, 1955.

[2] Baker Book House, pp. 15-22.

void." This view was first presented by Leucippus and Democritus, before the time of Socrates, and has held a place of prominence throughout the course of recorded history. Man is a machine whose functions are to be understood as the movement of bits of matter in space and time. Every aim and aspiration, every joy and every sorrow, is but an instance of action and reaction, attraction and repulsion, exemplary data of physical laws. The new, intricate, and fascinating electronic computers are not really different from the engineers who make them: they are just more crude, less sensitive in certain respects, and much more accurate. Every thought and every desire of man is merely the occasion of material complexes, logically no more nor less significant than the friction of two grains of sand in the Sahara Desert.

This view of man has been made popular and pervasive in the twentieth century in the area of academic psychology by Watson, and the behaviorists who have followed in his train, denying the existence of consciousness and the many personal human experiences, in their more extreme assertions, or else assigning them to a vague "epiphenomenal" status, which apparently has no "parts or passions." The important contributions of Pavlov and other reflexologists have made the study of man a safe and secure "natural science" which need not blush with embarrassment in the presence of its older brethren, physics and chemistry.

This satisfaction is short lived, however, when one considers the consequences. Those human treasures of ethics, ideals, and love, are exchanged for the fools' gold of a reductionism which changes them to mere moments in a field of material forces. This is not to say that man does not have an extremely important physical dimension, but rather that this dimension does not exhaust his nature and his potentialities. Neither does this assertion exclude the value and usefulness of the research of the behavioristic psychologists. It demands, however, that behaviorism shall not overlook that significant level of behavior which is evidenced when one tells a naughty child to behave himself. Conversely, only a fool would say the same thing to a watch which was not keeping good time.

In the field of mental health, the value of decisiveness and human aspirations ought to be too well realized to be beguiled into the inexorable and pitiable fatalism that is entailed in the theory that man is only a physical machine. It is a tragic joke that may be readily observed in the literature affirming such a view of man, which presents the physicalistic view as a *fact*, as something that *should* be believed, and marshals arguments in order to *convince* the reader. However, in the theory itself there is room neither for truth, obligation, nor decision. "At first man understood himself as a creature, and, to be sure, after the image of his creator, God. Then the machine age came, and he soon began to understand himself as a creator, and, strange to say, after the image of his creation, the machine!" (Viktor Frankl, *Das Menschenbild der Seelenheil kunde*, Hippokrates Verlag, Stuttgart, 1959, p. 46.)

The physical factors in human personality are very important. A small change in the secretion of a gland, or the function of a group of nerves, can greatly change the behavior of an individual. The field of chemotherapy will, no doubt, continue to be of inestimable value in psychotherapy. However, these factors should not be permitted to loom so large that they overshadow and obscure those essential characteristics of human personality which make man "a little lower than the angels" and give him a citizenship in a realm qualitatively far removed from sticks and stones and shifting sand.

2. *The Phylogenetic Model*

Another widely held view of man regards him as a complex biological organism. His physical characteristics are appreciated, but not permitted to obscure the fact that he has a feature which is not found in the complexes of matter, and is unexplained by the rules and principles of physical theory — he is alive. Though the gulf between the organic and inorganic has seemingly been narrowed by biochemical research, yet it is still wide and deep when one observes the difference between the living and the dead. While the inanimate slowly drifts in disintegration to an entropic wasteland, the living struggles to stem this tide by utilizing bits of this material world into means for survival and reproduction. This point of view was not unknown to the pre-Socratics, but it was Darwin, a century ago, who gave it form and impetus for our time. There is a great living evolutionary realm which had a modest and secret beginning in some prehistoric swamp and which, sometimes by slow, imperceptible, accidental variations, and sometimes by mysterious and sudden travail, through which offspring as "out of due time" appear, has eventuated in the vast interrelated complex kingdom of flora and fauna, with self-conscious and rational man upon its throne.

There is much to commend this description of man. The success of the Gestalt psychologists in biological and psychological research, and the "organismic" work of Goldstein and others, have made the "bundle hypothesis" of the physicalistic theory of man a bit difficult to retain. The "purpose" revealed in the metabolic process, and the "ingenuity" of the healing process in man, certainly demand a higher principle of explanation than mechanism. Thus in the biological view, the "dust of the earth" is transformed into marvelous organic entities, the highest of which, man, has created intricate social institutions and complex technological tools in his struggle to attain his goal in life. This goal, when viewed from that anthropological perspective which holds that man is essentially a biological specimen, is survival, accompanied by its necessary counterpart, reproduction.

Once again, however, man is presented in a truncated fashion. His highest achievements, and noblest aspirations, are reduced to the mundane plane of cellular activity. His social accomplishments are merely accidents of the instinctive drive toward his biological end. His rational movements, which burst the bonds of space and time, are designated as spatio-temporal instruments of the biological thrust. Even when he contradicts the basic thesis of survival by committing suicide, it is considered as one of those exceptions that somehow prove the rule.

3. The Rational Animal

Of those who thought the foregoing exceptions were too hard a test for the rule, the most familiar is Socrates of ancient Athens. Convinced that man was more than a complex of "flesh and sinew," he, followed by his student and literary spokesman, Plato, led the way to a view of man in which the highest and noblest dimension reflected and appreciated the good, the true, and the beautiful. The biological structure which provides the plaguing drives and passions is a "prison house" of the true aspect of man — the rational and immortal soul. Man is essentially man only when he is thinking. His defects and problems are erased when ignorance is eradicated. His true nature is expressed in the attainment of rational ends.

This "classical" view of man survived the middle ages and bloomed in the Renaissance, but has been hard put in modern times to survive the avalanche of enthusiasm for natural science. Anything that is not available to the traditional five senses has been ignored by the modern anthropologist and psychologist, as they respond to the "status drive" to Natural Science. Anything so resembling superstitious metaphysics might cost them their membership. In educational circles this anthropology has had a slight revival under the enthusiastic leadership of Mortimer Adler and his Great Ideas, but otherwise it has short shrift. In the field of mental health one may occasionally observe unconscious acceptance of a rational view of man in the abortive attempts to "educate the public." It is also sometimes presupposed in the therapeutic hour in the hope that when the patient "knows his own dynamics," then he will be all right.

The almost universal acceptance of a primary unconscious component of man in comtemporary psychology seems to obviate the possible resurgence of man as primarily a thinker. However, the increasing interest in Ego Psychology may be also increasingly fruitful if the rational aspects of the unconscious mental process receive due consideration. In any respect, "life is deeper than logic" and this necessary corrective to the view of man as exclusively physical and/or biological must not usurp the throne of a onesided anthropology.

4. The Image of God

Another view of man, which has had an even longer history than the foregoing, is that emphasizing his religious nature. Before the concepts of the Greeks were crystallized, a religious anthropology stemming from the Hebrew tradition was firmly established. This held that the truly important aspect of man was that he was a creature of a Divine Being, and in some way made in His image. Man's highest function and purpose in life is to worship his Creator and to serve Him. Various religious concepts from other cultures tended to blur this particular religious view of man, but it was this Biblical concept, as it was extended through the development of the Christian church, which by and large undergirded the cultural development of western civilization for the last two millennia.

The last century has witnessed a progressive repudiation of the spiritual nature of man, however, and an exclusive emphasis on his physical factors has taken its place. This emphasis seemed to be more in accord with the precepts of modern science, and seemed to offer a greater hope for new insights in the area of mental and emotional strength.

Such has been the secularization of our culture that Allport has noted the strange situation today whereby people will, with candor and without inhibition, discuss the most intimate details of sexual experience, but would blush to confess a religious impulse.

There has been of late, however, a surge of interest in the religious interpretation of man in the field of psychological and psychiatric research which, if not to the proportion of "turning the tide," is nonetheless receiving a wide and serious hearing. The sterility of theories and techniques based upon man conceived as a mechanism or psychological apparatus has given an air of necessity to the reviewing of what, until recently, was considered a dead option.

The Christian view of man is the sole perspective which adequately delineates the nature of man, affords a comprehensive account of his experience, and provides a proper goal of personality. Only the Biblical anthropology is broad enough properly to account for man with his physical structure, his biological needs, his symbolic experience, and, in addition, his unique moral nature. "Man cannot be explained — human personality cannot be understood — his struggles and strivings, his fears and his loves, his humility and his pride, his psychic efforts and his collapse — all these cannot in my opinion be understood without our having a well-founded view about the religious being of man."[3]

There is a difference of opinion among Christians as to whether man has to be regarded as a dichotomy (having two basic parts) or a trichotomy (having three basic parts), but there is full agreement that man has an immaterial as well as a material part. These components ideally function in an organic unity which is harmonious and productive. Actually, however, there are varying states of disharmony which individuals must strive to overcome. The uniqueness and great merit of Biblical anthropology is the recognition of the moral character of man's psyche (this term is used here to include whatever is meant by the Biblical concepts of heart, mind, soul, and spirit). The psychosomatic unity of man is a purposive organization, and Christianity teaches that this organization has an inherent and radical defect. Man is naturally self-oriented rather than God-oriented, and this is declared to be the chief root of his problems. The rectification of this defect is effected neither by biological maturation nor re-education, but only by a radical reorganization of his psyche. Thus, a Biblical view of man entails a remedy for social and personal delinquency not first of all in terms of an environmental change nor an internal resolution but rather in terms of a basic change in the organization of man's psyche whereby, through the supernatural power of God, he becomes both psychologically and metaphysically a "new creature."

---

[3] Waterink, "Man as Religious Being and Modern Psychology," *Free University Quarterly*, VI, i, February 1959.

BIBLICAL CONCEPTS RELATING TO THE PSYCHOLOGY OF PERSONALITY

Although the Bible is not a textbook in psychology, it does refer in many instances to basic psychological experiences. The problem for a person who holds the Bible to be authoritative is to know just how to relate Biblical concepts to contemporary theories of personality.[4] A superficial transposition of such concepts could very well miss the intention of the Biblical statements. In the field of theology there has been a good deal of discussion in terms of the basic components of human personality. From the point of view of dispensationalism there is a strong emphasis upon a three part anthropology (using as primary proof texts I Thessalonians 5:23 and Hebrews 4:12) as opposed to the Reformed tradition of a two-part dichotomy theory in which the basic distinction is between the material and the immaterial in man. John Laidlaw in his classic work, *The Biblical Doctrine of Man,* makes us well aware that we should proceed with caution. "To frame a complete and independent system or philosophy of man from the sacred writings is an impossible task. The attempt cannot commend itself to the judicious interpreter of Scripture. It is certain to foster one-sided views in theology, or to become a mere reflex of some prevailing philosophical school. It is an opposite extreme to say that Scripture affords us no knowledge of the soul's natural being — that the texts on which a so-called Biblical psychology has been founded, do not teach what the nature of man is, but only declared his relation or bearing towards God."[5]

I was recently informed by a graduate of a Christian college, a psychology major, that two of his psychology professors were

---

[4] For an interesting discussion of this point the reader is referred to an article by Edward Heerema, "Biblical Data for the Formulation of a Christian Psychology," *Proceedings of the Christian Association for Psychological Studies,* 1956.

[5] T. and T. Clark, 1895, pp. 3, 4.

at loggerheads concerning dichotomy and trichotomy and then asked me to judge between them. I responded that perhaps both were wrong inasmuch as the Biblical anthropology that is most accurate seems to be that which reflects man as a unity. A dichotomy is too simple; while a trichotomy tempts one to an injudicious use of the Biblical data. With reference to the latter, Laidlaw comments that "its crudest and most frequently quoted form is that which, taking *body* for the material part of our constitution, makes *soul* stand for the principles of animal life, and *spirit* for the rational and immortal nature. This is plainly not the construction which any tolerable interpretation can put upon the Scripture passages."[6]

The concept of "heart" as found in the Scriptures has often been used to indicate the nucleus, or core of personality, as well as being related to the concept of the unconscious. "Out of the heart are the issues of life; out of the heart come lyings, stealings, thievings, murder . . . the heart is deceitful above all things and desperately wicked . . . . believe in thine heart." Again quoting Laidlaw: "Its prominence as a psychological term in the Bible and in other books is due, doubtless, to the centrality of the physical organ which it primarily denotes, and which, according to the view of the ancients, bulked so much more in the human frame than the brain. Since, in the Bible phrase, 'the life is in the blood,' that organ which forms the center of the distribution of the blood must have the most important place in the whole system. By a very easy play of metaphor, therefore, 'heart' came to signify the seat of man's collective energies, the focus of personal life."

Philip Marquart, a Christian psychiatrist, reflects a similar opinion which makes an interesting parallel inasmuch as his training is in the field of medicine and his statement is more than a half century later. "The Basic Anxiety as well as the Sin

---

6 *Ibid.*, p. 68.

Nature come forth from the 'heart,' that core and center of man's personality. The 'heart' in Scripture seldom refers to the organic pump within the body (as it does in Exodus 28:29), but refers usually to that part of personality which was supposed to have a relationship to the bodily organ (modern psycho-somatics shows that it does have such a relationship). The heart is not the whole personality, but it represents the whole personality, for it is that point at which the whole personality converges to a focus. It is the very essence of personality — the real you inside — in contra-distinction to the various functions of consciousness and conduct which we usually study as psychology. Out of the heart come all the various activities of our personalities."[7]

The concept "spirit" is becoming often used in existential psychology but "soul" is still avoided so as to avoid the traditional religious connotation. A discussion of the spiritual dimension of personality will be given below. The term "psyche" which is a direct transliteration of the Greek word usually translated in English as soul, has been found more useful and better fitting into contemporary psychological terminology.

The above given Biblical terms are important in the development of a personality theory but when they are taken over as ready made components of the structure of personality, they may not serve so well as at first might seem to be the case. J. Waterink, of the Free University of Amsterdam, who uses the concept "ego" to describe "nuclear man," has a pertinent comment to this point. "There is, of course, no principal objection to calling this core of man's being the 'heart' or 'x' or anything else instead of the term 'ego.' But then it must not be claimed that such is the Scriptural definition of this 'core.' Care should be exercised that we do not read twentieth century content into Biblical terms."[8]

---

[7] "Basic Anxiety and Adamic Motivation," *Journal of the American Scientific Affiliation*, II, iii, September 1950, p. 4.

[8] *Proceedings of the Christian Association for Psychological Studies*, 1954, p. 10.

The important thing is that the truth about man as revealed in these Biblical concepts be also incorporated into any theory of personality. The anthropological concepts of the Bible such as soul, spirit, heart, and mind, have no precise scientific definition, but rather must be understood from their context. For example, sometimes soul and spirit are used synonomously, sometimes distinctively, and sometimes antithetically.[9] Ernest White, a Christian psychiatrist, puts the matter succinctly: "All the various functions of the mind as described in modern psychology are attributed indifferently to heart, soul, and spirit."[10]

Other Biblical theses are, of course, also important for a Biblically oriented view of personality. One which is very important in terms of understanding human personality is that of sin. This is seen in the Bible as a destructive, deteriorating, pathological force which is the basis for man's difficulties and conflicts. Although there is some controversy as to the origin and transmission of sin in the human race, there is very little controversy as to its penalty in human experience. "No longer do personality theories turn a deaf ear to the cry of the prophet of old, 'the heart of man is deceitful above all things, and desperately wicked; who can understand it.' The modern humanist wants no identification with earlier optimism. On the contrary, some point to a cess pool of impulses that threaten at every turn to break forth into overt action."[11]

O. H. Mowrer has made a strong plea for the recognition of

---

[9] Cf. Tweedie, *Logotherapy and the Christian Faith*, p. 161.

[10] "Preface to Biblical Psychology," *Journal of the Transactions of the Victoria Institute*, LXXXIII, p. 57. White also discusses in some detail Biblical anthropology in his book *Christian Life and the Unconscious*, Harpers, 1955.

[11] Jaarsma, Cornelius, "Toward an Anthropological Theory of Personality," *Proceedings of the Christian Association for Psychological Studies*, 1958, p. 37. It should be perhaps mentioned in this context that there is still a strong surge of optimistic humanism, in such prominent psychologists as Abraham Maslow and Carl Rogers, but in essence Jaarsma's statement is accurate.

sin as a prime psychopathological factor in mental disorder.[12] One should not be too eager to use the thesis of Mowrer, however, without careful consideration, for he repudiates a great deal of the Biblical account, especially the substitutionary atonement as well as the reformation principle of "grace alone." It will be interesting to see the impact that this famous psychologist will make in his writings in the field apart from his specialty, interestingly enough, in an area which should be the domain of theologians, but in which they have feared to tread. At any rate, sin is a very explicit concept in the Biblical account and one which the Christian ought well to heed in his examination of personality problems, or in the general field of psychology, for it may be that, as Mowrer has said, "Sin is the lesser of two evils."[13] Another psychologist supporting this point of view states that "consequently, in the light of this function of the feeling of sin and guilt as alerting man psychologically and spiritually, I wonder if anything would be accomplished by changing names. 'A rose — and sin — by any other name' would both come out to be the same thing after all. They are intrinsically bound up with both man's freedom and his responsibility."[14]

Another doctrine, that of salvation, which is seen to be the central thesis of the Biblical revelation, should be taken into account in any adequate personality theory. This concept has generally been avoided in the field of psychology, which has been very critical of conservative religious concepts for the most part. However, in recent times there have been many comparisons made between religious doctrines and the process of depth psychology and psychoanalysis. The id has been compared with the concept of sin, the superego with that of the conscience,

---

[12] *The Crisis in Psychiatry and Religion*, Van Nostrand, 1961. This volume is a collection of essays and lectures devoted to this thesis.

[13] *Ibid*, chap. 4; *The American Psychologist*, 1960, pp. 301-304; also note the reaction to this idea in *Time* and *Newsweek* for September 14, 1959.

[14] C. A. Curran, "The Concept of Sin and Guilt in Psychotherapy," *Journal of Counseling Psychology*, VII, iii, 1960, p. 194.

catharsis with that of repentance, and regeneration and sanctification with a successful psychoanalysis.[15]

A Christian psychologist should be wary of making any such
identifications which may be "psychologized" away, but should
be more careful to avoid the complete disregard of the inroads of
sin in the process of psychopathology, and the great potential of
regeneration as an aspect of psychotherapy. The bifurcation of
man into several parts and the relegation of sin to one of these
parts, and the setting it aside for the concern of the ministers
seems to me to be neither adequate Biblically, psychologically,
psychotherapeutically, or practically.

The Dimensions of Personality

Personality, though a common term, is an ambiguous one and
has extremes of variation in the psychological literature. For instance, in the classic work on personality by G. W. Allport[16]
there are some fifty different definitions of personality presented.
Two basic differing approaches to personality are those of psychoanalysis and behaviorism. These two approaches tend to
dominate the contemporary psychological context. The former
evaluates personality as the outworking of some deep unconscious instinctual drive and accounts for the different aspect of
personality through the use of the concepts of the id, ego, and
superego.[17] Behaviorism, on the other hand, sees man only as a
physical mechanism which "learns" a series of responses to environmental stimulations. The personality is the grand total of
reflex arcs of behavior. "Two trends can be clearly recognized
in the rapid progress of psychology. One trend can be broadly
called analytical psychology, the other behavioral psychology.
We must be aware at the very outset that neither psychoanaly-

---

[15] Barbour, *Sin and the New Psychology*. This is an older work, but it has
as a very explicit theme the point at hand.

[16] *Personality: A Psychological Interpretation*, Henry Holt Company, 1937.

[17] Cf. Tweedie, *Logotherapy and the Christian Faith*, p. 40. ff.

sis nor behaviorism is simply a scientific psychological doctrine: both represent a philosophy of man which strives to encompass man in the totality of culture. Contradictory as these two schools of psychology are in almost all their doctrines, they agree in some basic principles — just those principles which can hardly be accepted on evangelical-biblical grounds."[18]

There has been an attempt to modify behaviorism to account for the difference between physical relationships moving in space and time, and the complex differences found in biological organisms. The influence of Darwin has caused some to consider the uniqueness of life and the drive to survive and reproduce as the basis for personality theory. Other points of view with distinctives in terms of personality theory are proliferating. Some of those making a particularly significant impact on the contemporary scene are such as that of Adler, who believed the overcoming of inferiority feeling was of prime significance, of Maslow, with his theories of self actualization and self realization, Frankl[19] with the will-to-meaning, Jung and the impulses of the archetypes, as well as the Gestaltists with the drive for organizational completeness.

In conclusion it may be observed that there are a myriad of modern personality theories, stemming largely from the two basic trends, psychoanalysis and behaviorism. Few, if any, take into account the distinctive theses concerning man which are central to a Christian view of personality. These theories bypass what may be the most crucial components for an adequate view of personality for mental health and psychotherapy. "Most of the theories of personality have ignored the spiritual aspect of human nature and make naturalistic assumptions about man.

---

[18] T. T. Thienemann, "The Art of Counseling," *The Gordon Review*, September 1957, p. 95.

[19] The personality theory presented in this chapter, though significantly different, owes much to Frankl's "dimensional ontology." For a fuller discussion see Tweedie, *Logotherapy and the Christian Faith:* An evaluation of Frankl's Existential Approach to Psychotherapy; Chap. III.

The doctrines of man that ignore the transcendental dimension not only present truncated views of man, in failing to deal with an important aspect of human reality, but their greatest deficiency is related to the aspect of personality in which most emotional conflicts and disorders arise. Science offers certain insights applicable to the practice of psychotherapy, but has only proximate answers for the ultimate questions. When the practitioner moves into the areas of human freedom and responsibility, the canons of science are no longer appropriate."[20]

The Christian has a basic presupposition as he approaches the concept of personality for he believes that the Bible presents significant truths regarding man. Man is a spirit, made in the image of God, a religious organism. Thus we may regard the spirit as a person, a mysterious entity which is not subject to empirical research and/or empirical validation. The person expresses himself and makes a social impact as well as social communication. The personality is the expression of the spirit.

1. The Somatic Dimension

How does the spirit express himself; how does he make this social impact? At first, of course, he expresses himself through his physical body, or "soma." This is the first aspect of persons that we consider. They are extensive and they stimulate our sensory organs. Thus it is easy to see why some psychologists have presumed that personality is to be exhausted in the physical dimension. Though we would not want to agree to this, we would not want to overlook the very great importance of physical characteristics as the sensual aspects of personality development. People are tall and short and wide; they have brown, blue, or gray eyes; have red, blond, black, brown, or no hair; their skins are one color or another; they are both wrinkled and smooth; their faces are handsome, fair, ugly, plain; in short, there are

20 Walters, "The Psychiatrist and Christian Faith."

innumerable differentiating physical characteristics and these are important in any personality theory.

One makes a great error, however, if he, overimpressed by this aspect of man which stimulates his sensory organs, concludes that personality is nothing more than the physical characteristics of man. This is the behavioristic fallacy. As soon as he investigates these physical characteristics he discovers that he must go beyond them. There are factors beyond the actual physiological relationships which cannot be accounted for by these relationships themselves. He discovers that man has motivational forces or drives which are the underlying determiners of physical function, as well as other aspects of personality process. There are motivations and urgings to action which are much more important than the actual physiological structure in understanding what "makes him tick."

2. *The Psychic Dimension*

In this dimension of personality, which I call the psychic dimension, we see drives and motivation which are closely related to the physiological process, such as the tissue needs of food and drink, the needs for excretion of waste materials, and the strong procreative urges. These may be called physiogenic drives.

It appears that we can also distinguish other aspects of the motivation to action in human personality, which may be called psychogenic drives. These are the immediate reaction to man's encounter with different parts of his environment. For instance, in his experimental contact with the world, he has different emotional reactions to, or stimulations by, the objects in it. He finds that he is threatened by some of the objects of the world and he may adjust to this threat by either flight, which is a reaction of fear, or fight, which is an aggressive approach to destroy the threatening object. On the other hand, he may find a comforting secure stimulation by certain objects in the environment, with which he wants to unite. These may be referred to as emotional constellations inasmuch as most, if not all, of human emotional reactions can be categorized or grouped with reference to these three different types of reaction. In the constellation of anger we have a threatening object and an aggressive approach to it. In the state of fear we have a threatening situation and a withdrawal from it. In the constellation of love (this term may have too many other connotations to be useful in this sense) there is a non-threatening situation, a promising state of affairs to which the reaction is approach. It may be noted here, parenthetically, that this latter emotional experience is a characteristic experience for those persons enjoying good mental health. These psychic drives whether physiogenic or psychogenic are related to the emotional, non-logical, spontaneous reactions of man, and are very significant in the discussion of personality.

3. The Noetic Dimension

A third dimension in personality which one notices in regarding the expression of a person, or the expression of spirit, is that dimension which is neither physical, nor is it characterized by the non-logical instinctive thrust of emotional motivating forces, but rather is the dimension which may be called the noetic dimension after the Greek word *nous,* relating to the mind. Whereas the somatic refers to extending, and the psychic dimension to feeling, the noetic dimension is chiefly characterized by thinking and the accumulation of precepts and concepts into an organized unity. There is some historical precedent for calling this an "apperceptive mass" and it is roughly synonomous with the concept of mind. An excellent background for the study of psychology and personality from this dimension may be obtained from the classic work by Brand Blanshard, *The Nature of Thought.*[21]

---

[21] George Allen and Unwin, 1939.

The danger in approaching the study of personality is that one may become so fascinated with the data of one dimension that he overlooks or disregards the other dimensions. He thereby expresses or understands personality only with reference to a small portion of the information and thus distorts his personality concepts. The ever present dangers of psychologism (regarding only the psychic data), physiologism (the behavioristic regard for only the somatic data), or noologism (the regard only of the rational data) to account for the totality of personality.

It may easily be seen that all of the three dimensions must be incorporated into one unified view. As a matter of fact, although these dimensions, with regard to at least some of the data in them, seem to be very obvious and exclusive one from the other, we find that it is impossible to get specific and exclusive boundaries between the fields. When we investigate, for instance, the somatic dimension, we discover that it is impossible to understand where the physiological functions leave off and the physiogenic and psychogenic factors take over. The close relationship in emotional experience between the psychogenic drives and the physiological organism make them a part of a continuum rather than specific isolated dimensions.

So is the noetic dimension related both to the somatic and psychic dimensions. When there is a sharp blow to the physiological organ, the brain, it may well be that there will be either a permanent or temporary alteration of the rational function of man, or even a complete cessation for a period of time. However, no specific relationship between any neuron of the central nervous system and any idea or thesis of the noetic dimension has been found, or is likely to be found. Yet that there is a dependency of the latter upon the former cannot be denied. In the same way there is a very intimate relationship between the functions of the noetic dimension of personality and the psychic dimension, for not only are the data of the apperceptive mass organized in terms of their logical coherence and consistency within the total wealth of knowledge, but also a part of this rational organization is based upon the emotional significance of the experiences involved. An emotionally tinged value system is part of this mental construct. As a matter of fact, the emotional significance of certain of the data of the noetic dimension can cause, under the experience of threat, some of the data to be lost from usefulness due to anxious repression.

These factors should keep us both from disregarding any of the dimensions of personality by paying too much attention to any other, and also keep us from the opposite error of assuming that these dimensions are separate compartments, apart from one another and having little or no relationship with one another. We should emphasize that man as he expresses himself through his personality is seen to be a unity, a single entity, one organism with a manifold of unique characteristics. "Especially is psychiatry deeply divided into two enemy camps, the upholders of the psychogenic interpretation and those of the organicist interpretation. I am often classed with the former; I absolutely refuse to agree. For me it is neither the body which controls the mind, nor the mind which controls the body; rather are both at once the expression of an invisible reality of the spiritual order — the person."[22]

4. The Pneumatic Dimension

However, when we have concluded our discussion of the three dimensions of personality, we find that we have merely the shell of the human being and are in danger of assuming, because we have made a descriptive analysis of the different ways in which the spirit expresses himself, that there is no kernel, no nucleus, no person, no spirit at all to be accounted for in our study of personality. The spirit, the ground principle of the human being, the real person, is in a sense beyond explanation. The first principle of personality, like Aristotle's metaphysical

---

22 P. Tournier, *The Meaning of Persons*, Harpers, 1957, p. 104.

first principle, cannot be demonstrated. "The unifer, however, is always something that evades the process of being scrutinized. The most one seemingly can get of it is that by some sort of intuition there is an aspect of the 'core' which always remains the subject and at that moment eludes being its own object, as that which ties together and in the process is itself not tied, a analyzing and yet not at that moment analyzed, as a dreamer in his daydreaming and yet itself not at that moment in the dreamed."[23]

This "fourth dimension" of personality is as difficult to illustrate as is the fourth dimension in the field of physics. "One can make the body, soul and the understanding experimental objects. The spirit, on the contrary, is unreachable by science — it can only be intuited through inner sight (Innenschau) or, perhaps better said, perceived through grace."[24] It is well named as the pneumatic dimension of personality, for like the "wind" (pneuma), "it bloweth where it listeth and we hear the sound thereof but cannot tell from whence it cometh or whither it goeth." However we can infer from the activity of personality that the spirit is free, self-transcendent, and spiritual.

The person is free in that when he would turn to the right hand or to the left, he must make an explicit decision as to which way he will in fact go. Man has options for decision in spite of his inherited characteristics, the pressures of his environment, or the present state of his psychic drives. He can and must freely choose from the options at hand.

Man also has the peculiar ability to regard himself. It is as though he could rise above the confines of the three dimensions of his personality and stand apart for reflection and/or decision. In this regard one may note the aspect of awareness of consciousness as relating to this personal activity. This cannot for the most

---

23 John Daling, "Toward a Christian Concept of Personality," *Proceedings of the Christian Association for Psychological Studies,* 1957, p. 15.

24 P. Tournier, *Zwiespalt des Menschen,* pp. 66 and 67.

part be related to any particular dimension of personality for the conscious experience somehow integrates all the dimensions and is related to all of them. The unconscious level is that which is beneath the level of awareness and which contains those materials or aspects of personality which cannot be readily brought to attention. It is another question whether these activities of personality were so insignificant or so slightly perceived that they were not well organized in the apperceptive mass, or whether they are so distressing in the personality that some mysterious force of personal functioning, perhaps an activity of the spirit, must ignore or repress them from consciousness.

The next level of awareness is an abundant area comprehending a major part of the apperceptive mass. This construct covers all those things to which we are not presently attending in consciousness, but which we can bring readily to our attention by taking thought. Freud called this the preconscious or foreconscious.

Thirdly, there is the level of conscious awareness with which one is presently occupied. For instance, I am now gazing with some rapt attention at the tapestry on my wall.

Finally, there is a level of consciousness which pertains to the pneumatic or spiritual dimension of personality, which is not only a state of awareness, but rather an awareness of being aware. Thus as I gaze at the gallant stag which is the center figure in my tapestry, I may become suddenly aware that it is I who am gazing at this scene and I can, in some sense, reflect upon my motives and the activity of my personality as to why and how I am looking at the tapestry. I can become very conscious of the words I am writing and there is a certain sense in which this can be devastating and deteriorating. Dr. Zhivago was right when he said that self-consciousness is a poison, for it can frequently make my habitual motor activities become frustrated and make me function very inefficiently. This talent of self-consciousness in the spiritual dimension of personality enables man to rise above himself, to regard himself, and even to oppose himself. He can merely by a change of attitude change the three dimensional functioning of the personality.

Since the above material was written there has come to my attention the doctoral dissertation of John G. Finch[25] in which there is considerable evidence presented to support the above presentation. "The dimension of 'spirit' of the *Imago Dei* is a *sine qua non* of Christian anthropology" (p. 251). In addition, Finch presents a compelling argument that this spiritual dimension of personality has been either implicitly or explicitly incorporated in much of contemporary psychological theory, even when the context is somewhat anti-Christian as in the case of Freud. "It would appear as though, starting from radically different points of view, psychology from the standpoint of man and Christianity from the revelational standpoint of God, have converged toward the same point, spirit, and then diverged to a sort of hiatus. It would appear to this writer that any attempt at rapprochment between religion, or more specifically the Christian faith, and psychology will have somehow to go through this wicket gate. Or, if that time does not come, as Brunner seems to suggest, the regulative discipline of Christianity will be a valuable informant for the efforts of psychology to understand man" (pp. 252-3).

The spiritual dimension not only involves a free and self-transcendent expression, but also a spiritual expression. Within the spiritual realm of functioning (we must be careful not to consider the spirit as a different compartment apart from personality either, for the personality *per se* is nothing but the embodied expression of the spirit) there is also a reference point to a moral order. We have a moral consciousness, the consciousness which pertains to an absolute level of obligation which,

---

[25] *Some Evaluations of Freud's View of Man from Psychoanalytic Perspectives and Some Implications for a Christian Anthropology*, Unpublished Dissertation, Drew University, 1958.

though affected by the authority figures in our experience, cannot be accounted for by them. It rather seems to point to an external lawgiver who somehow places a condition upon the activity of the spirit. Thus personality cannot be exhausted either by the empirically examinable three dimensions of personality nor by the mysterious fourth dimension which somehow is the integrating factor of the other three, as well as that unique aspect whereby the person can make free decisions, and transcend or "stand off" from himself. However there is also need for an objective reference point to account for the religious orientation of the spirit. Human personality needs a divine reference point. "I do not mean to say here that the inmost being of man is capable of analysis. There always remains a mystery of the personality, which mystery cannot be understood, nor can it be analyzed, but can only be accepted in the meeting of the patient with God."[26]

CHRISTIAN ANTHROPOLOGY AND FREUD

A few years ago I attended a meeting of Christian college students at which a Christian psychiatrist lectured. In the discussion period which followed, a student asked if it were possible to discuss human personality adequately apart from the Freudian concepts of id, ego, and superego. The lecturer said that he did not think so. I recall reacting rather negatively to his reply. In retrospect, I think my reaction was not so much to his statement, as to the fact that he seemed to think that the psychoanalytic concepts were both useful *and* sufficient. I was rather in agreement with Runestam who made the following comments in a second edition of his work *Psychoanalysis and Christianity*, some twenty-five years after the original writing. "My chief objection to the *modus operandi* of psychoanalysis is that it is based on a faulty and shallow psychology with its superficial notion of

---

[26] Waterink, "Man as Religious Being and Modern Psychology," p. 30.

man's nature, and this in spite of its vaunted depth analysis."[27]

One does not have to agree with Freud to find the terms useful. Mowrer, a rather vocal and influential anti-Freudian, believes they are the most descriptive terms at our disposal and eminently useful. For myself, the only member of the trio that seems particularly helpful is "ego" which approximates "spirit" and draws less fire. The recent interest in ego psychology and the tendency to emphasize the ego as an instinct, rather than an outgrowth of the id, in recent psychoanalytic literature, may tend to support the characteristics of the "spirit."

The superego is the point of most opposition, for there is little fellowship possible between Freud's social-centered conscience, grounded in a sexual instinct, and the Biblical concept of a conscience. The Biblical view of conscience, while permitting of "cultural coloring" is explicitly related to a divine law and Lawgiver. Not necessarily a direct communication with God, but an essential aspect of the *Imago Dei* in the creature is manifest. "Conscience is thus not the echo or the abode of an immediate divine self-evidence, but an actual consciousness of a divine law established in man's heart. . . . that which is said by ancients and moderns of the conscience of God's voice in us, has in it this truth, that the testimony of conscience certainly rests on a divine foundation woven in our natural condition."[28] "Such a conscience certainly has larger dimensions than the Freudian superego can ever have. The very difference between the Freudian concept of the superego and the Christian concept of conscience dramatically distinguishes the religion that hinders from the religion that helps."[29] In addition, Freud's superego, an "anti-instinct," growing out of an instinctive drive, is not free of internal theoretical difficulties as Runestam points out: "He

---

[27] P. 176.

[28] Delitzsch, *A System of Biblical Psychology*, p. 165.

[29] Wayne Oates, *Religious Factors in Mental Illness*, Associated Press, 1955, p. 30.

[Freud] speaks of this as if it were a self-evident matter, easily understood, in spite of the fact that it is quite odd that out of the sexual energy mass suddenly can emerge a moral and aesthetic censor which is able to check or hinder the free flow of this energy mass."[30] Frankl often points out that this is as absurd as presuming a river can build its own power plant.

The practical problem with the "id" is that it may become identified with the unconscious aspect of personality and tend to obscure the fact that all personal dimensions have unconscious levels. The id is popularly conceived of as immoral and this obscures the fact that, at least for the Christian, there is both the old man and the new, who speak from the depths of the personality. Murray in his *Introduction to Christian Psychotherapy* has an interesting comment pertinent to this: "Sin, as we have seen, has roots in the unconscious; why not righteousness as well? Through what doors will the powers of God enter a man, entering, as they often do, long before he knows them, if not through the portals of the religious instinct, deep down in the unconscious with its neighbor instincts. . . . It is in the unconscious, that the creative work of God joins the creative impulse of man; and here psychology unites with religion, in the endeavor to find new ways in which these unconscious powers may be expressed."[31]

The unconscious is not some separate force in opposition to conscious levels of personal functioning, but rather a continuum. Ernest White asserts that much of the tension between psychology and religion is due to a fallacious assumption. "The fallacy lies in the false supposition that the unconscious is a separate department of the mind, a kind of water tight, closed system, entirely independent of the rest of the personnel."[32]

Thus one should exercise extreme caution when employing

30 *Psychoanalysis and Christianity*, p. 130.
31 Pp. 256, 257.
32 *Christian Life and the Unconscious*, pp. 22 and 23.

the common psychoanalytic concepts, especially in the context
of a Biblical anthropology. It is difficult to divorce the widespread materialistic connotation of these constructs from the
names themselves.

It would not be complete to conclude this discussion of a
Christian view of man in relation to Freudian concepts without
mentioning our attitude to one of the basic components of psychoanalysis — sex. Freud's theory is often called a pan-sexualism
bcause of the primary place of sex in the development of
personality, especially in maladjustments of personality development.

Some supporters of Freud like to insist that sex is to be understood as more or less equivalent to "pleasure," thus softening
the resistance to the process of infantile sexuality and at the
same time seemingly ameliorating the stark, stern dogma of
juvenile incestuous desires in the oedipal relationship. One is
hard put, however, to discover an illustration in the Freudian
literature of sex and the psychic process which does not refer
to genital sexuality even though implicit rather than explicit.

No doubt the psycho-sexual development begins long before
the pubertal changes of early adolescence. In addition, it is obvious that sex is an extremely powerful drive which must be
taken into account in an adequate view of personality. Stemming
from the somatic dimensions, it becomes a basic force in the
molding of personal characteristics, neither all-enveloping in its
compass, nor negative or vile in its function. "This sex instinct
... is at once one of the strongest of physical urges, and the
vehicle of deep psychic need. Rightly apprehended and used, it
can be made sacramental, and a measurable enrichment of life,
and a far greater thing than the mere blind procreative instinct
of popular thought."[33]

That sex is not made the central force of Biblical anthropology

---

[33] Murray, *An Introduction to Christian Psychotherapy*, p. 65.

is not that it is too shocking to discuss (for the Bible is most realistic in its presentation of the sexual function), but rather that the evidence seems to indicate that sex, though prominent in the symptoms of psychopathology, is merely one among many of the "instincts" of man.

SUMMARY

Our discussion of the nature of man from a Christian perspective has indicated that we must utilize the Biblical concepts which refer specifically to man and his functions. These alone give us the authoritative, inside information which reveals his essential spiritual characteristics. However, we must go beyond the Biblical terminology, which is often non-specific, and frequently conveys a historical connotation not pertinent to contemporary description. Caution should be exercised that in the process of utilizing new descriptions, we do not jettison the essential truths of the revelation.

There is a new mood in personality studies which tends to make easier the Christian psychologist's task. He is receiving increasing acceptance as a scientist and has the opportunity to utilize this new mood for the advancement of the Kingdom as well as psychological science. Both contemporary trends in the field of psychology and a re-evaluation of the data of the past seem to give empirical support to his thesis. A new look at man is providing opportunities to proclaim old truths about him and his teleological quest. "Careful and objective study of man's life reveals him in search, not only of immediate physical satisfactions, but beyond these in search of some sort of point and purpose in living at all. This search may take many forms, and may be conscious or unconscious, constant or fluctuating, but it is an inescapable aspect of human existence."[34]

Man's uniqueness is receiving careful consideration after sev-

---

[34] David Stafford-Clark, "The Nature of the Problem," *Christian Essays in Psychiatry*, (edited by P. Mairet), Philosophical Library, 1956, p. 14.

eral decades of down-grading to bundles of reflex-arcs or eddies
of blind libidinal energy. Once again there is the thought expressed that man may best be understood not in materialistic reductionism, but rather in the light of himself and his peculiar
characteristics. "A scholarly friend tells me that our word
anthropoid comes from a Greek word meaning, 'with the head
up.' And we are apparently in the process of discovering that
we cannot solve our problems by looking 'down' without also
losing perhaps the most distinctive aspect of our humanity."[35]

And when we try to interpret man in the light of his own
uniqueness, we are inexorably drawn to a higher plane of reference. We are directed to a metaphysical question which, in the
opinion of the Christian psychologist, can be succinctly and sufficiently (and exclusively) answered in two words — the Word
of God written, and the Word of God incarnate. Those who
have made the great impacts in the advancement of psychology
have hewn valuable building blocks for the construction of an
adequate anthropology (and credit should be given where credit
is due), but only the Christian has a blueprint. "We can but say
that this complexity we call man, enters time as an individual
bundle of individual capacities, weighted also with inheritance
and predisposition, uneasily poised between the subconscious
and the outer world, and receptive, if he will, of the intimations
of Divinity; and that his life is explicable only as the ante-cham-
ber of Eternity."[36]

Though the Christian psychologist is firm in his stand upon
a Biblical foundation, he does not demand that his fellow psychologists make a leap of faith apart from abundant evidence.
"The Christian view of man does not stand in conflict with any
established truth about human nature. Other doctrines of man
are not any more scientific. They are only rival affirmations of
faith and systems of belief. Since none is fully capable of demon-

---

[35] Mowrer, *The Crisis in Psychiatry and Religion*, p. 35.
[36] Murray, *An Introduction to Christian Psychotherapy*, p. 153.

stration in the scientific sense, that doctrine of man commends
itself most convincingly which has the strongest empirical foundation, illuminates the functions of personality over the broad-
est range, and offers a satisfying and verifiable solution to the
dilemma of human aspiration, evil and anxiety."[37] It is not a
plea to violate reason and common sense, but rather a challenge
to open one's eyes to the truth, and then use this truth to under-
sand and support man in the problems of life. Man stands, as
it were with one foot on earth and one in heaven, and the psychologists who would attempt to search him out, must both subdue the earth and hear the voice from heaven.

---

[37]Walters, *"Christian Faith in an Age of Anxiety."* Radio Lecture, University of Illinois, September 27, 1958 .

CHAPTER III

MENTAL ILLNESS

The definition of mental illness is not an easy matter. Although it is relatively easy to make a practical judgment with reference to the state of health of a sincere and co-operating person, the formulation of a theoretical statement is a more difficult task. The situation is similar to those with which Socrates had such little patience. People frequently use terms and concepts of which they have little or no precise understanding. It does not ease the situation to say that mental illness is a lack of health, for the latter carries an even less distinct connotation. There are some who believe that the scandal of psychology has been its inability to define the normal personality to the least common denominator.

THE DEFINITION OF MENTAL HEALTH

J. Bauma, at an annual meeting of the Christian Association for Psychological Studies, defined mental health as "the capacity to work, play, and love in the ordinary ways without an excessive expenditure of energy or by inefficient modes of living."[1]

---

[1] "Trained People Involved in Promoting Mental Health," *Proceedings of the Christian Association for Psychological Studies*, 1955, p. 16.

This, however, is not of much help unless we know with a little more clarity what "ordinary ways" are, and what the standards are by which we determine what "excessive" and "inefficient" mean precisely. E. A. Richardson, in a presidential address to this group a few years later, defines health as "the process by which an integrated life goes beyond itself, separates from itself and returns to itself in a reintegration."[2] This definition, also, helps us very little until we see it in the context of Richardson's thinking. He sees health to be properly understood only from an integrated view of man, who is seen as a "multi-dimensional unity." His concept recognizes both stability and movement in the integrated life. The healthy life is one which is open to new experiences even though this may involve the risk of starting a movement toward illness. In fact, one must take this risk in order to stay healthy, for the attempted withdrawal from experiences is in itself sickness.

Wendell Rooks indicates that health is not to be understood either in an individual or in a social sense apart from a divine reference point. The definition of mental health will, of necessity, be inadequate unless one takes into account "the matter of defining in all of life the forces of the one true ambivalence, namely, Thy will be done, or mine. This is absolutely fundamental for all of living, a principle to which all of our psychological and somatic functioning must become subservient if there is to be comfort. This means God-centered authority, Christo-centered thinking, and Spirit-motivated living, a faith-inspired sense of belongingness and adequacy."[3]

R. Van Zoeren, in a paper entitled, "Problems in Defining Mental Health" given at the 1958 annual meeting of the

[2] "A Unitary Understanding of Health," *Proceedings of the Christian Association for Psychological Studies*, 1960, p. 63.

[3] "The Place of the Christian Concept of Sin in the Theory and Practice of Psychiatry," *Proceedings of the Christian Association for Psychological Studies*, 1955, p. 35.

Christian Association for Psychological Studies, believes that there are roughly three choices of perspective from which to define mental health. The first is for the individual to have a free expression of instinctual drive, which Van Zoeren repudiates and declares to be a lay opinion falsely attributed to Sigmund Freud. One can, on the other hand, define mental health with reference to a culture pattern. This seems desirable, according to Van Zoeren, inasmuch as different societies have very different attitudes toward acceptable and desirable behavior patterns. He points up this difference in a quotation from Franz Alexander: "The average Balinese with his introverted, dreamy disposition would be considered in American society either a schizoid personality, a case of ambulatory schizophrenia or a prepsychotic personality. On the other hand, an American traveling salesman in the hands of a Balinese psychiatrist would run the danger of being incarcerated as a potentially dangerous hypomanic."[4]

The final alternative is a definition of mental health based on absolute standards. This point of view would hold that even though an individual were adjusted to his culture, the culture itself might be sick and, therefore, his adjustment would not necessarily indicate health. This seems to be what would follow from the statement of Dr. Rooks given above. Van Zoeren points out, however, the great difficulty of finding acceptable and convincing absolute standards by which mental health in an individual might be determined. He rightly doubts that this will come from any increased research in clinical psychiatry but rather perhaps must come from some other discipline such as theology. His conclusion is that "unless we are willing to accept the definition of mental health based on a relativistic concept, which for practical purposes asks only that an individual live in

---

[4] "Problems in Defining Mental Health," *Proceedings of Christian Association for Psychological Studies,* 1958, p. 62.

harmony with his drives, his conscience, and his culture — our definitions will continue to vary as the belief, ideals, and ideas of men vary."[5] It is interesting to note that his final statement as to an acceptable definition of mental health involves not merely the relativistic adjustment to one's cultural context, but also includes the individual matter of "drive," and "conscience." It also should be added that a definition of mental health which is relative to cultural patterns is no easier to apply in clinical practice than a definition which is based upon absolute standards. In both cases the empirical application introduces another relativity factor. And in either case the decision of a definition will be based upon one's philosophy of life rather than upon the clinical data.

A satisfactory view of mental health for the Christian will have to take into account three different directions or dimensions of personal encounter. A human being is called upon to come to terms with himself, with his cultural environment (primarily involving other persons), and with God. In the Biblical context this acceptance, or coming to terms, would be related to "love," or the positive response to the world of experience as was mentioned in the last chapter.

From a psychological perspective (reflecting the aspects of the psychic dimension previously discussed) this would mean that the individual, whether "inner," "outer," or "upper" directed, tends to anticipate from the experience of these directional encounters a positive growth in his personality, a fulfillment of the self. Inasmuch as every encounter involves an inherent degree of risk, then it follows that no person has perfect mental health through an extended period of time. Most clinicians, whether Christian or not, will accept the first two dimensions of adjustment, the self and its "horizontal" environment, but there are not many who will include the relationship to God as a con-

---

[5] Ibid., p. 65.

comitant of mental health. This is a crucial point for a Christian
view of mental health.

MENTAL HEALTH AND GOD

Is it necessary to be a "man of God thoroughly furnished unto
good works" in order to be mentally and emotionally healthy?
We would not hesitate to declare ill anybody who radically rejected himself or other people; but are we ready to affirm the
same for anyone who radically rejects God? This seems to follow
from a reading of the Scriptures; but can it be a respectable
point of view in the twentieth century? The prophets of Israel
seem to have had little difficulty functioning upon this foundation (it should be added that this was true only in the theoretical
aspect; socially it was much more difficult, for they were frequently stoned); but can a modern clinician adopt such a radical
approach?

If mental health has these three dimensions — self, environment, and God — we might visualize a hierarchial "ladder" leading up to the state of mental health. No doubt the specific rungs
of this ladder would be arbitrary, for they are of necessity
static samplings out of a fluid continuum between the extremes
of mental illness and good mental health. At the top would be
that healthy specimen, the dynamic Christian, who is well adjusted in all three directions of his life encounters. Next would
come those Christians who are properly related to God through
Christ, but who are ill adjusted in the horizontal relationships of
life. They have made a commitment to God, but have difficulty
in a commitment to self and fellow men. Their present life is a
burden to them, but at least they are directed toward the life
abundant. The next few rungs of the ladder are missing and
there is a "gulf fixed" between the top and the bottom "over
which no man can pass." This distance can only be traversed
by a leap of faith and a mysterious boost of grace. The third
step down is the level of those persons who are unable to find

a tolerable adjustment either on the vertical or horizonal axis
of life. They are crippled in personal-social relations as well as
estranged from God. According to this scheme there is yet another group, this fourth group consists of those individuals who
are satisfied with themselves and enjoy adequate inter-personal
contacts, but who are, in the words of the Scriptures, "without
God in the world." These are on the lowest rung. These are
the sickest!

Does such a hierarchy seem preposterous? To classify as the
most ill those whom secular psychology considers the most
healthy augurs ill for the establishment of a Christian witness in
contemporary psychotherapeutic circles. However the Christian
therapist of all people must be realistic; and if there is a personal Reality which provides and sustains the reality of the
material world, and which provides meaning and wholeness for
human personality, then this must certainly be taken into account. If reconciliation to this Reality is the sole means of the
fullness of life, a thesis which appears in accord with the teachings of the Scriptures, and estrangement from God leads to
misery and guilt in life, then those who are engaged in an effort to assist people in more abundant living ought to have such
a reconciliation central in their thinking. Even if the effects of
ill adjustment on this critical plane are successfully avoided in
life through the narcotic of activity, or some other ready means
of escape, there is a Biblical warning that the advent of death
for such a person does not disprove the validity of the above
proposed hierarchial scale of personal well-being. On the contrary, the Bible clearly tells us that there is a judgmental experience for the unredeemed to which death is merely the portal
and in which, whether taken figuratively or literally, is revealed
a perpetual state of terror, pain, and loneliness.

Thus if this be true, the man in the fourth category of the
scale, who in the eyes of the world seems to have the highest
level of personal adjustment, is actually in a dangerous pre-psy-

chotic condition. What irony if the community leader who promotes the local mental health drive should unwittingly harbor a
latent psychosis of the severest degree which will precipitate at
some time in his life, or at least early in the next! This would
be on the order of the socratic irony wherein Socrates found
himself to be the wisest of men in accordance with the revelation of the oracle at Delphi merely because he alone knew that
he was ignorant, and thus knew something; whereas other men
failed to place on the scale of wisdom because they supposed
themselves to be wise, when they were ignorant, and thus had
no knowledge at all. It may be that the individual who despairs
because he cannot accept himself, feels unaccepted by his neighbors, and is burdened by the weight of sin because he is not
reconciled to God, is nonetheless "nearer to the Kingdom" than
his well adjusted neighbor, whom he covets, but who has made
his adjustment to this world only. The latter, like the unsus-
pecting victim of a deadly cancer, is sickest of all because he
supposes himself to be well.

As I reread the above paragraphs, I become painfully aware
of two things. In the first place this hierarchial scale superfically
glosses over some of the major difficulties in the diagnosis of
mental illness and presents in static stages, or "rungs of a ladder," what is essentially a continuum from good to ill mental
health. Secondly, it seems to be a patent absurdity which is blind
to the practical problems of mental health — a topsy-turvy situation in which the well are sick and the sick are almost well.

Nevertheless it is the duty of the Christian to give heed to
the Biblical revelation, and if this seems to lead to a view of personality in sickness and in health which is counter to the viewpoint which is professionally popular and socially acceptable,
then he must swallow hard and stand firm. It would certainly be
folly for the Christian therapist to bow to a majority ballot and
participate in the seduction of men who are desperately ill by
encouraging them to believe that self acceptance and proper

social orientation will cure their ills. This will be further discussed in a later chapter.

I should like also to assert quickly that I have no special brief for the above "ladder of mental health" except for the didactic purpose of questioning the identification of those people comprising the first and fourth rungs. As a practical fact, neither of these groups seek the aid of the psychotherapist, nor are they statistics for a mental illness survey.

A WORKING HYPOTHESIS

At this point it would seem appropriate to present my own precise definition of mental health, but I am at a loss so to do. My formulation seems so imprecise and so difficult to posit in a scientifically respectable framework. The individual enjoying good mental health is "a man of God thoroughly furnished unto all good works." Here is the person who is at peace with himself, with his neighbor, and with his God. Each of us is continually moving back and forth on a continuum from this point to the point where man is at enmity in these three dimensions. In the light of both time and eternity, and in the Biblical imagery, each individual is on the road between heaven and hell. One goal or the other involves every man and leads him toward ultimate integration or ultimate disintegration. The direction one travels is determined by his relationship to Christ, the proximity to his goal is determined by his life experiences, and the attainment of his destination comes only at life's end — destiny is confirmed in death.

THE CLASSIFICATION OF MENTAL ILLNESS

The observation and classification of the symptoms of mental illness has always seemed to be a more fruitful procedure than the theorizing and defining of mental health. No matter how one defines mental illness, there is always an abundance of persons who bear the unmistakeable symptoms of mental ill health. For them life is a burden, weighted by fears, aggressions, indecisions, and regrets. Historically these "dis-eases" have been classified in terms of related symptoms. There is always the danger in coining words or phrases to describe these symptom groups that one will confuse them with specific diseases such as those in the physiological dimension of personality which are caused by invading micro-organisms. Terms used to describe emotional disorders are more like the common cold, which is used to describe a multitude of viral invasions having a more or less common group of symptoms in the respiratory tract.

It has been customary and convenient to describe mental "dis-eases" in terms of the defensive action of the human personality. The personality is conceived as an organic unity which in its life experiences must ward off those forces in the environment which threaten to destroy its unity. It finds "eternal vigilance as the price of freedom" and is continually being conditioned to defend itself as best it can, or, if invasion has been successful to make alliances with pills, professional counselors, or pastors, in order to throw off the yoke of bondage.

I shall present this defensive maneuver in terms of four lines of defense. These are more or less common divisions in the field of psychopathology, although one discovers upon entering the field that psychologists have a penchant for coining neologisms and a passion for reclassifying symptoms. This is, no doubt, an indication that there is even in this scientific era, post mid-twentieth century, a good deal of confusion as to just how to regard, and what to do with, the symptoms of mental illness.

These four lines, or levels, or modes, of defense of personal unity are: defense mechanisms, neuroses, psychoses, and psychopathic character disorders.

Defense Mechanisms

The first line of defense is traditionally known as the level of defense mechanisms. These are automatic, unconscious methods of defending the personality from the inroads of disintegrating conflict.

The relationship of the person and his defenses are sometimes likened to a mask behind which to hide. Jung called this the "persona," while Tournier has something of this idea in the "personage." Linquist, in discussing this relationship, sets the matter in a clear context: "The personage is a mask or front that everyone puts on. It is developed primarily because we think that the "person" is not adequate to be accepted as is, or else because the "person" is too tender to be exposed to difficulties of face to face relationships. The person is the true part of oneself. It is that which we are when our defenses are down, and when the personage is stripped from us. In a sense, I suppose, it is that which God sees when He views us — without the social amenities or the defenses we put up — the psychological 'fig leaves' that are part of us."[6]

1. Repression

The basic means of defense is called *repression*. This is the excluding of threatening experiences from conscious awareness. The imagery usually used to illustrate this mechanism is that of an active resistance to permitting those memories which cause anxiety of guilt feelings from rising out of the "deep places" of the personality, the unconscious, to the conscious level. They are contained by restraint. Repression is an unconscious selective avoidance of those past experiences which have disrupted the unity of personality and threaten to do so again.

In the Freudian terminology for personality factors, repression is the process whereby the impulses of the unconscious id, which would threaten the ego or offend the superego, are held back from consciousness. This makes an easy illustration although just what does the censoring is not clear.

Recently I was counseling with a young woman who in the course of an interview embarrassedly related a childhood incident for which she presently had guilt feelings and which "had never entered her mind since that time." Another recent client frequently mentioned that some of the incidents which he related to me in the course of some therapeutic sessions were interesting in that he was tempted not to tell them to me and also that he had not thought of them for years. He mentioned that they seemed to come out because he was trying to be honest. Repression is a face-saving defense as well as a protection against the memory of bitter and painful past experiences.

Freud seemed at times uncertain as to whether repression was one defense mechanism among many, or the primary defense which was manifested in a variety of ways. In any case, there are a number of terms to describe ways in which individuals avoid conscious confrontation with themselves. The intent here is not to decide for or against the supremacy of repression, but rather to familarize the reader with some of the common names of these defenses. All of these protect the individual from the experiences of anxiety and guilt. Various authors have various lists of such defense mechanisms. The following are an arbitrary few that are frequently mentioned.

2. Projection

Projection is the process of avoiding personal conflict by placing, or projecting, the sources of the conflict stimulus upon someone or something other than oneself. A few years ago I was in a minor automobile accident in which I was totally at fault. The memory is still vivid of a sudden realization of desperately trying to find the cause of the accident in the lady driver with whose car I had collided.

In a recent telephone conversation with the husband of a

client, projection was an obvious factor. He attributed to his wife the entire responsibility for a very difficult domestic situation and expressed himself as pleased that she was getting some help for her problems as he felt that she might affect the children negatively. This was in spite of the fact that he was an alcoholic, intemperate in language, berated his wife before the children, and refused to share any experiences with his wife, even to the point of seldom eating at the same time. Though her personal attractiveness and apparent willingness to co-operate in any way to save the marriage may have obscured her contribu tion to the difficulty, it was nonetheless obvious that the husband was projecting any fault of his own upon my counselee.

3. Introjection

Introjection, or identification, is another protective device. In this the individual avoids conflict, usually the anxiety of inferiority feelings, by "borrowing" the honors and attainments of his school, community, or of prominent people. A common mode of this mechanism is to "drop the names" of well-known famous persons, as though one had an intimate relationship with them. This elevates one to the same level of accomplishment and personal worth.

4. Regression

Regression to childhood reactions such as sulky withdrawal or temper tantrums, is a means of avoidance from the pain of present conflict. This usually involves a subsequent sense of shame, but this seems to be the lesser of two evils to the individual who utilizes this mechanism.

5. Reaction Formation

Reaction formation brings forth an extreme opposite of one's thoughts and emotions in order to cover over their unacceptability. A person who is resentful of another, such as an older child toward his younger sibling, may become oversolicitous and fawning; a selfrighteous prudishness in sexual matters may cover up a guilt producing prurience which threatens the personality.

6. Rationalization

Rationalism is the production of good reasons for bad actions. A justification is made for an indiscreet decision. This, like the other mechanisms, is usually held to be unconscious and to be distinguished from alibiing, its conscious cousin.

Other defenses, such as daydreaming (autistic fantasy), the use of alcohol and drugs, and a variety of divisions and subdivisions of those listed above are to be found in each of us and are means of personal equanimity in the face of the pressures of life. To be able to accept oneself is extremely important and these processes are attempts to make us more acceptable. Personal efficiency and personal adjustment is often maintained only at their expense.

7. The Value of Defense Mechanisms

Difficulties arise, however, in the excessive use of such defenses. It is not easy to state just how much utilization of defense mechanisms is excess, but a retreat to other lines of defense seems to be conditioned by a breakdown of the defense mechanisms, or as they are sometimes called, the mental mechanisms. Before we discuss the next line of defense, neurosis, two clarifying comments should be made.

The first is that defense mechanisms are essentially self-defeating and not to be construed as healthy processes. They are retreats from reality, avoidance of self confrontation. They are ostrichlike defenses which may hold off the day of reckoning, but which bear the seeds of their own destruction. Inasmuch as they do not really resolve personal conflict, but rather attempt to ignore it, these devices tend to fall into vicious cycles which make one more and more dependent upon them. This in itself may stimulate further threats of anxiety and guilt and lead to further personality disintegration.

None of the lines of defense are really healthy since they all are withdrawal tactics, efforts expended to avoid the truth. There is a saying that a good offense is the best defense and this may well be appropriated to the field of mental health. Direct confrontation of a conflict situation may seem more threatening than avoidance, but it tends to maintain the unity of personality in the long run rather than to be divisive. This is another facet of the fact that "the truth will make one free."

The second comment is to clarify the order of the personal defenses. The presentation of them in a series beginning with the defense mechanisms tends to give the impression that this descending order is the normal trend from bad to worse as the lines of defense break through. I am not sure that this is the case. Rather than to see the lines of defense as concentric circles, each perimeter becoming a more desperate attempt to preserve the personality as the preceding one capitulates (albeit an easily recalled illustration), it may be that when the defense mechanisms fail to maintain unity and relative freedom from conflict, the person may tend to retreat in any one of these three directions. Instead of concentric circles, there would be three smaller separates circles within the larger circle of the mental mechanisms. The inclination toward one defense rather than another is a mystery involving heredity factors, growth and development, as well as the pressures of the moment. These three directions are neurosis, psychosis, and psychopathic character disorder, or sociopathy. The descending order is probably more relevant to the difficulty of treatment rather than the degree of disintegration, or the sequence of psychopathological development.

NEUROSES

A neurosis, or neurotic conflict, is a state in which an individual is laboring under such a burden of symptomatic distress that he feels unable to carry out his role in the basic life adjustments. In our culture these adjustments usually relate to sexual maturation, courtship and marriage, vocation, religion, and growing old. The ego is bent under the weight of life's demands and the neurotic is fearful that it is about to break.

The point at which personal conflict becomes neurotic is difficult to determine in any precise means of measurement. Some persons function satisfactorily under an enormous burden of stress. Each of us has periods of conflict which, if persistent, would soon establish us as neurotics. As an arbitrary rule of thumb, I classify those as neurotics who, while having good reality contact, are so burdened with distressing symptoms as to cause them to despair to the degree of seeking professional help. Thus as a functional definition, the neurotic is a sane person wanting psychotherapy.

The neurotic is one who confesses the inability to cope with life. Since this is so often the case of one who is under the conviction of sin and under the suasion of an evangelistic appeal, there are those who consider a religious upheaval as basically neurotic. There may be something to this point of view. "To those who have had practice in psychotherapy there can be no surprise that some psychologists have classified conversion with the psychoneuroses. The conflict is identical; the incompatible motives, the sense of guilt, the sense of alienation from God, the sense of inferiority are similar in both."[7] However, the persistence of these symptoms usually determines whether the individual feels a need for psychotherapy and not their acuteness. In any case, whether neurotic or not, there is an obvious need of the Great Physician.

Parenthetically, the term *neurosis* and *psychoneurosis* are used synonymously here, though this has not always been true his-

---

[7] McKenzie, *Psychology, Psychotherapy, and Evangelicalism*, Macmillan, 1940, p. 97.

torically. There are some who make a distinction between the former as a malfunctioning of the neural system physically and the latter as a dynamic malfunctioning of "nerves" in the psychological (and hence, Freudian) sense. They are so interchangeably used in the literature of psychology that little gain is realized by separating them.

The symptoms most commonly expressed in neurotic adjustment may be conveniently classified in four groups. Once again I find this a didactic convenience rather than a dogmatic commitment. There are a multitude of ways to classify neuroses.

1. Anxiety State Reactions

These are neurotic conditions in which the individual is beset by a generalized anxiety. He is a "bundle of nerves," jumpy, fearful, and apprehensive. Fear crowds in on every decision and action, and makes life miserable. Two terms often associated with anxiety states are *neurasthenia* and *hypochondriasis*. Neurasthenia is characterized by general nervousness, acute fatigue, choking sensations, and shortness of breath. This is typical of the well, but not very precisely, known "nervous breakdown."

Hypochondriacs are characterized by the feeling that there is a malfunction or breakdown of some major physiological organ. The felt certainty of the patient is not backed up by any discoverable physical defect, however. The anxiety and conflict seem to be reduced somewhat and are somehow made more manageable when they are centered on some specific area. There seems to be less responsibility and guilt when there is something wrong with our bodies and not "ourselves." This condition keeps doctors busy and subsidizes a great industry for the production of pink pills and patented tonics.

The person in an anxiety state is permeated with the felt dread of imminent, unnamed catastrophe, and the helplessness to avert it. The total personality is threatened by the disintegrating force of this enveloping tension.

Last week I interviewed a woman who would sustain such a diagnosis. She was very nervous, given to weeping, and presented herself as totally misunderstood by a husband and daughter neither of whom appreciated her need for psychotherapeutic assistance. She was "doctoring" for several ailments and demanded almost daily interviews with her pastor. Her whole life is a desperate attempt to gain recognition and acceptance, coupled with a basic fear of accepting herself.

2. Physical Conversion Reactions

Often persons under stress have a tendency to convert, unconsciously, this stress into physical symptoms. This at least temporarily alleviates the pressure and averts the admission of personal responsibility for the conflict problem. There is a world of difference between what is my body's fault and what is my fault.

The symptoms may be functional such as muscle paralysis, blindness, sexual impotence, and speech disorders; or actual physiological defects such as skin eruptions, intestinal inflammation, stomach ulceration, and other psychosomatic problems. Why some particular organ is unconsciously selected, and not another, is unknown, although these hysteric symptoms often have symbolic meaning. Recently, for instance, I counseled with a young man bothered by a severe sexual impotence masking a rejection of his wife. At other times the problem seems to be only accidentally related to circumstances as in the case of another client whose sporadic and intermittent mutism had initially started when, as a young boy, he was told over the telephone that his beloved grandmother had died. This news had precipitated a momentary speech loss and this condition recurred whenever he was in a state of anxiety.

Neurotic conversion of anxiety states to physical symptoms reinforces the thesis of a mysteriously unified personality whose problems can effect any of its dimensions.

3. Depressive Reactions

A lady came to my office one day complaining of a persistent mood of depression which made life not worth living. She wept often, had suicidal thoughts, and found her home life intolerable. Our conferences revealed that she had recently patiently nursed her strong and independent husband through a severe emotional episode. She was unconsciously reacting to the fact that this had not been appreciated and that after he became well a socially distant relationship between them resumed. In addition, she was unwillingly working and continuing to supplement the family income. She felt that her absence from home might contribute to the possible delinquency of her children. These and other complications seemed to bring on a state of personal conflict characterized by a bleak, unrelenting depression.

Depressive reactions are frequent neurotic symptoms. They seem to reveal very explicitly the inner despair and "no way out" outlook of their victims. Inasmuch as suicide is an ever present possibility, disorders such as these are always critical.

4. Psychasthenic Reactions

One of the greatest fears of the neurotic personality is the fear of "going crazy." When emotional control is increasingly difficult and irrational impulses and fears thrust themselves into the field of consciousness, there comes to the individual the haunting thought that he is "losing his mind," that he is becoming insane. This *psychotophobia* is particularly true when the symptoms are those of *psychasthenia*. Literally this term means weak psyche. The experiences coming under this category are those in which conscious control of the thought process is partially lost. Three distinct but overlapping symptoms are involved:

a. Obsessions. Obsessions are persistent and uncontrollable thoughts which keep crowding into consciousness. Mothers sometimes have the thought of harming their children. Frequently persons with high moral standards and religious scruples will be obsessed with impure thoughts. A few months ago a young man came to me concerning an obsession of pushing girls into the mud. This had started accidentally one day while at work when he had seen a girl hesitantly skirt a mud puddle after the rain. The amusing thought came to him of how surprised she would be if someone had at that moment pushed her in. This generalized in the next few days so that he could not look at a girl, or even think of one, apart from this accompanying thought. This situation worsened to the point where he sought professional help. Hypnotic analysis of the obsession quickly revealed an experience of being seduced by a young matron when he was in his early teens. This series of incidents was fully repressed and came to light only when his vocational goal of the Christian ministry became both crystallized and threatened by his previous moral lapse. The obsession then made symbolic sense and bothered him no more.

b. Compulsion. A compulsion is the irrepressible impulse to perform some act. There are counting compulsions, touching compulsions, compulsions about stepping on cracks, compulsions for inordinate orderliness — almost any motor act can function as such. One of the most common is that of rechecking locked doors or gas stove jets. The urge to incessant hand washing is also frequently observed clinically.

c. Phobias. A near universal psychasthenic symptom is a phobic experience. This is an irrational fear. Usually the fear has as an object something or some situation which is in itself harmless, or at least having a danger potential far out of proportion to the fear. Very common phobic reactions concern being in a closed place (claustrophobia), in an open unprotected place (agoraphobia), or on a high place (acrophobia). At one time in the history of psychopathology it was popular to coin a new phobic name for every possible fear object. Such a burdening of the vocabulary is now, fortunately, out of fashion, though one sees many a glamorous diagnostic phrase in the older literature. After all, *rhomophobia* sounds much more professional, and mysterious, than just plain "fear of worms."

A recent patient of mine had such a dread fear of leaving her home town that she would become ill at the moment she crossed the boundary line. A young man with a similar symptom would drive more than a mile in order to avoid going a few yards across the borders of the neighboring city near which he lived.

In an actual confrontation with a neurotic patient the situation is more apt to be a mixed neurosis, involving symptoms from several of the above groups, rather than monosymptomatic. Just last night I interviewed a client who had acute symptoms from all four major groups.

It will be advisable, perhaps, to reiterate at this point that most of us at one time or another have, in a normal context, one or more of the above mentioned experiences. Students often make false inference after a discussion of neurotic symptomatology that inasmuch as they have had such experiences they must be neurotic. This does not follow at all and I would deem it unfortunate if such were the case after reading this section. It is the persistency of these experiences, leading to an interference with the necessary adjustments in life, which leads to the land of neurosis. I find it practical to assume that one has entered that land when he appeals to me for help.

PSYCHOSES

Whereas the ego is said to be bent in neurosis, in psychosis it is "broken." There is a basic disorientation that breaks contact with reality and sets the sufferer adrift on a confused sea in a private world of mysterious origin. "The cardinal features of psychosis are abnormal perception and thought disorder."[8] This becomes true only in terms of a persistent, change resistant state,

8 Walters, *The Academy Reporter*, Academy of Religion and Mental Health, March 1959.

however, for each of us has experienced these "cardinal features" either in a condition of sleepiness, fever, or day-dreaming.

The psychotic is subject to being declared legally incompetent, or insane, and may be incarcerated for his erratic behavior. He is often a social leper, observed and dealt with in fear and trembling.

The psychotic is not only erratic in his social behavior but also in his thought and perception. At times he may appear to be very normal and then gradually slip into his fantasy world so that the observer is often taken unaware. Often only certain areas of experience are aberrated, while others seem to fit a normal pattern. A very bright student of mine who was assigned to do a case study of a chronic psychotic hospitalized patient marvelled at the ease with which the patient bested him in a series of checker games.

As in the case of the neuroses, psychoses are traditionally classified in groups having similarity of symptoms. In a like manner also, this procedure has a dubious value, for individual reactions are unique and it is difficult to find persons in the flesh who fit the neat categories. Armed with the descriptive characteristics it would seem relatively easy to place an individual case; but such is not the case, for the individual patient's symptoms uniquely fit his own personality. The conferring of a technical name upon a symptom pattern sometimes gives rise to the fallacy of assuming that a specific disease entity has now been isolated. It seems to me that here is an area that is in serious need of demythologizing.[9]

Psychoses are generally divided initially into two categories; those which are organic, and those which are functional. Organic psychoses are those which are related to a physiological defect in the central nervous system, due to such factors as alcoholism, old age, venereal infection, or cranial injury. These

---

[9] Cf. T. Szasz, *The Myth of Mental Illness*, Harpers, 1961.

conditions are usually irreversible. Functional psychoses are those which have not as yet been convincingly related to a physical factor. Thus they are classified in terms of the functioning deviation, or symptom pattern of the individual. It is this latter group with which we shall be concerned.

The classification, once again, is arbitrary and based upon practical and educational considerations:

1. Manic-Depressive Psychotic Reactions

These so-called affective disorders are characterized by extremes of mood and by loss of reality contact. The mood changes may be cyclical, alternating from high elation to black depression. The mood may remain either manic or depressed, however, with no changing sequence. Asocial behavior and the possibility of self-destruction in the depressive phase usually indicates the need for hospitalization. This week I conferred with a young man in a manic episode. He was so keyed up with enthusiasm that he could not sit down. His ideas were coming so fast that he could not finish with one before another came out. This gave his conversation a level of incoherence, though each item was related to his "exploding" theme. His intention was to solve all the problems of the world. The scheme was rationally conceived with a correct geographic division and a program that included economic, political, educational, and religious reforms which he would personally institute. He was very concerned with dates and believed his program would not get fully under way until he was thirty, which was Christ's age of action. He also suggested, with an air of modesty, that he had been selected for the messianic return of Christ.

Shortly thereafter, I interviewed a young woman in a severe depression. She had been hospitalized for some time during a series of electro-convulsive therapeutic treatments. She had recovered rather well and was making progress until she had a relapse at the onset of a menstrual period. Depression is a total personal experience. Her walk, talk, posture, gestures, ideas, eyes — her total behavior — was flat, dejected and depressed. Suicidal thoughts and self-punishing impulses were frequently on her mind. She spoke of an overwhelming hopelessness. Interestingly, at the same time she spoke of her hope in Christ, and mentioned her determination to refrain from suicide because of her daughter and her Christian faith.

Often a separate category is presented for individuals, usually females, who are experiencing an emotional disorder during the climacteric, or change of life. This appears to be functional although it is closely associated with the physiological changes taking place in the onset of sterility. This disorder, called *involutional melancholia,* is symptomatically similar to psychotic depression in general.

2. Schizophrenia

The schizophrenic disorders cover the largest single grouping of psychotic illness. Schizophrenia, which means "divided mind," is identified by a radical disturbance of the thought process, which may deteriorate into a disjointed "word salad" of incoherence. In addition, the affective states, though varying from high elation to depressed moodiness, are superficial and transient. A tendency to apathetic withdrawal is characteristic.

The schizophrenias are traditionally sub-divided into four groups, according to the chief symptomatic behavior pattern:

a. Simple schizophrenia. This is chiefly recognized by increasing apathy, social withdrawal, and general personal deterioration along with the fantasy thinking.

b. Hebephrenic schizophrenia. This means literally, "youth mind," and is a disorder occurring shortly after puberty. (Schizophrenia was formerly known as *dementia praecox,* or premature dementedness, due to the high incidence of these disorders among adolescents.) Symptoms often include "kicking over the traces" morally and socially, a very erratic and regressed behavior pattern, along with a rapid deterioration of the personality.

   c. Catatonic schizophrenia. Catatonic schizophrenia is characterized by the behavioral and postural tension of the individual. It frequently involves extreme variations in muscle tension, from an agitated incessant pacing or gesticulating to a withdrawn, statuesque, waxy flexibility. Either of these extremes may continue for long periods of time.

   d. Paranoid schizophrenia. This disorder involves a persistent persecution complex in addition to the major schizophrenic symptom pattern.

3. *Paranoia*

Paranoia is a deceptive disorder due to the apparent logical cohesion of the thought pattern of the sufferer. There is a systematic delusion of persecution and the whole "meaning mass" of the individual is oriented with, and motivated by, this defensive need. Excessive suspiciousness and a tendency to generalize the circle of persecution is often noted. This was the case of the celebrated "Mad Bomber of New York," a mild appearing, unobtrusive Connecticut commuter, who had brooded over his felt injustice at the hands of a New York utility company and had enlarged his enemy to include the whole metropolis. The tight systematic delusion of the paranoic is difficult to penetrate and expose to the patient, for any agreement on the part of the therapist reinforces the symptoms, while in the case of non-acceptance one is quickly regarded as an ally of the persecuting forces. The situation is not so much a withdrawal to a fantasy world, but rather a bizarre interpretation of the real one.

   A woman was referred to me for diagnosis who revealed classic paranoid patterns. She was in charge of the family finances and had, in filing the federal income tax report, listed as a dependent her aged mother-in-law while at the same time knowing that her sister-in-law, who shared in the care of the old lady, had done the same. This violation of her ethical standards greatly disturbed her and she developed a subsequent pattern of ideas in which the Bureau of Internal Revenue had solicited the aid of the whole neighborhood and had assigned a special agent who kept her under surveillance day and night for several months. They were watching in order to prevent her escape while they finished "getting the goods on her." This seemed to be a living illustration of that homely couplet — "Oh, what a tangled web we weave, when first we practice to deceive."

Paranoia is distinguished from paranoid schizophrenia by its logical and systematized delusion. The latter has obvious thought disturbance and the persecution usually involves hallucinatory perceptual disturbances with threatening voices and the presence of the enemy.

Psychosis is that line of defense in which the individual redeems the unity of his personality at the high cost of withdrawing to a world of his own creation. The rigors of life are resolved by releasing one's grip on reality and emigrating to that fantasy land where, in a vivid and terrifying sense, dreams come true.

PSYCHOPATHIC CHARACTER DISORDER

The fourth and final defense of being human which we will mention is that of the psychopathic personality, or sociopath. This is the shadowy area free from moral inhibition and social restraint, or at least a sphere of pretending to be free from it. The "cardinal traits" of the psychotic are missing, but evidence of illness is at every hand. In the past often called "moral insanity," psychopathic character disorder is the plight of those whose conscience is "seared over as with a hot iron" and who resist any help by virtue of a bland blindness to their need. Hervey M. Cleckley in his monograph, *The Mask of Sanity,*[10] sets forth a fascinating series of case studies of psychopaths.

---

[10] 3rd. edition, Mosby Press, 1955.

They are intelligent, beguiling people from all walks of life (including a psychiatrist) who are entangled in asocial escapades which stymie both the mental health experts as well as the criminologists.

The psychopath seems inexorably bent on the task of bringing about his own downfall. He does that which will serve him worst and seems to need the masochistic rewards of his deeds. As in the case of the neuroses and psychoses, psychopaths are unique individuals and only arbitrarily subject to classification. The following is an outline of my own grouping of psychopathic character disorders.

1. Psychopathic Personality

This person is an anomaly in social relations. The psychopathic personality seems unbound by moral fibre or ethical ideals: a chronic liar when the truth would be better, with ease and conscience free entering into immoral activities, a beguiling character who convincingly vows a change of behavior and then blithely ignores his promise. They are frequently from good homes, have above average intelligence, and possess apparent qualities of leadership. They run the gamut of emotions, but these are shallow and transient. They engage large debts with no intention of payment, steal that for which they have no use, and face exposure with the insistent denial of the obvious followed by an indignant demand for others to stop making tempests in teapots.

Barry J. was an early adolesecent when he was first referred to me by his distraught parents. I saw him in a juvenile detention center. He had stolen cars for pleasure rides, broken into homes for no apparent reason, and chronically lied about his escapades. When he was apprehended by the police after he had wrecked a neighbor's car, he vehemently denied any involvement even though caught at the scene of the accident and having been seen by several witnesses. He then blandly argued that the neighbor did not care anyway and that he had intended to return the car after a brief ride. His bed was in a locked cell when I visited him and he calmly told me that he preferred it there, had wanted to sleep in as a reason for not being with the other boys in their daily duties, and would go home after some minor misunderstandings were cleared up. He mentioned his firm Christian faith and supposed that his difficulties with unreasoning officials were times of testing. Later I discovered that he had escaped from the center on the previous day in a laundry cart and had been a continual problem to the authorities in his brief residence there.

2. The Homosexual

The homosexual individual, a member of the major group of a variety of sexually perverse persons, is sexually stimulated by those of the same sex, and seeks sexual expression through an alliance with such. In spite of this situation which is inherently frustrating — biologically, socially, legally, psychologically, and theologically — he seeks to defend his personality as being normal though misunderstood and mistreated by society. Cleckley has written another monograph in this area entitled *The Caricature of Love*,[11] which details a variety of individual studies and reveals the pathetic paradox of homosexuality.

Though the homosexual is inherently unhappy, he clings to this defensive adjustment with a tenacity which usually defies law enforcement agencies and psychotherapeutic treatment alike. An account of an attempted hypnoanalysis of a young professing Christian who had deep homosexual attitudes will be given in a later chapter.

3. The Alcohol and Drug Addict

The problems of the alcohol and drug addict are some of the

---

[11] Ronald Press, 1957.

greatest social problems of our day, causing instability and fracturing of the basic family unit. They are increasingly recognized as being psychopathically oriented, and intensive research is engaged in with the hope of discovering the developmental factors related to such personality defects. Though the state of drunkeness has an obvious physiological relationship with alcohol, the alcoholic may return to drink after a long period of withdrawal from alcohol, with the full consciousness that the pleasant euphoria of the early stage of drinking is transitory, that the "hangover" from drunken states is frightfully unpleasant, and that his major social and personal problems are directly related to his use of alcohol. The gross irresponsibility of the alcoholic and drug addict places them among the psychopathic character disorders.

4. The Chronic Criminal

The habitual criminal seems unable to abide by the social norms of vocation and income. The rebellion manifest in his attitudes toward law and order indicates a basic psychopathological disturbance. This attitude usually resists change and persists even when there is ample opportunity to "go straight" and when the bitter rewards of crime in the isolation of hiding, the fear of discovery, and the punishment of capture provide ample evidence that "crime does not pay."

The person with the psychopathic character disorder is beset by a chronic need to violate the mores of his society and a defensive development that represses the voice of conscience. These constitute the greatest difficulties in psychotherapy due to the lack of insight, and the lack of motivation to change. The "rebels without causes" really do have causes, but such threatening ones that they do not dare to search them out.

Mental and emotional disorders and maladjustments have been presented as means of defense against personal disintegration and as a retreat from the rigors and stress of life. Inasmuch as such stress is a universal phenomenon and that these defensive retreats are essentially self-frustrating, and, paradoxically, lead to a distintegration of the unity of personality, there has been a good deal of thought and research applied to the etiology, or causation, of these disorders. Some discussion concerning conclusions that have been drawn about etiological factors is now in order.

THE CAUSES OF MENTAL ILLNESS

There is a long standing debate as to whether the causes of mental illness are to be found in physical or psychological components. The non-Freudian European tradition has generally tended to classify neuroses as psychologically based, or psychogenic, and psychoses as physically caused, or physiogenic. Freudian dynamic psychology has tended to psychologize most disorders, while behavioristic psychology has inclined toward a physiological basis for all psychopathological problems.

Caution would no doubt dictate some sort of a middle of the road perspective holding that both physical and non-physical bases are significant for the functional problems. Orville Walters, a Christian psychiatrist, takes this stance: "Both views of schizophrenia (physiogenic-psychogenic) may be correct. Perhaps habitual fear, anger, or other stressful experiences upset an already unstable body chemistry inherited by the schizophrenic, thus bringing on the characteristic disturbance in the thinking. If this be true, the basic defect is a chemical one and the trigger mechanism is psychological stress."[12]

In the psychiatric tradition of Europe there is a strong philosophic foundation that underlies the diagnosis of neurosis. R. Allers avers, "At the bottom of every neurosis there is a metaphysical problem."[13] Waterink, a conservative Christian psy-

---

[12] "Faith: A Built-In Psychotherapy," January 1959.
[13] "Psychiatry and the Role of Personal Belief," in *Faith, Reason and Modern Psychiatry* (ed. by F. Braceland), P. J. Kennedy & Sons, 1955.

chologist in the Netherlands, believes that "many neuroses are
the expression of a more or less unsuccessful attempt at attaining
the realization of one's own self, from the perfection of one's
own potentialities."[14] Frankl, while insisting upon the physical
basis for psychotic reactions, convincingly argues for a "noogenic
neurosis" which takes root and flourishes in a meaningless life.[15]

Walters mentions four probable causes for mental illness in a
recent article: *organic* (due to structural changes in brain cells),
metabolic (from a disturbed brain chemistry), psychologic
(based on emotional disruptions), and *developmental* (faulty
childhood patterns of behavior persisting into adult life).[16]

Heerema sees the roots of mental illness as an imbalance in
developmental years. "The affective roots of most mental illness
we have found to be in faulty conditioning in earlier years. The
two main factors bearing on the proper actualization of the personalities affective energies are control and expression, or discipline and emotional security, or determination or freedom.
These two forces must be in the proper balance in the molding
of the young affective life."[17]

A conflict theory of mental illness is also held among Christians. Ernest White in *Christian Life and the Unconscious* holds
that the degree of conflict modified by inherited characteristics
will determine the emotional disease. "It is a law of the mind
that conflicts tend to be externalized. It depends very much on
the inherited disposition of the individual how far this externalization proceeds, and at what level it occurs. With some it goes
no further than their conscious emotional states. With others it
is projected into their bodies, producing various disturbances of
bodily functions. With others again, their conflicts are projected

----

[14] "Man as Religious Being and Modern Psychology," *Free University
Quarterly,* vol. VI, No. 1, p. 59.
[15] Cf. Tweedie, *Logotherapy and the Christian Faith,* p. 93ff.
[16] *Ibid.*
[17] "Christian Faith and the Healthy Personality," p.30.

on to the outside world, and delusions are the result of this externalization."[18]

It should be emphasized, however, that it is not tension, stress of conflict *per se* which causes mental illness. Stress which is not intrapersonal may mobilize the dimensions of personality and tend to unify and integrate it. Frankl stresses this point in his writings, for he observed numerous instances in the Nazi concentration camps where persons stood up under the pressure of all manner of stress and then broke down when liberated. Just as an old structure may be reinforced by adding weight, so may the burdens of life reinforce the unity of personality.

As White mentions above, the disruptive forces may externalize in personality deterioration at any level. In my presentation of the dimensions of personality, this means that the primary symptoms of mental illness may be released through any of the four dimensions (physical, emotional, intellectual, and spiritual), but that all dimensions are involved.

We have already seen support cited for the etiological significance of the first three dimensions and it remains to be investigated whether the spiritual, or pneumatic, dimension is also causally involved in mental illness. There is an increasing acceptance in evangelical and humanistic circles of the spiritual dimension as a factor in understanding mental illness (of course a majority of persons in the area of psychology would not admit the existence of a spiritual dimension at all, and the humanists have a much different conception than do the evangelical Christians). V. E. Frankl has insisted that an adequate understanding of mental and emotional disorder involves this spiritual dimension, but is equally adamant in his assertion that the spiritual factor of personality could not be itself involved in the pathology. His reasons are philosophical and based upon the fact that then there would be no core of personal integrity

---

[18] P. 18.

to which to appeal in times of illness. His Logotherapy rests upon such a foundation.[19] I. Progoff, another of a growing number becoming sensitive to the spiritual needs of man, asserts "I have found the evidence accumulating that modern man is suffering much more from the repression of his spirit than from the repression of sexuality as Freud once said. It is because traditional beliefs and symbols have lost their inner content, that it has become commonplace for modern persons to feel ashamed of their spiritual feelings and spiritual language. They treat the religious strivings within themselves as throwbacks to primitive times, as superstitions unbecoming to a scientific age."[20]

Runestam, a Christian, suggested the same possibility several decades ago. "Is it not conceivable that the subdued murmur which emerges from the innermost recesses of the souls of men, distorted in every manner, and which in our day especially expresses itself in the much publicized general nervousness and anxiety, finally, however muffled, becomes the threatening language of the enclosed, forgotten, and suppressed religio-moral needs?"[21]

Thus we note the fact that the spiritual dimension is critically related to mental health is accepted by many, both in and outside the Christian camp. Whether the spiritual dimension itself is directly and causally involved in mental illness is another matter. Jacob Mulder, longtime superintendent of a Christian neuropsychiatric hospital, concludes, "My own view is that mental disturbance is due to disease of the body. . . . In what manner and in how far is this spirit of man affected in mental disease? It is my own view that this spirit is not affected in a destructive sense. When we speak of sickness of the spirit

---

[19] Cf. *Der Unbedingte Mensch*, Deuticke, Vienna, 1949. Also, Tweedie, *Logotherapy and the Christian Faith*, p. 105ff.

[20] "Psychology as a Road to Personal Philosophy," *Journal of Individual Psychology*, vol. 17, no. 1, May 1961, p. 47.

[21] *Psychoanalysis and Christianity*, Muhlenberg Press, 1958 (Rev. ed.) p. 42.

we are using a figurative language. The spirit's disease is of an ethical nature and concerns man's relation to God. The Spirit or psyche requires perfect functioning organs, however, to obtain knowledge and understanding and to perform that most intricate function, rational self-expression."[22]

The relationship of the spirit of man and psychopathology, or mental illness, brings us back to the question of religion and mental illness. Most Christian psychologists do not worry about the now nearly passé theory that religious experiences cause mental disorders — "the fact that the mentally disturbed so frequently demonstrates a religious content merely proves that man is fundamentally religious"[23] — but they like to keep, if possible, religion and psychopathology in separate categories. Orville Walters holds[24] that the association of the two is unwelcome, for it tends: (1) to blur the boundary between the normal and abnormal in religious expression, (2) to derive religious generalizations and universals from the pathological, (3) to become judgmental too hastily about deviant forms of religious expression, and (4) to equate sin with psychopathology. That these may be significant dangers if carried to an extreme seems obvious, but equally dangerous is the ignoring of the spiritual nature of man and his illnesses.

To this point we have discussed the nature of mental illness, its common symptom patterns, and the fact that primary symptoms can stem from any of the dimensions of personality. The etiology of emotional disorders is but little known except in terms of obvious, though nonetheless mysterious, connections between the illness and physical injury or invasion, and/or disintegrating developmental stress. In contemporary psychological

---

[22] *Psychiatry for Pastors, Students, and Nurses,* Wm. B. Eerdmans Publishing Company, 1939, p. 153.

[23] *Ibid.,* p. 170.

[24] "Religion and Psychopathology," *Academy Reporter,* Academy of Religion and Mental Health, March 1959.

circles there is a tendency to find causal factors, at least for the functional disorders, in two conflict experiences. These are easily related to the spiritual dimension of personality (and not easily understood apart from it). I refer to anxiety and guilt. For some they are identical, others conceive them as entirely distinct. Most see them as intimately related to psychopathology.

ANXIETY

Rollo May, who has written a monograph on the subject, defines anxiety as "the apprehension cued off by a threat to some value which the individual holds essential to his existence."[25] Anxiety is usually considered an essentially human experience which is a necessary function of being human. Kierkegaard and Heidegger have brought it to the contemporary scene with their intense, often inscrutable, and influential works.[26] Anxiety is an objectless fear, a nameless dread that a future decision may be disastrous, a felt imminence of destruction, a paralyzing uncertainty about the yet unveiled future.

Although anxiety is almost universally accepted as a pathological factor in mental health, there is some difference of opinion as to whether it is not also a possible asset. P. Marquart, a Christian psychiatrist, apparently thinks not — "The real cause of Basic Anxiety is the Fall of Man, whereby he sinned against God, and has transmitted to us in some way, the sin nature with its inevitable accumulation of sin acts. Guilt and fear and over compensatory strivings are all involved in its origin and inevitable continuance."[27] On the other hand, Walters considers it a valuable asset in the advancement of the Kingdom — "There is an irreducible minimum of anxiety for every person. A part is the residual anxiety written into the nervous system by the

---

[25] *The Meaning of Anxiety,* Ronald Press, 1950, p. 191.

[26] Cf. Tweedie, *The Significance of Dread in the Thought of Kierkegaard and Heidegger* (unpublished doctoral dissertation), Boston University, 1954.

[27] "Basic Anxiety and Adamic Motivation," *Journal of the American Scientific Affiliation,* vol. 2, no. 3, September 1950, p. 2.

events of his past life. Another part is the by-product of day-to-day living, as heat is generated by friction in a machine. Anxiety accrues for the Christian when ventures are taken in the name of faith, as when a chastened Saul made himself available on the Damascus road for a life-time of uncertainty and hardship. Anxiety accrues when compassion outruns one's reach, as when John Knox cried, 'Give me Scotland or I die.' Anxiety accrues in a world where there is perpetual tension between the holiness of God and the selfishness of man, and realization is always short of aspiration.... Such anxiety is creative and leads to growth.... thus Christian faith, far from being a ticket to security, as Freud and Marx both contended, has always produced insecurity.... Mature Christian faith offers courage to master the anxiety of spiritual emptiness, of moral guilt and even the anxiety of fate and death in an era of atomic threat. But faith also generates an anxiety of discontent that has moved and continues to move a daring and creative minority in a world that is largely preoccupied with a search for security."[28] In spite of this rather optimistic assessment of anxiety, analysis of the anxiety experience reveals the seeds of paralysis rather than of progress. Paul himself advised us to be anxious for nothing, while Christ preached that peace and security came through Him. Fear and trembling may point up a crisis situation, but only hope and confidence can resolve it.

Robert White in his classic text in abnormal psychology, *The Abnormal Personality,*[29] uses the concept of anxiety as the basic causal factor in psychopathology. The increase of anxiety is an increase of disintegrating stress and pathological pressures. The circumstances which will stimulate anxiety are relative to the personality development of the individual and his genetic in-

---

[28] "Christian Faith in an Age of Anxiety," *Christian Century,* September 20, 1958.
[29] Ronald Press, 1956 (2nd. ed.)

heritance. Whether anxiety is the exclusive pathological agent in functional disorders is another matter.

GUILT

Another pervasive and universal human experience is that of guilt. It has the same crippling effect as anxiety and has always been considered a factor in psychopathology. "There is no worse suffering than a guilty conscience, and certainly none more harmful. It has not only psychological effects — it acts as a clog upon vitality, and has far-reaching repercussions on general health."[30] "Guilt is fundamental to almost every problem of the human personality; it begets anxiety, is manifested in the inferiority complex and follows resentment. Any counseling — whether it is religious or secular — that is going to succeed in helping people with their problems must know what to do with the problem of guilt."[31] "A sense of guilt has a peculiarly damaging effect upon the personality. It may best be described as a wound. Guilt cuts deeply into the emotional and spiritual nature. At first this personality cut may not cause suffering and one may feel that 'he has got away with it.' However, if, like the history of some physical diseases, the development is slow, nevertheless the time comes when this guilt malady begins to cause trouble; all of a sudden it may 'break out'. . . . Guilt is an unclean wound. Sorrow, for example, is a clean wound. It pains deeply but being clean the wound heals according to the process of nature. . . . Guilt festers and becomes an infection center; as in the body, so in the mind and the spirit."[32] "It is a fact that the psyche is much less indulgent to unconscious breaches of its own laws and demands (which also are an expression of the 'eternal law' of God) than is the instructed confessor; it will re-

[30] Paul Tournier, *A Doctor's Casebook in the Light of the Bible*, Harpers, 1950, p. 210.
[31] C. T. Hulme, *Counseling and Theology*, Muhlenberg Press, 1956, p. 156.
[32] N. V. Peale, *A Guide to Confident Living*, Prentice-Hall, 1948, p. 37.

venge itself for their disregard no less than will the stomach
for the consumption of indigestible food stuffs, whether that
consumption be conscious and deliberate or ignorant and com-
pelled. For the psyche has its own pattern and laws of origin
and growth of functional compensation and order, which cannot be flouted without producing psychopathological symptoms,
of which the guilt-sense is the most common."[33]

Whereas anxiety is a dread of the future, guilt is a dread of
the past. In the former the wrong decision might be made, in
the latter the despair is based upon the fact that the wrong decision has already been made. The clock of reality cannot be
turned back, and there is no undoing of the deed.

Freud posited guilt as not being due to a violation of the eternal moral law of God, but rather to the superego. This personality component, originating from the restraints and con-
demnations of authority figures in the life of a child, tends to be
oppressive if the social environment was too condemning. Christians tend to waver between this naturalistic concept and the
Biblical concept of guilt as a result of sin against the moral law
of God. The resultant is the difficult eclectic idea that guilt is
either false, coming from the superego, built up by the traditions of the elders, or true, coming from a violation of God's
law. The former is neurotic guilt and is to be analyzed away,
while the latter must be dealt with theologically. One is potential
sickness, the other is sin. One calls for the psychotherapist, the
other for the pastor. A complicating factor enters, however, when
one tries to separate the two kinds of guilt. "It is absolutely impossible by intellectual processes to separate that of which we
are the victims from that for which we are to blame. It is not a
matter of analysis; it is beyond all analysis."[34]

A surprising voice in the affirmation of guilt as a psycho-

---

[33] Victor White, "Guilt: Theological and Psychological," *Christian Essays
in Psychiatry* (ed. by P. Mairet), Philosophical Library, p. 165.

[34] Tournier, *A Doctor's Casebook in the Light of the Bible,* p. 190.

pathological force is that of O. H. Mowrer, internationally known leader in the field of psychology and much more noted for his behavioristic studies of learning theory than for a theoretical foray into the existential realm of sin and guilt. Mowrer sees the difficulty of the dichotomy of guilt into false and true guilt not so much in the inextricability of neurotic and true guilt, but rather in the conviction that the former is not a fact at all. False guilt is a fantasy of Freud! The mentally ill person in the view of Mowrer has a problem of guilt not because he is sinned against, but rather because he is a sinner. "The Freudians, of course, recognize that guilt is central to neurosis, but it is always a guilt of the *future*. It is not what a person has *done* that makes him 'ill' but rather what he *wishes* to do but dares not. In contrast, the emerging alternative — or, more accurately, the re-emerging one — is that the so-called neurotic is a *bona fide* sinner, that his guilt is from the past and real, and that his difficulties arise not from *inhibitions* but from actions which are clearly proscribed, socially and morally, and which have been kept carefully concealed, unconfessed, and unredeemed."[35]

To a lesser degree this "guilt theory" of mental illness has been posited by at least some Christians for generations. There is a recurring conviction that the Biblical emphasis upon sin and guilt as crucial in human problems must be realistically considered. Closing one's eyes to the potentially significant data is unjustifiable, even if done in the name of science. The following pair of citations reflect the attitudes of many Christians professionally involved in the mental health problem. "A sense of guilt plays a surprisingly large part in the mental life of many people suffering from mental ill-health."[36] "When the counselor reaches the bases of varied neuroses of the human personality he usually finds the presence of guilt.... The feeling of guilt may

---

[35] *The Crisis in Psychiatry and Religion*, p. 126.

[36] E. White, "Spiritual Factors in Mental Disorders," *Journal of the Transactions of the Victoria Institute*, LXXI, no. 49, p. 112.

be focused upon one particular area of life and be known as the guilty conscience; it may also spread itself thinly over life as a whole and be known as the inferiority complex. Inwardly we know that we have failed to live up to expectations — our own, other people's, and ultimately God's. We also know both from internal and external witness that we live in a moral world and that there are consequences of our failures."[37]

SIN AND PSYCHOPATHOLOGY

Since the concept of sin is so central to Christian teachings and Biblical doctrine, it is of paramount importance for our study that we carefully consider its relationship to mental health. One great theme of the Christian evangel has been its proclamation of the cure for sin. If in some way this involves a cure for psychopathology, then it certainly should be fully investigated. E. White points up this crucial relationship in the following quotation: "We see then that guilt is a widespread and deeply rooted emotion, producing much discomfort and anxiety. Although psychiatry may be of great assistance in modifying or removing abnormal or pathological guilt, it does not, in my judgment provide a final answer and satisfactory solution. Christianity, and Christianity alone, provides a complete answer to this problem."[38]

Inasmuch as Mowrer's thesis is the focal point of our discussion, it will be well to reiterate it in his own words. "In psychopathology the trouble arises, not from what is being repressed, but rather from what, in the form of a wrathful conscience, is being expressed. *Past* disregard, denial, or 'repression' of conscience may, to be sure, account for the present outbreak or 'attack'; but the very presence of disturbance means that the repression has broken down. And the psychotherapeutic task, it

---

[37] Hulme, *Counseling and Theology*, pp. 175-6.
[38] "Guilt," *His*, April 1959, p. 9.

would seem, is much less the releasing of the repressed than of helping the individual to *understand* what is happening to him and how he can help make the final outcome constructive rather than destructive."[39] There are those who believe that Mowrer is entirely unrealistic and cite the fact that many people live in gross violation of social and personal morality and are not psychologically ill. Mowrer does not make the error of fallaciously converting his 'A' proposition: All psychopathology is (due to) sin, to the generalization that: All sin is psychopathology; however, for he carefully points out that only particular kinds of moral lapses are necessarily psychologically negative. "Personal sin occurs, as I see it, and sows the seed of psychological destruction when and only when the individual violates a social injunction or regulation but *pretends that he has not.*"[40] Victor White, a Roman priest-psychotherapist, expresses this same point: "Indeed, it may happen that while external nonconformity with accepted morality brings no accompanying moral anxiety, external conformity with it may bring serious breakdown with strong guilt-sense."[41]

The reaction to Mowrer from his erstwhile theoretical colleagues (behavioristically and psychoanalytically oriented psychologists) has been sudden and sharp. His symposium on "Sin as a Concept in Psychopathology" at the annual meeting of the American Psychological Association in Cincinnati in 1958 raised a furore and made *Time* magazine.[42] This was followed by "Sin, the Lesser of Two Evils" in the *American Psychologist*,[43] the basic journal of the American Psychological Association in which Mowrer set forth the challenge of disinterring sin from the graveyard of liberal theology and ancient psychology, and re-

---

[39] *The Crisis in Psychiatry and Religion,* p. 35.
[40] *Ibid.,* p. 147.
[41] "Guilt: Theological and Psychological," p. 164.
[42] Sept. 14, 1959, p. 35.
[43] Vol. 15, No. 5, pp. 301-304.

establishing it as a meaningful psychological concept. He argued
that this is necessary on both theoretical and empirical grounds.
Typical of the reaction, though perhaps a trifle extreme, is that
of Albert Ellis. "If, in this thoroughly objective, non-guilty manner, we can teach our patients (as well as the billions of people
in the world who, for better or for worse, will never become patients) that even though human beings can be held quite ac-
countable or responsible for their misdeeds, no one is ever to
blame for anything, human morality, I am sure, will be significantly improved and for the first time in human history
civilized people will have a real possibility of achieving sound
mental health. The concept of sin is the direct and indirect
cause of virtually all neurotic disturbance. The sooner psychotherapists forthrightly begin to attack it the better their patients
will be."[44] Here is an interesting turn of events! Instead of sin
being the basis of psychopathology, *the belief that this is true* is
the basis for psychopathology.

There is some support for Mowrer, both in the present and in
the past. Shoben[45] attempts to modify the brunt of the attack
in an article accompanying Ellis' and to set the hypothesis as one
to be empirically supported or dropped. Some of Mowrer's associates at the University of Illinois [46] have presented experimental confirmation of his thesis. In addition, there are important prior writings from which Mowrer claims to have
gained insight, though he learned of these after he had inde-
pendently arrived at his conclusions. He is particularly impressed
with Anton Boisen, a rather humanistically oriented theologian

[44] "There Is No Place for the Concept of Sin in Psychotherapy," *Journal of Counseling Psychology*, vol. 7, no. 3, 1960, p. 192.

[45] "Sin and Guilt in Psychotherapy: Some Research Implications," *Journal of Counseling Psychology*, vol. 7, no. 3, 1960, p. 198.

[46] D. G. Peterson, "The Insecure Child Over-socialized or Under-socialized?" Cf. also C. H. Swenson, "Sexual Behavior and Psychopathology: A test of Mowrer's Hypothesis" (1962 — to be published) and P. L. Berger, *Verification of Two Theories of Neurotic Anxiety: Freud vs. Mowrer*, University of Missouri, 1962.

who has been a primary mover in the movement for clinical training for ministers and institutional chaplains. Says Boisen, "Psychological conflict, even in its schizophrenic manifestations, has religious significance."[47] Orville Walters, a Christian psychiatrist who is in charge of student health services on the same campus at which Mowrer serves, also gives some historical support. "Stekel, a pupil of Freud's, called neurosis 'the disease of a bad conscience' and believed that the remedy lay not in relaxing the demands of conscience but in restoring ethical ideals. Pfister, a Swiss clergyman, and one of the early pupils of Freud, believed that restoring the voice of conscience was a most important step in treating neurosis. O. H. Mowrer, of this campus, has convincingly elaborated this theory of neurosis."[48]

Many Christian therapists, who have an essential interest in, and commitment to, the theme of sin and redemption, do not see such a theory as Mowrer's as a light breaking through the darkness. Vander Linde, before Mowrer aired his views, spoke rather sharply in an article in the *Gordon Review* against the point of view that sin is the basis of psychopathology. "Those who see faith as the complete answer to the achieving of mental health often have as a basic assumption the equation: illness equals sin. Thus, in the case of maladjustment or more severe mental problems such people attribute the cause to bad thinking or bad feelings, which are regarded as sinful processes... while mental illness may be a part of the consequences of sin, each individual case is certainly not to be attributed to a particular sin of the people in question. Jesus took the trouble in His day to correct the people concerning the naivete and oversimplification involved in such an idea. The psychological tendency in all of us to consider any illness, misfortune or unpleasant

[47] "Religious Experience and Psychological Conflict," *American Psychologist*, vol. 13, no. 10, October 1958, p. 568. See also *Exploration of the Inner World*, Harpers, 1962.

[48] "Christian Faith in an Age of Anxiety," Radio Lecture at the University of Illinois, September 13, 1958.

event as a punishment is an easily observed phenomenon. Such attitudes are emphasized in the training of children, especially in the homes of the more pious. But, if the relationship were such a direct chain of cause and effect, then obviously the more seriously ill would be those with the greatest sin or least faith. On a common sense level we would and do reject this notion as absurd or nonsense."[49] It may be noted, parenthetically, that Vander Linde does not avoid the fallacy of illicit conversion (as Mowrer does) in moving from the thesis that: "Illness equals sin" to his concluding remarks.

Another Christian psychologist says of Mowrer, "his reaction to Freud's psychologism carries Mowrer to an exclusively moralistic evaluation of mental illness, which I think will turn out theoretically as well as practically to be untenable."[50]

Many who hold to the Biblical authority would see weight in Mowrer's hypothesis but would hesitate to go all the way. They do not want to commit themselves to accepting sin as an exclusive cause for psychopathology though they readily admit a frequent causal relationship. The last of the following supporting quotations, in particular, graphically portrays emotional symptoms as foolish attempts at self-atonement for sin. "Repression of conscience, as well as repression of sexuality, engenders a disturbance in the person. In an endogenous depression guilt feelings and delusions of sin can arise, but conversely we are acquainted with depressions which arise from a realistic guilt."[51] "Twenty years of study and nearly that time in actual treatment of psycho-neuroses have convinced us that we shall not make progress in the treatment of mental conflicts until we have taken full cognizance of the fact that there is a factor involved in all

49 "Christian Faith and Mental Health," *Gordon Review*, September 1956, p. 100-1.

50 R. J. Bijkerk, "Reactions of a Psychologist," *Proceedings of the Christian Association for Psychological Studies*, 1960, p. 27.

51 J. Kingma, *Proceedings of the Christian Association for Psychological Studies*, 1956, p. 13.

conflict in the moral and spiritual spheres."[52] "A bad conscience can, over a period of years, so strangle a person's life that his physical and psychical powers of resistance are thereby impaired. It can be the root cause of certain psychosomatic affections. It is like a stopper which can be pulled out by confession, so that life begins at once to flow again."[53] "Many of the symptoms of neuroses and psychoses are attempts to satisfy the demand of conscience for atonement. Though the animal sacrifice was primitive it was a far more therapeutic form of atonement than our modern forms of self-atonement. There are people who because of feelings of unworthiness are subconsciously bringing on their own failures; others who are torturing themselves with anxieties and worries; others who enslave themselves to a rigid and compulsive pattern of self-denial, not for any altruistic purpose but to obtain a semblance of mental peace. In all these forms of self-atonement — often stimulated by a pusillanimous religion — there is a self-inflicted suffering which becomes meritorious in balancing the budget of just desserts. They are, figuratively speaking, crosses which these individuals erect for themselves on which they can regulate their suffering to the extent that they can tolerate their right to existence. The doctrine of justification is the glad tidings to these sufferers that atonement has been made and that God accepts them as they are. When an individual is convinced that God accepts him as he is, he is encouraged to accept himself. Those whose consciences demand punishment can see that justice has been satisfied: the love of God is demonstrated in sacrifice and in suffering."[54]

Unfortunately, Mowrer repudiates the latter part of Hulme's statement as "cheap grace" and pursues his research in the hope of establishing self-atonement as the answer to the psycho-

---

[52] McKenzie, *Psychology, Psychotherapy, and Evangelicalism*, p. 15.
[53] Tournier, *The Meaning of Persons*, p. 15.
[54] Hulme, *Counseling and Theology*, p. 158.

pathological effects of sin. Even the Christians who are influenced by Mowrer's theory, will repudiate his hope for a humanistic resolution of the problem of sin. The evening on which I received his controversial monograph, *The Crisis in Psychiatry and Religion,* was spent in a high level of interest, reading it until the not so wee hours of the morning. The stimulus for the first half of the book was a positive interest, bordering on enthusiasm, for his historical critique and constructive hypothesis of the cause for mental illness — a realistic view of sin in human behavior; the last half maintained the stimulus level of intensity but rather from acute disappointment as to the projected solution to the problem. I suppose, among Christians, that my reaction was not unique.

Anyone who has been psychotherapeutically related to persons suffering from mental illness needs no convincing that at the root of every problem lies a significant amount of sinful action. The anxiety and guilt which have disorganized the personality are results of decisions and actions which were made for selfish goals. Usually this is the irresponsible action of the sufferer; sometimes he is more victim than villain. In every case, sin is at the door. Every emotional problem is a spiritual problem. Problems can always be projected into secondary components such as the physical, emotional, and intellectual dimensions, or to the environment; but resolution of them comes only when personal responsibility is borne. This is a hard saying, but I believe that progress in mental health will be proportional to the number who can hear it.

CONCLUSION

Mental illness arises from a disruption in the process of personal growth and personality development. It is a disintegration of personal unity. This conflict state is characterized by feelings of threat and the reaction to the threatening situation either by fearful withdrawal or angry attack. The degrees of mental and emotional disorder are not clearly defined but are best conceived as points on a gradual continuum ranging from confident adjustment to life's challenges in good health to the total disorganization and withdrawal in the state of extreme illness. We have discussed the individual's resistance to disintegration in terms of lines of defense: defense mechanisms, neuroses, psychoses, and psychopathic character disorders. These defenses are essentially negative and self-defeating for they generate further defensive needs. The symptoms revealed in these defensive adjustments are expressions of the underlying causal forces which motivate the negative trend to mental illnees. A great deal of research has been undertaken to identify these etiological, or casual, factors. In organic illnesses they seem to be the reaction of the physical dimension of personality, the body, to the stresses of the physical enviroment. Since this is the only dimension with empirically verifiable attributes, many have generalized these casual components to the whole range of mental illness. In our view of personality, these are seen rather as the deterioration of the personality due to the breakdown of the vehicle of the spirit, not the exclusive causal factors of mental illness.

The functional disorders are those in which anxiety, the threat of the future, and guilt, the threat of the past, have broken down the positive functioning of the individual. There is both Biblical and empirical evidence to support the view that these can best be understood in terms of sin and its consequences in the executive function of the spiritual dimension of personality. If this be true, then it also involves the factor of personal responsibility which is necessary for the successful psychotherapeutic treatment of these disorders. If this be true, it is also a significant challenge for the Christian psychotherapist, for he alone has the insight and assets by which to redeem the wages of sin.

CHAPTER IV

PSYCHOTHERAPY OR CHRIST— TO WHOM SHALL WE GO?

Christianity and healing are essentially related. The term "salvation" itself is rooted in the concept of healing and making whole. Christ is often referred to as the Great Physician. These factors have a bearing upon our study in two ways. The first is the question as to whether any illness, physical or emotional, can, legitimately, be treated in any manner apart from the "the prayer of faith" in the light of the Biblical teaching. The second relates to the application of Christian faith to mental illness, especially if our analysis of the causes of functional disorders as being primarily anxiety and guilt is significant, as a psychotherapeutic measure.

The first item has been discussed to some extent in the first chapter. Perhaps it will be sufficient at this point to summarize my own attitudes to divine healing. They are somewhat as follows: God can heal any manner or mode of human defect; He is sovereign over His creation. He has done so in the past according to the Biblical records. He is apparently doing so in the present, according to reports from many sources — some

111

of them from men and institutions of indubitable integrity. I have witnessed no incidents where dramatic miraculous healing has taken place. God will presumably continue extraordinary works of grace in the lives of broken human beings, and has left a prescription for the prayerful request of such assistance (James 5). It is interesting to note that the historical denominations, as well as the so-called "fringe groups" of the church, are becoming intensely interested in the provisions of this Scriptural passage.

At the same time, there is a natural (though no less divine, and no less mysteriously marvelous) means of healing which has been made more efficient through such means of grace as modern medicine and psychological research. It is, in my opinion, gross presumption to ignore them. On the other hand, in the area of psychotherapy one must exercise special caution, for the changes in attitudes involved may have implications much farther reaching than the change of tissue in some physiological process.

The problem of the relationship of the Christian faith to psychotherapy will be the burden of this chapter. At first glance it seems to be as clear as the title of an unpublished manuscript written by P. B. Marquart, entitled *Psychotherapy or Christ?*[1]

This mimeographed pamphlet consists of a number of case studies reported by Marquart from his experiences as a military psychiatrist during World War II. He presents several instances of the futility of secular psychiatric procedures and, conversely, the healing force of Christianity in the life of the emotionally disordered individual. The symptoms are traced to sources of guilt and anxiety and then these roots are destroyed by the healing force of "grace through faith." "Psychology and psychiatry ought to be taught right out of the pages of the

---

[1] Wheaton College, Ill., no date given.

Bible — for there is a psychology there which needs to be gathered and worked up into a course of its own, separate from the rudiments of men."[2] The method of treatment is not unlike that of an evangelistic counselor — "I don't ever use the non-directive kind exclusively, because a Christian has to be directive in his method — at least in his ultimate objective. Whenever it becomes apparent that a man needs Christ, I insist on pointing him the Way."[3] There seems to be little doubt that Marquart chooses the second part of his title for his psychiatric approach.

This attitude is not exclusive to Marquart, though it is a distinct minority group among Christians professionally related to this field. Clyde Narramore seems to support this point of view in both his periodical *Psychology for Living*[4] and his recent volume, *The Psychology of Counseling*.[5]

Paul Adolph, in *Health Shall Spring Forth*, also evinces a similar point of view — "It is the author's conviction on the basis of experience that Christianity, conscientiously applied to the emotional tension problems of our era, offers complete and satisfactory solution, not only to these tensions, but also to the disease symptoms which they so often produce."[6]

The opposite tack is taken by N. L. Peterson, a Christian psychiatrist prominent in the Christian Association for Psychological Studies and the American Scientific Affiliation. He chooses the former horn of our mild dilemma and distinguishes psychiatric problems from spiritual or physical problems. For him, Christianity has no more bearing upon his psychiatric practice *per se* than does it have upon the practice of a plumber who is a Christian. "That we have a physical body which relates

---

[2] *Ibid.*, Foreword.
[3] *Ibid.*, p. 25.
[4] Published at Pasadena, Calif.
[5] Zondervan Publishing House, 1961.
[6] Moody Press, 1956, p. 11.

to a physical world is certainly a reality, and this part of us is the province of the physician. But that there is a corresponding component, the spirit, which must relate to God, is also reality. This is the minister's province. The sector of the spectrum between these two realities, the physical and the spiritual, is the sphere of the psychiatrist. There is so much to be done by these three professions that there should never be any conflict or competition."[7] Thus Peterson would change the title to *Psychotherapy and Christ,* but would tend to keep them in separate spheres. Paul Tournier would be somewhat adverse to this approach — "A human being is a unity, body-soul-spirit, with reference to somatic medicine, psychological medicine, and soul-healing. Medical science is, in my opinion, all three and it is only a doctrinaire prejudice to erect boundaries within this unity."[8] (One of the blessings of the Christian life was reinforced to me recently as Drs. Tournier, Peterson and I sat around a dinner table discussing these theoretical problems in an atmosphere and attitude of harmonious Christian fellowship.)

Runestam seems to support the viewpoint of the distinction between psychotherapy and Christianity, while providing a closer co-operation than Peterson apparently affords, and at the same time recommending caution. "One must bear in mind that just as analysis can prepare and otherwise set the stage for a richer spiritual life, just as easily can it set up insurmountable barriers against its coming into being. As a matter of course, this applies somewhat to spiritual ailments. The closer these approach the nature of religio-moral conflicts, the more indeed must one be cautioned against seeking to alleviate them by

---

[7] "Psychiatry and Christianity," *Christianity Today,* November 9, 1959, p. 10.

[8] *Krankheit and Lebensprobleme,* Benno Schwabe, Basel, 1941. (This and other quotations from German editions of Tournier's books were translated by me. My introduction to Tournier was through his German works and several of these citations were collected before I came in contact with the later English translations).

mental release of energy in terms of psychoanalysis. But where the conflicts have so completely eclipsed the soul that the sun rays of grace cannot penetrate the darkness, there a psychic preparatory function is needed."[9]

Rather than choosing either horn of the dilemma: psychotherapy *or* Christ (or in the case of Christians who choose the former, converting the phrase to psychotherapy *and* Christ), there is a *tertium quid,* a third viewpoint, which attempts to transcend the dilemma and, in the words of T. Jansma, to "Kill the Conjunctions."[10] He asserts that the situation calls not for a critical choice between psychotherapy and Christianity, or a questionable alliance of the two, but rather the application of a psychology which is basically Christian. "We are engaged in Christian Psychiatry, not pagan-rooted psychiatry. The person we treat is the image bearer of God. His functional sickness is related to the sickness of us all: our fundamental alienation from God, our proneness to hate God and our fellow man, the disintegration of the personal self, the tension of the fallen world of nature and man. We must be more bold, nay, more godly, in applying clinically what we profess creedally."[11] William Goulooze expresses a similar sentiment in his *Pastoral Psychology*: "We need to have the aid of psychology for an effective ministry, but it must be a psychology that will recognize the place of the Bible as God's revelation and the place of Christianity as God's work of redemption."[12] J. A. C. Murray also echoes such a thesis throughout his *Introduction to Christian Psychotherapy*: "Modern medical psychology can indeed unveil the shadow side of life, and explicate the complex, but

---

9 *Psychoanalysis and Christianity,* Muhlenberg Press, 1958 (rev. ed.), p. 170.

10 An address given at the 50th Anniversary of Bethesda Hospital, Denver, Colo., August 24, 1960.

11 *Ibid.*

12 Baker Book House, 1950, p. 86.

only a religious psychology can give meaning and unity to life, and explain man's deepest desires to himself."[13]

Only from such an approach as this, it seems to me, can we be realistic concerning an adequate view of man and mental illness. Only through a Hegelian-like synthesis of transmuting the data of psychology into a Christian world view can we avoid the subtle hypocrisy of divorcing belief and action in a psychological vocation, and the irony of offering the hungry stones instead of bread.

PSYCHOTHERAPISTS: THE NEW CLERGY

A widespread phenomenon in the twentieth century has been the transfer of pastoral functions to the psychotherapist. Personal problems and difficulties which formerly would have been discussed in the pastor's study are now the topics of psychiatric consultation. A recent article by C. Wallace and P. London in the *Christian Century* with the intriguing title: "Psychotherapists: the New Clergy" discusses this rather well established modern practice, coming to the following conclusion: "We do not wish to argue whether therapist or pastor is the more appropriate agent for such ministration, nor for that matter to assess where actual competence might lie . . . . Our purpose is rather to emphasize the fact that churchmen have been rather uncritical in their championing of the psychotherapeutic priesthood."[14]

It is true that some ministers have made psychotherapeutic referrals to avoid responsibility but more often it is due to a felt incompetence to deal with the problem. Occasionally catastrophes have given impetus to this movement. "One lesson we must draw from at least one of the tragedies (two prominent British churchmen had committed suicide) is that more often than we thought technical psychiatric treatment is indispens-

---

13 P. 8.
14 April 26, 1961, p. 516.

able. Earnestness in personal prayer, sacramental grace and counseling by richly experienced pastors—all, no doubt, have their place in the Christian cure for mental illness, but the Christian who believes that these means of grace leave little or nothing else to be desired lays himself open to disaster. Too often it is assumed that Christian faith renders it unnecessary, perhaps indeed disgraceful to turn to a psychiatrist for systematic treatment."[15]

McKenzie believes that modern psychology has taken the steps to research and to gain experience in areas where the minister had the theoretical equipment but did not think it a vocational obligation to carry it through. "We must confess that modern psychology and psychotherapy tell us no more about the incompatible motives that tear the human soul asunder than was already in the Scriptures for all to read; but we lacked the perceiving eye and the understanding mind and the believing heart. Modern psychology has elucidated how human motives work, how they become perverted, how they 'split' our personality into flesh warring against the spirit and spirit against the flesh. It has added no knowledge of new motives; albeit it has helped us tremendously to realize how motives in the unconscious may work their havoc in our spiritual life."[16]

Mowrer seems to see the inroads of the contemporary psychotherapist into human affairs as being mostly negative. He believes that this has transformed "sin" into "sickness," missed the point of diagnosis, and has engaged in making both individuals and society sicker. The following quotations will make clear his objections to the passing over of spiritual problems into the hands of secularists. This objection is of particular interest coming from a famous scientist hitherto identified with

15 D. L. Edwards, "The Twentieth Century Sickness," *Frontier*, Spring 1960, p. 38.
16 *Psychology, Psychotherapy, and Evangelicalism*, p. 218.

the secularist. "In the past we had, it seems, a sort of tacit understanding: the theologians would leave the question of facts to the scientists if the scientists would leave the question of values *to them*. This won't do, because it results in unconcerned scientists and uninformed theologians."[17] "Most pastoral counseling, as we know it today, therefore falls short, as does secular psychotherapy, of the crucial and ultimate step in the quest for salvation and personal wholeness. If one takes the neurotic's guilt seriously, that is, if (as now seems likely) 'neurosis' is just a medical euphemism for a 'state of sin' and social alienation, therapy must obviously go beyond mere 'counseling,' to self-disclosure, not just to a therapist or counselor, but to the 'significant others' in one's life, and *then* on to an active redemption in the sense of the patient's making every effort within his power to undo the evil for which he has previously been responsible."[18]

Most of Mowrer's criticism is devoted to the psychoanalytic movement, with which he is intimately familiar both theoretically and experientially. "Psychoanalysis as a movement is in trouble. Church attendance in this country, by contrast, is rapidly increasing, well beyond population growth. In other words, Freud's 'reality principle' appears to be doing less well than the 'illusion' with such an unpromising future. Perhaps Freud was still, in one sense, right; maybe he was only wrong in his estimate of man's growing capacity to live *without* illusion. Or, can it be that he himself misperceived 'reality.'"[19] "From testimony now available from both the friends and the foes of analysis, it is clear that, at best, analysis casts a spell but does not cure. By aligning himself with the patient's id, the analyst (devil?) may indeed succeed, as Bakan puts it, in *suspending* the superego; but the superego (or conscience), more

---

17 *Even There, Thy Hand* (unpublished manuscript), Urbana, Ill., p. 10.
18 *The Crisis in Psychiatry and Religion,* p. 108.
19 *Ibid.,* p. 10.

commonly than we might wish to believe, is a reflection of enduring social realities; and the advantage we gain by overcoming it in analysis is dearly paid for later, many times over. Man's salvation must surely come, not from his looking and moving *downward,* but from an *upward* reach, toward reconciliation and community, made by means of confession and manifest restitution."[20] "I don't know how often, when I have criticized psychoanalysis, the protest has come back: 'But isn't it true that the superego *is* overly severe in the neurotic individual and needs to be softened, made less harsh and demanding?' It is true that this is what Freud *said,* and a lot of people have tried to believe and apply this doctrine. But it is public knowledge that both therapy and prevention which are based on this premise lead only to the most dismal consequences; and one might suppose that it was time that we stopped, for purely pragmatic reasons, accepting the premise itself. If it doesn't *work,* what is there to make us think it is *true,* especially when it contradicts some of the most basic principles of the Judeo-Christian ethic?"[21]

Mowrer's negative criticism of contemporary psychotherapy is not exclusively reserved for Freud, however, and the approach of Carl Rogers gets some attention. "The non-directive or client-centered type of therapy which is associated with the name of Carl Rogers will, of course, be immediately thought of by many as 'non-Freudian.' But as I am using the term, I would say that Roger's approach is deeply 'Freudian.' Like classical psychoanalysis, it begins by not holding the individual personality responsible for his difficulties and gives him no prescription for dealing with them on his own initiative. Rogers views the individual as inherently good and holds that he is corrupted and diverted from his indigenous growth tendencies along normal and healthy lines by the untoward actions and

---

[20] *Ibid.,* pp. 121-2.
[21] *Ibid.,* p. 158.

attitudes of those around him. Here the encouragement of self-pitying and hostile tendencies within the client is hardly less direct than it is in psychoanalysis."[22]

Thus Mowrer sees the root of mental disorder to be in sin, and the person with the best potential for treating the problem as the pastor. The modern movement from the priest to the psychotherapist is motivated by the unwillingness of the patient to confess his responsibility and to reveal his sinful action, as well as the readiness of the minister to "pass the buck" of responsibility to the therapist, even though the latter undermines the principles which the minister professes to hold dear. Mowrer believes that the answer lies in a clinically trained ministry, whose clinical training is oriented to the application of a religious view of man. Evangelicals will, perhaps, tend to become enthusiastic about Mowrer's thesis, but they had better be cautious in judgment for they are held to be equal, or nearly so, in ineptitude along with the contemporary psychotherapist. Of the neurotic personality, Mowrer says, "What, now, can a person in such a predicament do to be 'saved'? It would appear that two equally misleading answers have been given to this question in our time. Protestant theology has preached a doctrine of 'justification by faith.' Place your *trust* in God and *believe* in Jesus Christ, we have been urged, and your sins will be immediately *forgiven*. And for those who prefer a 'scientific' rather than a 'religious' approach, there has been the doctrine of 'justification by insight.' In the latter approach, one comes to see that his sins are not real and that he doesn't really *need* forgiveness. It is hard to determine which of these doctrines has been the more pernicious."[23]

In any case, Mowrer's revolt against the "priesthood of the therapist" has a strong argument for a Christian psychotherapy in spite of the fact that he obviously repudiates such a per

---

22 *Ibid.*, pp. 164-5.
23 *Ibid.*, p. 232.

spective. It is clear, though unfortunate, that he does not know of the potential personal power that is inherent in the "cheap grace" of reformation theology. I challenged him at a luncheon discussion to make an empirical study of the redemptive values of the Christian faith in an evangelical rescue mission, such as the Pacific Garden Mission of Chicago. Here, if at all, would be a crucible in which his hypothesis might really be put to the test.

CHRISTIAN PSYCHOTHERAPISTS

We have asserted that it is not a matter of choosing between Christianity and psychotherapy to meet the pressing needs of mental health, nor is it to make an uneasy alliance between faith and secular psychology. A Biblically oriented psychology, a Christian psychotherapy, appears to be the theoretical and practical answer. I would like to present three men who have attempted such a program and give the reader insight into their attitudes and aims.

1. Paul Tournier

Paul Tournier is a Swiss psychiatrist-internist who is well known through his practice, as a Bible teacher, and in his many writings. Three volumes recently translated and printed in this country by Harper's are: *The Meaning of Persons, A Doctor's Casebook in the Light of the Bible,* and *Guilt and Grace.* They reflect a warm Christian approach to personal problems, Biblically based and carried out with no artificial dichotomy as to the roles of a therapist and a Christian. In short, an attempt to formulate a Christian psychotherapy.

"The analysts really practice soul-healing when they bring more clearly to the attention of a person the past events which influence his psyche, the drives of impurity and self seeking, which are basic to their therapy; for they help him to be more honest with himself. Therein consists, from my standpoint, the secret of their successful treatment. For to help a man to be more honest with himself is to bring him nearer to God."[24] "To treat the sick person and not the sickness is to help our patients solve their life problems. This solution lies, for the most part, in the spiritual sphere."[25] I have sometimes been accused of not recognizing the frontier between these two (psychotherapy and soul-healing), and of being in danger of confusing them. It seems to me that the real danger is that of mixing them without realizing it, and not in intermingling them openly and consciously as I do. For in practice all psychotherapists do intermingle them. The one who does not recognize the frontier is in fact one who sincerely believes himself to be still a psychotherapist, and who claims to confine himself to the scientific realm of psychology, when actually he has entered the field of soul-healing."[26]

"Every psychotherapist sooner or later goes beyond the strictly psychological sphere — even the Freudians, in spite of their principles. The recounting of a life story, a mind thinking aloud, freed from the bonds of formalism, leads one inevitably to the consideration of problems which are no longer psychological but spiritual problems such as the meaning of life and of the world, of desire and of death, of sin and of faith, or one's own scale of values."[27] "Further, I have a threefold vocation: medical, psychological and spiritual. It is bad enough to fall into a technical routine as a doctor or as a psychologist; it is much worse to turn soul-healing into a matter of routine. I confess that it is the spiritual vocation which interests me most, for the very reason that all my experience has taught me the limitations of medicine and psychology, and because the supreme

24 *Krankheit und Lebensprobleme*, p. 250.
25 *Ibid.*, p. 16.
26 "The Frontier Between Psychotherapy and Soul-Healing," *Journal of Psychotherapy as a Religious Process*, no. 1, January 1954.
27 *The Meaning of Persons*, p. 109.

and universal need of man is to find God."[28] "Soul-healing consists in putting men in touch with Christ."[29]

2. Ernest White

Ernest White, a British psychiatrist, has made a significant impact not only upon his patients, but also upon the Christian public through his various writings, especially *Christian Life and the Unconscious* (Harpers, 1957), and his function as the executive secretary of the Victoria Institute, a group of scientific men of Christian faith similar in composition to the American Scientific Affiliation mentioned in the first chapter. His reliance upon a Biblical foundation for his vocation as well as in his personal life seems to identify him as a Christian psychotherapist rather than a Christian who is a psychotherapist.

"The experience nearest to Christian conversion in its effect on life and character which I myself have observed is the striking change which sometimes occurs in people as the result of psychotherapy. It is really remarkable to see the liberation which follows treatment in some cases. People are literally transformed in character and outlook. But however great and radical the change, psychotherapy does not create saints. Christian conversion is, in essence, turning to God. Psychotherapy, as such, knows nothing of this, and neither does nor can effect it. It may enable a patient to adjust himself successfully to the main tasks of life on a material plane, but it cannot from its very nature, satisfy the deeper spiritual needs of the questing spirit. The non-Christian psychiatrist may lead his patients along the road to health and enable them to lose their neurotic symptoms, but cannot deal with the sick and hungry spirit."[30]

"No one who has intimate dealings with men and women such as occur in psychological analysis can fail to discover the

[28] *Ibid.,* p. 37.
[29] *Krankheit und Lebensprobleme,* p. 232.
[30] P. 60.

THE CHRISTIAN AND THE COUCH

important part played by religious questions in the minds of those who consult him. Spiritual factors, that is, factors concerned with morals and religion, and ultimately with a man's relationship to God, must be taken into consideration if we are to deal adequately with any individual who is sick in mind."[31] "We are all sinners in one way or another, and it is not the function of a psychologist either to condemn or to absolve the sinner. His purpose is to seek to understand the sinner, and to show him the path to a better way of life."[32]

3. Orville Walters

An American psychiatrist who shares the same campus with Mowrer (University of Illinois), but also shares the convictions of a Christian psychotherapist is Orville Walters. He is a frequent conference speaker and has published numerous significant articles which support and promote this point of view. To have a man of such sterling character and with clear Christian convictions in charge of student health services at a major American university is, perhaps, a harbinger of good tidings to our culture which usually manifests rather grim evidence of moral decay.

"To ignore or minimize the field of metaphysical concern in favor of sexual conflict or any other predetermined framework may leave untouched the most important cause of difficulty . . . . The frequent concern of the religious-minded patient and his family over the therapist's attitude toward religion is not without relevance. The naturalistic orientation not only includes certain beliefs, but excludes others."[33] "Ethical neutrality is an abstraction that does not exist in fact. Every man has his

[31] "Spiritual Factors in Mental Disorders," *Journal of the Transactions of the Victoria Institute*, 1949, p. 109.

[32] *Christian Life and the Unconscious*, p. 152.

[33] "Metaphysics, Religion, and Psychotherapy," *Journal of Counseling Psychology*, vol. 5, no. 4, 1958, pp. 249-50.

own hierarchy of values and in the process of psychotherapy, where understanding of deep motivation is sought and where issues of ultimate consequence are faced, the value systems of both therapist and patient are inevitably implicated. When the psychiatrist offers to pit his professional knowledge, skill, and time against the patient's illness for a fee, his activity is no longer heuristic, but therapeutic. He may try to preserve the objectivity of a scientist, but he now has an interest in the outcome."[34] "The hidden hungers of the human spirit can never be satisfied by psychotherapy as long as it tries to maintain ethical neutrality. The stability that Freud and others have observed in Christian people can never be fully understood in scientific terms."[35]

"But even psychotherapy cannot bring peace of mind until there is first peace of soul. As Gordon Allport has asked, 'Can a person ever really attain integration until he has signed and sealed a treaty of peace with the cosmos? Religion and experience both answer, No."[36] "Jung is neither correct nor realistic when he says, 'We cannot expect the doctor to have anything to say about the ultimate questions of the soul. It is from the clergyman, not the doctor, that the sufferer should expect much help.' The statement is unrealistic because there are few psychiatrists who do not directly or indirectly influence their parents' choice of life philosophy . . . . Jung's pronouncement is wrong because it is inconsistent with the Protestant tenet that every man is a priest. Theology may have its technical aspects, just as medicine does, which would make unwise any indiscriminate trespass upon another's professional field. There is no such restriction upon the essentials of victorious Christian

---

[34] "The Psychiatrist and the Christian Faith."

[35] "Faith: a Built-In Psychotherapy," *Christian Herald*, January, 1959.

[36] Christian Faith in an Age of Anxiety," A radio lecture, University of Illinois, September 20, 1958.

living, which the wayfaring man may share and to which he may bear glad witness."[37]

These three men set forth lucidly, both from an experiential understanding of the Scriptures and a wealth of practical psychotherapeutic experience, the conviction that a Christian psychotherapy is the answer to the question of relating Christianity and psychotherapy, and to the needs of modern man in his illness.

"CHRISTIAN" PSYCHOTHERAPY

There are many who would object to using the term "Christian" as an adjectival modifier for psychotherapy, on the grounds that it leads to the reduction of this science to an absurdity.[38] This would imply that there is a special kind of procedure that a Christian should employ for every action; Christian surgery, Christian transfusions, Christian anesthesia, etc. It also leads to the inference that there is a Buddhist psychotherapy, a Mohammedan psychotherapy, and a Roman Catholic psychotherapy, etc.

If this be absurd, then I suppose that we must make the most of it, for it is certainly to the point. This radical approach is a central component of Christianity. Christianity is radical; it penetrates to the *radix*, or root, of everything. It maintains that the God and Father of Jesus Christ is the sovereign Creator and Controller of heaven and earth. Therefore, no vocation or vocational art is exempt from His jurisdiction. Every hypothesis and each instance of hypothesis testing flows from a basic philosophy of life. Each scientific observation is affected by the subjective experience and frame of reference of the observer. Each subject taught is modified by the philosophical perspective, whether conscious or unconscious, of the teacher. Every field

---

37 "Spiritual Malpractice," *Action*, May 1, 1954, p. 8.

38 Cf. T. Jansma, "Christian Psychotherapy," *Christianity Today*, June 20, 1960, pp. 9-10, for a discussion of this point.

of science is relative to the philosophical foundation of the one
who articulates the field. We must be careful that we do not let
"science" become a sacred cow; as every scientist knows well,
the absolute certainty of his discipline exists only in the mind
of the layman.

Objectivity and stability in the world is in Christ, according
to the Christian *Weltanschauung,* or world view, and this
implies the validity of using the term, Christian psychotherapy.
Inasmuch as every datum finds its significance in the personal
values of the observer, the term Christian psychotherapy is not
only not absurd, but a direct implication, if Christ really is the
Way, the Truth, and the Life.

I do not wish to argue further for the non-existence of
scientific neutrality. The philosophical apologetic for such a
viewpoint is easy to discover. The works of Cornelius Van Til,
Edward John Carnell and Gordon Clark are profound analyses
of this point from the perspective of evangelical Christianity.
Non-Christian sources which support this argument also abound.
Just yesterday I was reading a fascinating and convincing book[39]
by an experimental psychologist and psychiatrist, Erwin Straus,
which completely undercuts the myth of complete objectivity
and the fallacy of positivism which prevails in the behavioral
sciences today.

It is, of course, not only non-Christians who would oppose
the concept of "Christian Psychotherapy," for there are many
evangelicals who maintain the validity of scientific neutrality.
S. Norborg, in his interesting answer to William James' classic
work, *The Varieties of Religious Experience,* strongly supported
this—"We are not seeking any 'Christian' psychology. Psych-
logy is psychology just as geology is geology or medicine is
medicine. Psychology can never become 'Christian' or 'Bud-
dhistic' or 'Mohammedan,' as long as we cling to an objective,

---

[39] *Vom Sinn der Sinne,* Springer Verlag, 1956.

scientific conception of psychology."[40] The evidence underlying the following comment from Runestam, a contemporary of Norborg, points out what I believe to be the dubious vantage point upon which Norborg would encourage us to cling —"Christian theology has its own psychology, and it own conception of man's essence and basic constitution. Psychoanalysis and Christianity: this is not only psychology versus theology; it is also *psychology versus psychology*."[41] Christian psychotherapy is not merely a possibility, but rather a necessity if there is validity to the reality presented in the Scriptures.

PSYCHOTHERAPY AND VALUES

This myth of neutralism and objectivity has been a common belief of psychotherapists. The purpose has been to elevate their art to the lofty plane of science, understood as an objective description of physical processes, and to avoid any hint of value judgments with their patients. To the uninitiated, who is not aware of the surging drive for scientific status in this field, this seems to be a strange situation, for nothing would seem more obvious than that the individual with a mental disorder is having a serious value problem. His value system, his ethical ideals, his moral standards and his world view are all involved in his personal problem and threaten to totter and fall. As we have previously mentioned, there is much evidence to suppose that an unstable set of values is the root of his illness.

There are many psychologists who are recognizing the necessity of a changing attitude to the whole concept of values in psychotherapy. The recognition that value neutrality is an impossibility, and that value change in the life of the person is a positive goal, is becoming increasingly defended in the literature. "The therapist, whatever his pretenses, is not ex-

---

[40] Augsburg Publishing House, 1937, p. 9.
[41] *Psychoanalysis and Christianity*, Muhlenberg Press, 1958 (rev. ed.), p. 7.

clusively a scientist — in practice he is an active moral agent."[42] "There are other psychologists, however, who feel that this quest for objectivity represents a spurious goal, that there is no such thing as a psychotherapy unconcerned with values — only one that is *blind* to them, that we need to be aware of our own values and the role they play in the therapeutic work. As Sol Ginsburg has pointed out 'in the last analysis, adjustment is a name for the process of living up to a set of values.' "[43]

"An amoral therapy is a contradiction in terms. What therapist of any school is prepared to accept with complacence the decision of an alcoholic patient to go back to the bottle, of a male homosexual to seduce a small nephew, or of the apocryphal Rogerian patient to jump out of a skyscraper window?"[44] "In helping the patient to reformulate his personal philosophy, the therapist encourages him to think of other postulates that he could substitute for his unfunctional ones, and to discover new ways of thinking and acting to sustain his new, more functional philosophy. This must grow out of his own unique personality and experiences rather than being imposed upon him by the therapist. If the patient cannot be encouraged to take the lead in reformulating his personal philosophy, the therapist makes suggestions, but keeps these to the minimum necessary to stimulate the patient."[45]

Likewise does the Christian psychotherapist have a specific set of values which can give meaning to living and dying. It is folly to try to carry out an interview in an atmosphere of value neutrality or complete scientific objectivity; it is double folly for

[42] C. Wallace and P. London, "Psychotherapists: the New Clergy," *Christian Century*, April 26, 1961, p. 516.

[43] H. Feifel, "Symposium on the Relationship between Religion and Mental Health," *American Psychologist*, vol. 13, no. 10, October 1958, p. 566.

[44] G. Watson, "Moral Issues in Psychotherapy," *American Psychologist*, vol. 13, no. 10, October 1958, p. 575.

[45] D. Lynn, "Personal Philosophies in Psychotherapy," *Journal of Individual Psychology*, vol. 17, no. 1, May 1961, p. 53.

the Christian to try so hard to do so that he manifests a subtle secularism which is foreign to his faith. This is just what the attempt to relate to others without significant values is, a secular and vain value.

Thus a Christian psychotherapy embodies a positive set of values as well as the cure for the great disvalue, sin, so prominent in the lives of all of us, particularly in the problems of the emotionally disturbed. Here lies the solution to the negative stimulus directing the hapless down the road to mental illness and the positive power that can redirect and motivate him toward the goal of mental health. We would beguile ourselves if we supposed that the whole psychotherapeutic movement is coming to this or a similar point, however, for there is a multitude, like Ellis, who think that such a trend would be catastrophic. "Because of these most serious disadvantages of giving individuals a serious sense of sin and because any deity-positing religion almost by necessity involves endowing those members who violate its god's laws with a distinct concept of blameworthiness or sin, I am inclined to reverse Voltaire's famous dictum and to say that, from a mental health standpoint, if there were a God it would be necessary to uninvent Him."[46] However the Christian therapist must have the courage of his convictions and stand firm in the authority of the Scriptures, and his personal experience of the power of Christian faith, in his diagnosis and prescription for those in distress and despair.

THE VALUE OF CHRISTIAN PSYCHOTHERAPY

Since our project was to survey the writings in the field of mental health of those who have a Biblically oriented point of view, it will, perhaps, be of interest and significance to present at this point some citations with reference to the validity and applicability of a Christian psychotherapy.

---

[46] A. Ellis, "There is no Place for the Concept of Sin in Psychotherapy," *Journal of Counseling Psychology*, vol. 7, no. 3, 1960, p. 191.

"We Christians have another unique criterion. We believe that a person must know and feel the proper relationship to his Divine Creator — this is both the first step as well as the epitome of mental health."[47] "Attempts to achieve this by self-atonement bring only a temporary acceptance which is broken anew by anxious doubts at each new outcropping of guilt. It is only an experience of justification by grace through faith that can sustain a relationship with the heavenly Parent in the face of repeated sin. It is this concept of justification or parental *agape*, that is conveyed in the revelation of God in Jesus Christ, and gives to this 'image of the invisible God' its dynamic for the release of the creative powers of personality that are blocked in conflict with their destructive counterparts."[48]

"To reawaken the psychopath to beauty, charity and holiness, and to show him those incarnate in a Person; to touch his maladjusted life to the finer issues of loving his neighbor and loving his God, are the unique prerogatives of a Christian psychotherapy, and it is high time that they were exercised."[49] "When the mind is blocked and warped, all its perceptions blunted, and its powers alienated and misused, we shall best make straight the way for the Gospel, if we first remove, by the new powers committed to our hand, the obstructions which thus hinder it. *We* do not heal, anymore than does the physician heal the body; it is the inscrutable *vis medicatrix Christi* for which we do but open up the way."[50] "We see that the Christian psychiatrist can make an important positive contribution in his chosen field by the application of the doctrine of the atonement in dealing with the problem of guilt reaction. With the knowledge of sin forgiven and with the assurance of salvation there comes a complete release of tension to the tortured soul. Anxiety

---

[47] J. Bauma, "Training People Involved in Promoting Mental Health," *Proceedings of the Christian Association for Psychological Studies*, 1955.

[48] Hulme, *Counseling and Theology*, p. 184.

[49] Murray, *An Introduction to Christian Psychotherapy*, p. 174.

[50] *Ibid.*, p. 176.

and fear are abolished and into the heart of man is born 'that peace which passeth all understanding' (Phil. 4:7). Then, and then only, is it possible to forget 'those things which are behind' and to reach forth 'unto those things which are before' (Phil. 3:13) in the Christian life. This is true mental hygiene."[51]

"We must, as Christian psychiatrists, help the patient to differentiate the so-called good Baals from Jehovah-God. We must strive to point out the need for dethroning Baal with all of his cohorts and humbly to enthrone Jehovah-God with saving grace. We must attempt to free the patient from the prostitution of his religo-psychological mechanisms and direct him to the use of these forces for his eternal welfare."[52] "While we do not doubt what pills and psychiatrists can do for mental illness, the only sure and lasting cure for psychosis is to be found in Paul's exhortation to bring every rebellious thought into captivity and subjection to Christ (II Cor. 10:5). When He is absolute Monarch of the entire life, the mind is at peace with God and with all around."[53]

These reports reflect the concern and activity of men knowledgeable in the field of psychotherapy and at the same time knowledgeable in the Christian faith. They reveal something of the potential of a psychotherapy integrated in Biblical truth. One should exercise care, however, not to make the hasty generalization that the psychotherapeutic task is easy, that a Christian psychotherapy is an automatic panacea for all problems, and that to be a therapist one needs to be armed with the "Sword of the Spirit." "Christians who suppose that neuroses are automatically cured in the new birth believe in a myth. I have observed deeply Christian and devoted pastors who were splitting

---

51 John Howitt, "The Guilt Reaction," *Journal of the American Scientific Affiliation*, vol. 3, no. 1, March 1951, p. 16.

52 Rooks, "The Place of the Christian Concept of Sin in the Theory and Practice of Psychiatry," p. 34.

53 H. Lockyer, "The Most Effective 'Mind Pill,'" *Evangelical Christian*, February 1957, p. 67.

their churches because of uncommon conflicts and neurotic trends which made them suspicious and hostile against the very souls they should have been helping. It is a fallacy to reduce all the ills of Christ's people to a few alleged causes in order to apply doctrines and warnings which may be harmful because they are positively irrelevant."[54] Perhaps some of these doctrines and warnings are more relevant than St. Clair thinks, but his admonishment is timely, for they are so frequently irrelevantly applied, minus the non-condemning love and therapeutic skill of the well-trained Christian psychotherapist. The next chapter will be occupied with the discussion of the role and responsibilities of the Christian psychotherapist, and the training requisite for him to fulfill them.

THE GOSPEL AS A TOOL

A frequently voiced objection, at least it has been frequently directed to me, is the fear that the concept of a Christian psychotherapy essentially contains the degradation of the gospel to a "tool," an instrument for the alleviation of personal problems. It is held that the Good News is rather the revelation of God, for His glory, an end in itself, and not to be used instrumentally for some other purpose. There may be technical subtleties involved that exceed my layman's grasp of systematic theology, but the divine disclosure in the prophecy of Isaiah — "The Spirit of the Lord God is upon me because the Lord hath anointed me to preach good tidings unto the meek; he hath sent me to bind up the broken hearted, to proclaim liberty to the captives, and the opening of prison to them that are bound ... to comfort all that mourn" (Isa. 61:1, 2), which is fulfilled in Christ (Luke 4:18, 19) — seems to blunt this objection. It is true that a therapist might have the motives of Simon the Sorcerer (Acts 8:18, 19) in his activities, and use the Christian faith as a basis for self-

---

[54] Robt. J. St. Clair, "Salvation Through Self-Realization," *Action*, June 1, 1957, p. 4.

glorification, but he would not, at least in this instance, be a Christian psychotherapist. The Christian psychotherapist is professionally committed to the diagnosis and treatment of mental and emotional disorders. He is unique in that his theoretical foundation for the understanding of man, and the goals of therapy, as well as much practical advice as to how to attain these goals, are rooted in the Biblical revelation. This in no way implies that he is perfect, that he has a perfect understanding of significant factors, or even that he is very successful in his vocation. It does imply, however, that he stands on a "firm foundation."

In addition to the possibly selfish motives of the therapist in a Biblically related therapy, there is always a possibility of devious motivation in the patient. There is the possibility that the neurotic person may develop neurotic religious adjustment. There is, of course, danger, and possibilities of foiled intentions, in every significant path of life — psychotherapy is least of all an exception. "Some Christians have an infantile conception of God. I do not mean to be derogatory. However, I do mean that their concept of God is a 'gimme' concept. They look for 'pie in the sky.' Whether it is an easier life here or hereafter that they want, their attitude is that God exists primarily to meet this need. Their faith in God is pure dependency and at least that is something. However, these people are psychologically vulnerable when disappointed."[55] However, the foregoing pretty much describes us all at times and it should be pointed out that Christ's gesture to the weary and troubled individual was an offer to make his burden light (Matt. 11:28). I do not know about pie in the sky, but the Bible does offer personal peace in the present life and eternal felicity with Christ in the next. I do not remember that an utter altruism was the condition for acceptance.

---

[55] McNeel, "The Relevance of Christianity of Life Adjustment," Lecture given at Emmanuel College, University of Toronto, n.d.

The God of the Christian psychotherapist is the God who can exercise sovereign grace over the motives and moments of both the therapist and the patient, the suffering one, and guide the outcome of therapy. "Only such a God can direct his sovereign imperative to men — 'My son, give me thy heart.' Man is made for self-surrender. This surrender involves his total self, and this totality experience of a complete surrender can truly be ours only if our God is great enough to compel such surrender. Such a surrender of the whole being to the sovereign God serves as a powerful restraint upon the development of those subtle, self-centered tricks that are involved in the forming of morbid mental states. For such a soul is laid bare in unqualified self-committal to the great God who looketh on the heart. God so conceived and so adored will hardly be used as a crutch in an abnormal religious adjustment, in which the self, failing to find satisfaction in some desired experience in life, seeks to make God a substitute for the consciously or unconsciously desired object. A truly sovereign God will not play second fiddle."[56]

SUMMARY

In the last chapter, anxiety and guilt were pointed out as two basic causal factors in functional, emotional disorders. Anxiety is the apprehension of the imminent disaster of the future; guilt the despair concerning the decisions of the past. A Christian psychotherapy alone can resolve these tensions at their foundation, for it alone can give confidence of the future — "In the world you shall have tribulation, but be of good cheer, for I have overcome the world"; forgiveness of the past — "sins removed as far as the East is from the West"; and hope and comfort for troubled souls in the present — "Come unto me all ye that labor and are heavy-laden and I will give you rest."

Whether this potential will be realized in our times to meet

---

[56] Heerema, "Christian Faith and Healthy Personality," pp. 25-6.

the need of mental health will depend upon the number of dedicated Christian men and women who develop the skills and experience requisite to deal with those who have slipped from the path along life's way unto the morass of mental and emotional despair.

In the light of the extent and nature of mental and emotional disturbances, the question was raised as to whether Christianity, or modern psychotherapy, is the indicated source of aid. Our conclusion was that neither this alternative choice, nor an uneasy alliance of the two was the answer, but rather a psychotherapeutic theory and method which is an outworking of Biblical truth, a Christian psychotherapy. Such a therapy would meet the basic needs of man and cut away at the very roots of mental illness. It would reassert the need of man to confront himself in his illness with honesty and responsibility, an approach which such a prominent psychologist as O. H. Mowrer deems secular psychology long since to have abandoned.

A radical therapy based upon the tenets of evangelical Christianity would certainly have difficulty in making inroads in a secular society, but several prominent persons in the field of clinical psychiatry and psychology are already successfully carrying out a vocation of Christian psychotherapy.

Values and value judgments are seen to be necessary and desirable in a psychotherapeutic relationship, in spite of the vain attempt of modern psychology to maintain a value neutrality. The Christian therapist forthrightly and unapologetically points the patient to those values by which he can live and die, and the means by which he can live again.

Such a program calls for trained personnel who are called of God. A discussion of such persons and their training will occupy us in the next chapter.

CHAPTER V

THE CHRISTIAN THERAPIST

CHRISTIAN VOCATION

There is a widespread secular belief that Christian vocation refers only to ministers and missionaries. Those Christians who are not called to such activities are left to find something for themselves to do, so that they can get subsistence for their families as well as make some contribution to the support of the "called Christian." Such an attitude is secular for there is no vocation that does not come under the sovereignty of God. Every life task should be directly related to the work of the Kingdom of Christ.

A part of my activity is in conjunction with a senior liberal arts college which has a basic Christian philosophy of education. A prominent businessman of my acquaintance who was invited to speak at chapel, queried me as to the nature of the school. He said that he had heard that many of the students were studying for other than church related careers, and that many secular subjects were taught. I replied that the first part of his statement was accurate, for a large variety of vocationally preparatory programs are offered, but that there was some misunderstanding about the latter for there are no secular subjects *per se.*

There are many secular attitudes which generate secular theories about specific subjects. A pastor may have a secular attitude concerning his work (I have several acquaintances who are secular ministers), while a truck driver may have a sacred vocation. It depends upon the commitment of one's life and the purpose of one's work.

Many evangelical Christians, whose sincere faith is undoubted and whose general helpfulness in the Christian community is hailed by all, miss a Christian vocation because they find no relevance between their work and the Christian faith. They see their tasks merely as means for economic support. Professional people are probably more culpable than most others in this respect. For a variety of reasons and mixed motives they have a tendency to be "vocational hypocrites." Psychologists are no exception.

There is a world of difference between the Christian who is a psychotherapist and the Christian psychotherapist. The latter have not only clarified their calling but also realize the power potential in dealing with men in the light of the Bible. If what God has said concerning the nature of man is true, then it should follow that what is revealed concerning the needs of man, and the resolution of these needs, must also be true. Fritz Kunkel gives a lucid account of the secularizing of the social sciences: "The prophets of the Old Testament were practical sociologists. Jesus of Nazareth was the greatest psychologist of all times. But the riches of traditions, accumulated in religious literature and art, were neglected, and theology made no attempt to fight. It gave in, ignoring for many years the new sciences as they in turn ignored theology. Later, however, the ministers began to realize that they needed more knowledge of the human mind, as well as of social relations. So they began to study the secular psychology and sociology as they found them—instead of creating their own Christian sociology and psychology and teaching their secular colleagues the deeper truth and the stronger power that was entrusted to Christianity from the beginning."[1] A belated rectification of this situation is one of the tasks of a Christian psychology.

THE REQUIREMENTS FOR A CHRISTIAN THERAPIST

The first requirement of a Christian psychologist is, of course, that he be a Christian. A personal experience of reconciling faith in Jesus Christ, being "born again," is a necessity. Unless he has found his own personal needs met, then he has little ground upon which to try to meet the needs of his client. The non-Christian therapist, especially the one who would attempt to apply Christian principles in his work, is a blind leader of the blind. There is little to protect the both of them from falling into the ditch. It is like a non-swimmer who jumps into the water to save another, a tragicomedy in which both founder.

The personality of the therapist is extremely important in psychotherapy. Not only must the Christian psychotherapist have experienced the transforming power of regeneration, but also must have matured in the faith. He has obtained the potential for personal maturity but must actualize this in growth and development. He must himself be enjoying good mental health, accepting not only God, but himself as well as others. (It is alarming how many individuals enter the field of counseling, psychiatry and clinical psychology in an unconscious effort to find the solution to their own personal problems.)

At this point the potential Christian psychotherapist has the requisite talents to enter a period of training for this career. When he has the "love of God shed abroad in his heart" and is able to manifest this to his neighbor as himself, then he has the basic equipment for a Christian vocation. This is a particular necessity in a Christian psychotherapy. "Success in psychotherapy depends, of course, on accurate knowledge of the mind's

---

[1] *In Search of Maturity*, Scribner's, 1943, p. 12.

disorders, their symptoms and their cure, but much more, upon what the patient sees of a strength and rightmindedness in his therapist. There is no one so sensitive to atmosphere as your neurotic, and good character is its own infection; you cannot cleanse a wound of mind, as of the body, unless you yourself are aseptic."[2] If, then, *agape* is the active therapeutic agent in neurosis as it is in sin, this would place a premium upon the therapist's having a source of *agape* to draw upon that does not fail at critical points in therapy. No therapist can be unfailingly kind, understanding and forgiving. But God can. And if the therapist can make manifest the presence and love of God in the relationship, acceptance assumes a vertical and eternal significance which, we believe, adds significantly to the potential of the therapeutic relationship to effect healing and transformation."[3]

It must not be presumed that a particular experience of conversion is the only religious moment for the foundation of a Christian psychotherapy. The Christian life is a day by day experience of walking with God, repenting for alienating actions, and renewing one's dedication to his Kingdom task. W. S. Reed expresses this clearly in terms of medical practice. "The Christian discipline of medical practice may require the physician's re-evaluation of his work in terms which are supra-Hippocratic. There is a sense of eternal purpose in his work. It allows him to accept Christ, and then to find Christ walking beside him in his rounds, and standing beside him in his surgeries. It shows him that his practice has a divine purpose, and that he is not merely to save his patient from one disease so that later he can develop another disease and die. Christ sends the physician to present Christ to his patients. In this encounter they have the

[2] Murray, *An Introduction to Christian Psychotherapy*, p. 258.
[3] L. Granberg, "The Personality Theory of Carl Rogers," *Proceedings of the Christian Association for Psychological Studies*, 1958, p. 31.

opportunity not only to be saved from disease, but to receive life eternal, which ultimately is the greatest consideration."[4]

When the young person is redeemed, mature in the faith, and has a sense of Christian vocation—the conviction that God has a task for him in the world—he has the fundamentals upon which to begin a specific career preparation. It is difficult in this day, when there are thousands of occupations through which to bear witness and by means of which one may investigate God's Word and His world, for a young person to make a vocational decision. Need is a factor in vocational choice but not the decisive factor, for everywhere there is a need. It seems to me that a sense of desire and a sense of destiny, stimulated by providential, though seeming accidental, incidences, must challenge the Christian youth. If this desire accords with the Scriptures, persists through seasons of prayer, and is correlated with one's abilities, then this is ample evidence upon which to launch forth in preparation. If one believes that God wants him to know His will, even more than he, as an earnest seeker, wants to know it, then he can be confident that He will open and close the appropriate doors of opportunity.

TRAINING

Christian psychotherapy branches out into three vocational areas which are directly involved in the field of mental health. All three — psychiatry, clinical psychology, and pastoral psychology — are rapidly expanding fields, offering unlimited opportunity. They require four to eight years of intensive theoretical and practical training beyond a senior college bachelor's degree, before one can enter these respective areas of activity. There are those who function with sub-minimal training, but this is bcoming more and more difficult due to the crystallizing of social, institutional, and legal restrictions upon

---

[4] "Developments in Christian Healing," *Christianity Today*, January 30, 1961, p. 14.

these roles. Professional psychotherapy is a demanding occupation and one that ought not to be, and cannot be, lightly entered.

It is my opinion that the undergraduate training ought to be in a Christian college of the arts and sciences. Only in such an institution is it possible to become thoroughly acquainted with the Biblical knowledge in conjunction with the necessary science and humanities areas in a context of consciously attempting to integrate all data into a Christian world and life view. It does not follow that one could not be a Christian psychotherapist if he attended a secular institution, nor that he would automatically be one after attending a Christian school, but the encouragement, confidence, and curriculum available on the Christian campus are invaluable in the preparation for a Christian vocation.

Institutional competency in terms of standards, faculty, and facilities are of great importance, but of equal importance is that the theoretical and applied training should be integrated in the molding of a mature educated Christian person. There is much room for improvement in all phases of contemporary Christian collegiate education, but the administrators of the few accredited Christocentric colleges, and those just short of accreditation, are painfully sensitive to these deficiencies and are pursuing these problems with wisdom and dispatch. The time worn epithet of "hot house" education is rapidly losing any vestige of relevance on the contemporary conservative Christian campus. One sees rather, an allegiance to Biblical authority, an alertness to social change, and an eagerness to make an impact for Christ in the modern world.

In spite of the growing strength of the Christian witness on the secular campus, I am convinced that the obstacles to preparing for a Christian career in an institution dedicated to a secularism, which subtly attempts to cut away the very foundations of the Christian faith, are almost insuperably great, even though the Christian student come through with firm religious

convictions. The Christian scholar is in another category altogether than the scholar who is a Christian. I have listened to
most of the arguments pro and con with reference to Christian
education, have visited many Christian and non-Christian cam-
puses, have attended two Christian schools of higher education
and four secular universities, and have taught a decade in a
Christian college, and a half decade in a non-Christian school.
These experiences have led me to conclude that a basic Christian
education on the collegiate level, while not a panacea to all the
problems of preparing for a Christian career, is a near necessity
for an effective ministry as a Christian psychotherapist.

This is especially true in the field of psychology. Here, perhaps
above any other discipline, the theoretical and practical thrust of
the program tends to be anti-Christian rather than "neutral" or
non-Christian. Many are the young Christians in this field who,
under the peer pressure, the suasions of personable and learned
faculty, and the barrage of question begging literature, fall by
the wayside.

The undergraduate collegiate training should be a progressive
development of personal maturation and the obtaining of a
great fund of information carefully integrated in terms of the
Christian faith. This is probable on a carefully selected Christian campus, and possible, for the mature student, on a non-
Christian campus, though I often feel that the story of the
camel and the needle's eye is somehow pertinent in this latter
case.

With the exception of theology, there is very little opportunity for a Christocentric graduate education.[5] This is especially
true in the area pertaining to psychotherapy. There is presently
a concerted effort to establish a Christian university in this

_____

[5] A notable exception is the Free University of Amsterdam. During a recent
visit there, I was favorably impressed with the excellent opportunities for
graduate clinical training in an institution with a basic Christian philosophy
of education.

country, which would, presumably, have a graduate department of psychology, but apparently the lack of economic resources, and the disunity concerning the patterns of social behavior to be required, make its establishment doubtful, or, at best, distant in the future. Reports of a graduate Christian school of clinical psychology being established on the West Coast have foundation in fact, but there are many obstacles to overcome. This is the most hopeful sign for the growth of a Christian psychotherapy even though it will, if realized, meet but a small portion of the need for training Christian therapists.

It may be in order to delineate briefly the differences in the three psychotherapeutic areas listed above and to indicate the general formal requirements of preparation.

1. Psychiatry

The psychiatrist has a medical education and is a physician. His period of training usually involves four years in medical school after college, followed by two to four years of supervised hospital residency. It is the psychiatrist who is utilizing the new mental health "wonder drugs," for he alone, of the three principle mental health vocations, can prescribe drugs and "practice medicine." There is a tendency in psychiatry to emphasize physiological factors in mental illness, presumably due to the intense physiological training.

Psychiatry is a very active specialty in the field of medicine today, but it still falls far short of the need. Psychiatrists are generally concentrated in high population centers and there are many communities without psychiatric services. I am writing this chapter while on vacation in a rural New England area, a distance of one hundred and fifty miles from the nearest psychiatrist!

There is some pressure from the American Psychiatric Association to maintain psychotherapy as a medical term and to exclude any persons from this field who do not have medical training. The unmet need, coupled with the widespread establishment and acceptance of clinical psychology after World War II, has, at least to this point, thwarted such pressure. It has brought about legislation in many states, however, which tends to exclude quacks and irresponsible persons from being active in the mental health field.

2. Clinical Psychology

This term refers to those in the field of psychology who specialize in the diagnosis and treatment of mental and emotional disorders. The clinical psychologist generally works under medical supervision. This is always true in hospital settings, where he is often restricted to administering and interpreting diagnostic psychological tests, though private practice of psychotherapeutic counseling among clinical psychologists is becoming rather widespread.

The educational period to the doctoral level takes a minimum of four years after college, including one year of hospital or clinical internship. The usual time of study, and the interneship, often exceeds this minimum by double this amount of years. The emphasis in training is often on psychological and functional factors in mental illness, rather than physiological.

In order to avoid the accusation of illegally practicing medicine, the clinical psychologist often carefully refers to his counselees as "clients" rather than "patients," though, since the latter means "suffering one," it seems rather more appropriate. Increasingly the role of the psychologist as a professional in mental health treatment is replacing that of a supportive research function. Clinical psychology is a rapidly expanding field. The tension between this discipline and psychiatry seems to be lessening somewhat, though each believes its training to be best suited for the problem of mental illness.

3. *Pastoral Psychology*

The entry into the field of mental health of the clinically trained minister is a relatively new phenomenon. Such persons have a regular theological seminary training of three years after college in addition to a program of theoretical psychology and clinical experience during the summers, or after the theological degree. Such persons are usually certified either by the Institute for Pastoral Care, or the Council for Clinical Training, as well as by their denominations. The role image of these individuals range from that of a pastor who is prepared to minister to the emotionally troubled in his parish to that of a religiously oriented psychotherapist.

The clinically trained hospital chaplain is making a significant impact psychotherapeutically. In some state hospitals, where the medical and psychological departments are understaffed, it is the chaplain who is really carrying on the necessary psychotherapeutic function, when it is carried on.

There are some, such as Mowrer, who sees the solution to the problem of mental illness as appropriately and best realized through the parish pastor. He believes that the clergy are returning to a role that it, unfortunately, had abandoned. But, regrettably, the return is more often in the name of Freud than in the name of God. "It would appear that the church must become concerned, in a new and more vital way, with the problem of mental illness. No longer should it take a position of subservience to a profession which, by its own admission, has failed to solve this problem; instead, it must approach the problem indigenously, that is, in terms of religion's own great insights and authority. And its present precepts and principles are not sufficient to this task, they must be modified and revised until they are."[6] "I have previously argued, as Anton Boisen has done for the past thirty-five years, that the church

---

[6] *The Crisis in Psychiatry and Religion*, p. 137.

loses its very excuse for existence and cuts itself off from
essential sources of inspiration and validation as soon as it
refuses to go all the way with the person who is in that emotional and moral crisis which we call neurosis and psychosis."[7]

The above mentioned vocational roles have their individual
strengths and weaknesses in terms of dealing with the full
scope of mental health problems. An excellent compromise
would be local clinics established with each of these persons
on the staff, supported by competent social workers. (Psychiatric
social workers should, perhaps, have been added to the list of
primary personnel in psychotherapy. Omission is more a function of my lack of information concerning their training and
responsibilities, rather than of any intended implication of their
secondary importance. Social workers are an extremely significant part of the psychotherapeutic team in the Veterans' Administration Hospital station at which I am presently engaged
in a research project. Present trends in institutional group
therapy and intensive rehabilitation programs, indicate an increasingly prominent role for the social worker in the future.)
Such a team, integrated in the Christian faith, and, perhaps
sponsored by large urban churches, or groups of smaller
churches, seems to be a solid foundation for effective action for
mental health.

TECHNIQUES OF THERAPY

Often in therapy there is an overemphasis on techniques.
A therapist cannot carry out a therapeutic program without
employing some method of treatment or interviewing, but care
must be exercised not to make any particular techniques ends
in themselves. Our view of man and human personality for-
bids an attitude toward the patient as though he were an
object to be manipulated. The emotionally ill person is not

[7] *Ibid.*, p. 168.

like a broken down automobile which can be fixed with certain
tools and by replacing certain parts. He is, rather, a despairing
human being, with potentials of personal power far beyond
his fondest dream, who believes that his present situation of
suffering is the best adjustment to life that he can presently
make. More basic to his recovery than specific modes of treatment is a therapeutic relationship which communicates love
and acceptance, a supra-technique relationship which is the
substance of therapeutic success.

However, counseling apart from specific techniques is both a
hazard and a haphazard. The counselor must be able to modify
his approach to the uniqueness of the patient and the problem
in each counseling contact. Nonetheless, experience with as
wide a variety of techniques as possible will furnish confidence
and a sense of competence to the counselor, which will, in
turn, flow to the counselee. The important thing to remember
is that a counseling process is not exhausted in its techniques.
"Counseling is not simply a technique. It is an art, a specific
form of spirtual creativity. We are not satisfied with being a
Christian in one aspect of life and being psychologist or counselor in another."[8]

Techniques are necessary to the therapist's activity but they
can become, apart from due caution, opportunities of avoiding
inter-personal confrontation and the demands of a mutually responsible relationship. On the other hand, apart from a specific
therapeutic program, psychiatric counseling may deteriorate into
a mystic meandering, frustrating both participants, neither art
nor science, nor a composite of the two.

There is a certain sense in which there are no specifically
Christian psychotherapeutic techniques. Many methodological
approaches are equally well adapted by various theoretical viewpoints. Frequently therapists with a Christian orientation dis-

8 Thienemann, "The Art of Counseling," p. 95.

tinguish between psychoanalytic methods and psychoanalytic theory. The latter is held to be counter to Christianity, while the former are eminently useful. "Much confusion could be eliminated if people would see more clearly the distinction between psychoanalysis as a technique and as a theory."[9]

Such therapeutic activity as prayer or the use of the Bible would be exclusive to a Christian, or at least religious, therapy, though other techniques are somewhat "neutral." On the other hand, the attempted relaxing of some moral attitudes and the encouragement to "live less rigidly" in these areas, though not widespread, nonetheless occurs and would be opposing to a Christian therapy. Many other faddish techniques that come and go are either so inane or so indiscreet that they would be practically excluded from the repertory of the Christian therapist.

However, neutrality of techniques is an abstraction which never really exists, for techniques exist only in action. They are not stockpiled in some platonic world of Ideas, but rather are found only in therapeutic activity. This activity is always intended to be the means to some therapeutic goal. And every therapeutic goal entails a philosophy of life and a value system which either correlates with the Christian world and life view, or does not.

Thus techniques are therapeutic necessities serving as the content of a therapeutic program. Their significance is found in supporting a personal relationship between therapist and patient, in sustaining a developing context of understanding, confidence, and decision. They are steps that hopefully will lead even the sickest individual toward a life of health.

Before discussing the techniques of counseling as they apply to a Christian therapy, it would be strategic to make some dis-

9 R. Jaarsma, "Psychoanalytic Theory: Misunderstood or Resisted?" *Proceedings of the Christian Association for Psychological Studies*, 1955, p. 7.

claimers. There are some unfounded attitudes that tend to be organized into a caricature of the Christian therapist.

Magic, for instance, may be imputed to the Christian therapist, and may be the unconscious hope of the counselee. There is a wishful element in every psychotherapeutic patient that the therapist will have a magic wand, but there is a further danger that the Christian therapist will be selected for this specific reason. "These people expect me to be a magician. They think that I 'possess,' in virtue of my religion, insight or powers which would be lacking in a non-Christian colleague. This notion of 'possessing' spiritual power is the mark of the belief in magic. These patients imagine that I am going to sweep away their difficulties, free them from their bonds without much effort on their part, save them from error, from stumbling, from the suffering and darkness which are still a part of human life."[10] Progress comes only after this attitude has dissipated.

The Christian therapist is also sometimes construed as one who is equipped with the "whole armor of God" and nothing else. He is represented as a cloying consoler or a curt condemner; one who believes personal problems are resolved merely by citing Bible verses or leading in prayer (practices which are, at times, very pertinent to psychotherapy). His competence is evaluated by his personal faith rather than his training and experience. I hope that these are not characteristics of actual Christian counselors, and that this projected image of the Christian therapist will soon be changed.

1. *Diagnostic Instruments*

Of the tools and techniques of psychotherapy, probably none are more widely discussed and debated than psychodiagnostic testing instruments, or, as they are more popularly known,

---

[10] Tournier, *A Doctor's Casebook in the Light of the Bible,* p. 122.

psychological tests. The most popular of these are the "pencil and paper" personality inventories and the projective techniques, such as the Rorschach diagnostic inkblots. These "tests" are receiving a great deal of attention in research and are often hailed as the key to effective psychotherapy. Many psychologists on hospital staffs do little but obtain these test results in order to fill files and to provide a scientific atmosphere for the practice of psychotherapy. Research possibilities of psychological tests are significant, and should be pursued, but the diagnostic benefits are dubious.

Carl Rogers is the vanguard of contemporary psychotherapists who repudiate diagnostic testing as a prelude to therapy. In his opinion, the testing procedure disrupts the therapy relationship and transfers to the therapist both authority and responsibility. The results contain little useful information that will not be obtained in the interviewing, and they tend to impede the therapeutic progress. My observations lead me to the conclusions that while carefully introduced and conducted psychodiagnostic tests do not detract significantly from the therapeutic relationship, the data derived are not significantly valuable. Diagnostic psychological tests, though used for many years, are hotly debated both as to theory and interpretation of the results. As I sit here typing this manuscript from my hand-written notes, I am reminded that I will attend a weekly Rorschach seminar this afternoon conducted by a man widely believed to be one of the great American experts on this particular instrument. Though the discussions are fascinating, and this man's ability to "tease out" of a protocol a wealth of data is amazing, yet I am unconvinced that our work is more than interesting personality research or *ad hoc* and *post facto* diagnoses significantly dependent upon information not gained through the test itself.

Though frequently I employ such instruments for research purposes; as tools for psychotherapy, they seem to me to be of little value. When the symptoms are subtle, the tests are not reliable, and when they are obvious, then an elaborate test is superfluous. Several therapists, avid supporters of psychodiagnostic testing, whom I have challenged with regard to the practical application of test results to psychotherapy, have confessed to me that the tests have really no bearing upon psychotherapeutic decisions. Whenever there is a conflict between test results and "clinical intuition," the latter seems always to win out. Therapists who regularly employ psychodiagnostic measuring procedures other than for research purposes, not directly relating to the therapy program, employ them, in my opinion, as scientific "emperor's clothing." Psychodiagnostic testing has yet to be demonstrated as necessary or even helpful for the practice of psychotherapy.

Intelligence testing, for persons with problems relating to successful educational experience, is a tentative exception to the above evaluation. I occasionally find these tests (I use the Wechsler Scales) useful in the counseling context.

2. *Interview Data*

The keeping of records of interviews is another practical consideration for which there is no unity of opinion. The easiest method is to tape-record, but the cost in time to utilize this method is prohibitive except as a training device. In case the interview is electronically recorded, it should be done only with the patient's knowledge and consent. Attempted deception is a most dangerous element in the counseling context. Note taking rarely raises an objection from the counselee and is the most practical procedure. I find it convenient to take rather full notes during the anamnesis, or brief life history recited by the patient; brief notations during ordinary interviews; and almost verbatim accounts of hypnoanalytic sessions. Each therapist must discover the procedure which best suits his personal needs. An adequate file on a patient should include the salient facts of his life story and the significant details of the therapeutic process. These are invaluable aids, in the light of inevitable memory distortion and lapse, for the successful functioning of the busy therapist. It goes without saying that these files, as well as any of the data of the counseling session, are to be kept in strictest confidence and revealed only with the express consent of the patient.

The duration and frequency of the counseling interview is also a rather arbitrary matter. The traditional "fifty-minute hour" seems to be the most satisfactory. It allows for an un- hurried appointment and a ten-minute buffer period in which to terminate any unanticipated problems, to make and receive phone messages, and to "get set" for the next client. Some therapists report a successful program with half-hour periods, but I have been too aware of the pressure of time under such circumstances. It is important that patients are not permitted to overrun the time allotment or compensate for lateness unless an unusual situation prevails.

The frequency of interviews is a variable factor. Traditionally psychoanalysis has called for an intensive therapy with five or six daily interviews each week. This seems to me to be too intensive and goes beyond the point of diminishing returns. It is too costly in time and money for the average person, does not allow a sufficient period in which to consolidate therapeutic gains, and greatly limits the contact potential of the therapist. I find that twice weekly appointments during the period of acute symptoms, and weekly interviews thereafter makes for the most efficient practice.

It is interesting to observe the client's reaction to the tradi- tional piece of psychiatric furniture, the couch. Some are very threatened by it, while others find it a haven of rest and relief. Many contemporary counseling offices do not even contain one. This is not so much due to a reaction to psychoanalysis as it is to the symbolic defeatism of "lying down on the job" or

facing life's problems "lying down." However, I find that as
soon as a good counseling relationship is established, a reclining
position is the most relaxed and relaxing situation for what
I shall describe later as the analytic phase. A comfortable variable position chair which can be adjusted to an upright position, as well as reclining, is a practical compromise for
counseling furniture.

THE COUNSELING PROCESS

The counseling program may be conveniently divided into
four phases: introductory, analytic, synthetic, and terminal. In
actual practice the boundaries of these phases are very indis-
tinct and considerable overlapping is the rule rather than the
exception. They are frequently clearer in retrospect than in
the present. There is no timetable which can be arranged for
the various phases of psychotherapy since each program is a
unique experience with a unique personality. An interesting
observation of every therapist is the experience after a successful
therapeutic program, when he becomes confident that his
procedure is the indicated one for any such cases. Then when
confronted with what at first seems almost identical symptoms,
he rediscovers that the previous procedure has little or no relevance, for each individual presents a special case.

1. The Introductory Phase

This phase of the counseling process has a fourfold function.
It is a period of "sizing up" of each other by counselor and
counselee. Here first impressions develop into a relationship
of rapport. This mutual trust and confidence is necessary for
effective counseling. The introductory phase is an opportunity
for the client to recite his symptoms as he explains his reason
for requesting an appointment. The level of emotional control,
the severity of symptoms, and the duration of the illness are
important observations to obtain.

A brief life history also is involved in the introductory phase. The important factors are the significant people in the patient's life, as well as the significant incidents, especially those which were traumatic. I do not use a formal outline but rather suggest that the individual tell me about himself and his family. At any point digressions relating to the emotional disturbance are permitted. It is important to try to see the patient as he sees himself.

The final aspect of the introduction might well be termed the diagnostic decision. This is not to be construed in the sense of giving some technical name to the patient's problem (though he often requests it), but rather as a time of decision as to whether a counseling program is indicated and would be beneficial. Economic factors, available time, and severity of illness are considerations of this decision. Occasionally the presence of psychotic symptoms, or physiological factors, indicate a medical referral for hospitalization and/or chemotherapy. It is important for the non-medical psychologist to work closely with the medical profession so as to fulfill the best interests of the patient.

When a decision is made to begin a psychotherapeutic program, it is well to avoid any promise of success or shortness of time involved. My own practice is to indicate that these factors are impossible to determine predictively, but that the decision of the client to do something constructively about his problem is in itself a significant element of a good prognosis. If he feels that he can trust me, and is willing to reveal himself and his private world to me, then there is ground for optimism that, working together, we can both experience personal growth and emotional maturity. It seems to me advisable at this point to set specific goals of therapy. The patient is requested to do so and I also supplement his hopes for the future with the goal of a "man of God, thoroughly furnished unto all good works." The degree of specificity must, of course, be carefully correlated with the religious insight and experience of the client.

The introductory phase usually lasts through two appointments, although occasionally it requires only one. Sometimes a very digressive anamnesis or an intensive and long symptom recital will extend this to three sessions, rarely more.

2. *The Analytic Phase*

The analytic phase is a series of interviews which attempt to analyze the symptoms and their development as well as basic factors in the development of the personality. It is an endeavor to bring to light the underlying experiences which have made the individual's world one of sustained fear and/or anger rather than love and confidence, a threatening world rather than a challenging one. Since I hypothesize much of this "material" to be unconscious, either repressed or forgotten, the analysis is usually carried out as an analysis of dreams, fantasies, or recent moods of stress or elation, and often under hypnotic relaxation. The time of analysis is so variable as to make impossible even vague time limits. In my experience it has varied from one interview to twice (and occasionally thrice) weekly interviews for ten months. A successful analysis usually involves the nonrecurrence of symptoms, the feeling of the patient that he "understands himself," and the feeling of the therapist that he knows how the personality of the patient developed and how the person felt in his symptom sickened world.

3. *The Synthetic Phase*

This phase of therapy is directly related to the goals of therapy. The analysis of personality may be in itself depressing apart from a transforming synthesis. I do not view this change in which the person becomes confident and decisive in his life experiences as a reconstruction of personality factors, or a redirection of basic attitudes, but rather a transformation of the personality. For the Christian, it involves the discovery that "all things work together for good for those who love God" and that there is power in positive action. The non-Christian learns that the transformation of personality is dependent upon a transformation of the person.

In the synthetic phase it is of particular importance for the client to face, and to bear, the responsibility of his condition. Others have entered significantly into the experiences that have formed the malfunctioning of the personality, but only the patient can make rectifying decisions and attitudinal changes. Many analyses are unsuccessful because the patient is encouraged to see his problems as arising from the actions of emotionally significant persons in his life. While this is frequently, too frequently, true, and invariably half true, anything short of shouldering the responsibility by the patient will obviate any attempted synthesis.

In the synthesis, the therapist often makes suggestions concerning the grounds upon which an effective personal adjustment can be made and sustained. It is in this phase that the Christian world view and Christian faith become pertinent. The personal fragments derived from the analysis are poor building bricks for personality reconstruction. New materials and a new architect are needed. Murray lucidly describes the goal of synthesis in Christian therapy as it is related to analysis. "Unlike other systems, a Christian psychotherapy has a twofold aim. In the first place, it shares with materialist psychology the technique of tidying up the mind. It, too, uses every discovered probe and pointer to the subconscious — analysis, dream-analysis, association, suggestion, and the like — but it uses them with a greater purpose in view, and its special function only begins where other psychologies stop. Even while fulfilling this first purpose, it never loses sight of its greater purpose, which is, to make health and salvation synonymous;

any lesser aim leaves the sufferer uncured and endangered."[11]

The Christian therapist forthrightly suggests the healing force that enables unity and maturity of personality, the power of God. Rather than being professionally unethical and therapeutically unwise, this is responsible action which leads to a positive, constructive goal and avoids the onus of precipitating and perpetuating an "analytic wreck." "For a humanistically-minded therapist or counselor to prolong the wallowing and floundering of a confused soul in the morass of his own frustrations and conflicts — when he needs the regenerating grace of God — is like unto a physician stubbornly withholding a proven remedy because of his own prejudice or ignorance, while the patient suffers or dies."[12]

The synthesis always gradually emerges from the analysis. Sessions become more future-oriented. Plans and hopes are discussed. Termination becomes an imminent possibility through the content of dreams as well as the conscious thoughts of the client.

4. The Terminal Phase

Termination of a psychotherapeutic program is a mutual decision, just as are the other decisions in therapy. Usually the topic of termination comes out of the counseling context. Either the client will suggest it or it will become an obvious factor in dream fantasy. The following is a termination "dream" during a hypnotic session:

"I'm starting to feel a little 'high.' I can see myself lying down on a cloud in the bright sun. Way above the earth — resting — satisfied. It's starting to get dark underneath — it's raining under the cloud. It's dark and black. Something is happening — I'm falling through underneath. I keep alternating from being on top to underneath. I'm trying to climb up a rope

---

[11] An Introduction to Christian Psychotherapy, p. 177.
[12] Walters, "Spiritual Malpractice," p. 8.

that is hanging down — very different — someone's helping me.
It looks like Robin Hood. He has a long staff and he's pulling
me over the top with it — like a shepherd's staff — probably
from the twenty-third Psalm [smiling]. I wonder why I thought
of that. I have one leg and knee over the top — going very
slowly — now on top. He has a Tyrolean hat on—now it's a
monk with a brown robe— he has a hood on — a rope belt—
a bald head like Friar Tuck [smiling], or maybe Dr. Tweedie.
He looks like you. Now we're [smiling] — I don't know whether
to say you or he — standing at the edge of the cloud —you're
walking off and waving goodbye. I don't want you to go and yet
it feels comfortable here and you're still going away — I feel
kind of good now. This probably means that I feel confident
enough to go off on my own — to carry the ball myself."

This fantasy was discussed briefly and a decision was made
to terminate after two more sessions. A slight threat with
reference to the termination was experienced, so the client
extended the appointment for two more weeks.

The termination phase ordinarily involves less frequent interviews, usually bi-weekly, so that a period of personal growth
can be observed and reinforced. Sometimes termination is a
unilateral decision of the patient, before the therapist deems
it a wise decision. I do not resist such a choice for at least it
is a significant decision which the client is making. He will
likely return if his symptoms return or else seek help elsewhere.
Therapy with an unwilling client is largely wasted effort.

The Christian therapeutic process is a process in which an
ill and confused person, living in a threatening restricted world
is transformed into a healthy and confident individual with
challenging tasks to perform in an open and ever widening
world of opportunity. This is made possible through the future directedness of the Christian faith, which gives significance to the present and makes assets out of the crippling
liabilities of the past. The mysterious grace of God, working

160   THE CHRISTIAN AND THE COUCH

through a well-trained and dedicated Christian therapist, enables the ministry of psychotherapeutic healing.

RAPPORT AND EMPATHY

An extremely significant factor in the therapeutic process is *rapport*. This is an interlocking of mind and emotions between the counselor and the counselee. Rapport is the establishment of mutual trust and confidence. Apart from this, emotional healing is practically impossible. It is a relationship of love in which the patient dares to come out from behind his desperate defenses, while the therapist extends courage and strength for the difficult task.

Rapport is not a once and for all time event, but a continuing state which must be continually reinforced. It can be broken through the shifting moods of the counselee, if the counselor is immature or improperly motivated. Abiding love and acceptance by the Christian therapist is a major component in sustaining rapport. The counselor who has many prejudices and "can't stand" certain people has personal problems himself and will frequently have a difficulty becoming and remaining *en rapport*.

A related element in therapy and the key to counseling is empathy. This is to be distinguished from sympathy, which is a sharing of the emotional states of the counselee, or an involvement in similar moods as the counselee. Sympathy puts too much pressure upon the counselor and is too threatening to the relationship of rapport. It is like the lifeguard who jumps into deep water to rescue a person in distress instead of throwing him the life ring or pulling him out with a pole. Circumstances alter cases, but lifeguards such as this often lose their lives by drowning. The therapist who becomes sympathetically involved in the problems of his patients is himself in danger of becoming a patient.

Empathy is imaginative identification with the counselee:

a sort of controlled sympathy by which the counselor experiences the world of the client, yet is not entangled in it. He suffers not with the patient, but through him. He is so close to the patient's problems that he is intensively involved in the patient's experience, yet distant enough so as to withdraw easily when the interview is ended and prepare to enter into the life of the next client. This *participations mystique* is difficult to describe, but is the most treasured talent of the competent therapist. The extent of establishing and sustaining empathic rapport is directly proportional to the maturity and wide life experiences of the counselor. It is a natural component of confident Christian faith.

Thienemann discusses this relationship of patient and therapist as the difference between explaining and understanding. The Christian therapist does not attempt to explain the patient as an abject object, but to understand him as a man. "There is a difference between understanding and explaining. The immediate grasp of understanding comes from love, sympathy and identification; on the other hand explanation involves rational thinking in terms of cause and effect. The psychoanalyst tries to explain, the Christian counselor tries to understand his fellow man ... the healing process supposes a total change of personality, a conversion, a rebirth of man — all beyond the limits of analytical psychology."[13]

DIRECTIVENESS AND VALUES

There is a great deal of discussion in contemporary psychotherapeutic circles of non-directive versus directive counseling. This is largely due to the influence and impact of Carl Rogers, whose theory is popularly known as non-directive psychotherapy. Rogers refers to his therapy as "client-centered therapy" and this is more realistic. The reaction of the non-directive approach against the doctrinaire authoritarian coun-

---

[13] "The Art of Counseling," p. 98.

selor role is justifiable if not carried to an extreme. Non-directiveness, just as value neutrality, is an impossible ideal. The personality of the counselor will influence the direction of therapy in a multiude of ways. The point is not to close one's eyes to this influence but to make it positive and supporting of the therapeutic goals.

The Christian therapist is neither passive nor authoritarian. He is permissive while yet suggesting limits that the patient might well consider for his life. He accepts the person of the client unconditionally but does not hesitate to suggest to him (what he already knows so well) that "whatsoever a man soweth, that shall he also reap."

The difference between presenting values to the client, and imposing them upon him, is extremely important. Critics of the value-oriented psychotherapy frequently make the accusation of value imposition. They are right in pointing this out as a folly, for it would increase the immaturity of the client and deepen his neurotic dependency. This may be a straw man argument, however, for it is doubtful whether it is really possible to impose values and basic decisions upon another person. It certainly is possible (and I think foolhardy) to try, but this will either break rapport or else force into the patient's unconscious the conflict generated whenever man is treated as a manipulable thing. The Christian therapist is not to take away the patient's freedom, but rather to encourage him to exercise this freedom responsibly. The problem of the patient is that he has never learned to live in the dialectic of freedom and responsibility. The Christian therapist believes this can be accomplished only in Christ, but he also knows that this must be by a free choice of his client.

"We are not called upon to impose our scales of values on our patients. But if we help them to recover this fundamental function of life, namely choice, sooner or later they will raise the question of values—the dialogue will become spiritual. I

cannot at this point break off the dialogue on the grounds that
I am neither a philosopher nor a theologian, but merely a
doctor. What I must do then is to know what my own convictions are, and take responsibility for them, without attempting
to impose them on others."[14]

It seems to me that at a certain point in the therapeutic
program it becomes not only an opportunity but also an obligation to present value options to the patient. In any case it will
be done either with one's eyes open or blindly, either as fundamental to therapeutic goals or inexorably out of the sheer
fact that the counselor is also a human being. Christian therapy
entails an exposition rather than an imposition of values.

At this point it is, perhaps, appropriate to mention the problem of the counselor bringing in his own personal history as
an element in the counseling program. Many therapists are
adamant in the conviction that this is absolutely contraindi-
cated. This appears to be an artificial and arbitrary denial of
the personality of the therapist, however, and a very dubious
procedure. In the analysis phase of therapy, it appears to be
neither appropriate nor helpful, but in the synthesis (and occasionally the introductory phase) my observation and experience leads me to agreement with Tournier—"I believe that
nothing is more fruitful than to speak to the patient about our
experiences."[15]

The Christian therapist attempts to effect a careful compromise between the extremes of non-directive counseling, in
which the counselor tries to be a passive mirror of emotional
behavior, an amoral, objective, impersonal person, and authoritative directiveness, which tends to usurp both the freedom and
the responsibility of the patient. In the light of effective psychotherapy, these extremes are both fallacy and folly. The
Christian counselor engages as a person in a living dialogue with

---

[14] Tournier, *The Meaning of Persons*, p. 209.
[15] *Bibel und Medizin*, Rascher, Zurich, 1953, p. 267.

the client, a mutual enterprise for the purpose of finding for
the emotionally disturbed client an effective way of life. It is a
process which flows from client-centeredness to Christ-cen-
teredness.

CATHARSIS

A fundamental need for every emotionally ill person is to
get "something off his chest." Much of his misery is due to experiences which cause him conflict and confusion, and he in-
ternalizes them in order to defend his personality. Conscious
misdeeds and traumatic experiences concealed from the public
eye, take their toll in anxiety and guilt. Unconsciously repressed
experiences also are creating the stress which is being revealed
in the patient's symptoms.

The relief of catharsis, or cleansing, of these emotionally
charged events is commonplace in counseling, but always a
wonder to behold. The individual is really confronting himself
and in a way, before a witness, that makes his immediate decision to "come clean" irrevocable. The silly fears, secret sins,
and hidden hates, which hold him in bondage, are exposed.
Instead of the anticipated condemnation and increased burden
by virtue of the revelation, there is a wonderful feeling of cleansing and strengthening of personality.

An interesting incident which forcefully conveyed the
cleansing and healing power of an honest confession occurred
in the case mentioned previously of the client who was relieved
of an oppressing obsession through a hypnotic analysis of the
symptom (see page 83 above). After he had made the painful exposure and while still under hypnotic relaxation, he said (I
thought), "Open the window." I started to do so, inasmuch as
the office did seem at the time to be a bit stuffy, then discovered
that he had asked, rather, "Did you open the window?" for he
continued by saying, "I feel so cool now — so cool — so *clean,*
I mean cool." This "Freudian slip" revealed just how his con-

fession had effected him. He now felt clean and honest. The symptom never returned and this confession was a stimulus for continuing personal Christian growth for this young man.

It is doubtful if there is really any psychotherapeutic process between counselor and client, unless the analytic phase significantly contains confession and catharsis. The Christian counselor must be prepared to accept calmly and confidently from the most unexpected sources, sordid details of personal defeats. No condemnation will enter into the relationship except the self-condemnation of the counselee, which has already exacted its "pound of flesh" in symptomatic suffering and the burden of guilt. Above all, the Christian counselor will remember "to judge not lest he be judged," for honesty requires him to assent to the fact that "in that which he judges, he is also guilty."

If rapport and empathy are established, catharsis will follow after. It is to this experience of personal sin and despair underlying the need for catharsis, that a Christian psychotherapy can deal directly. The Christian therapist will rejoice in the catharsis for he knows that this is a necessary prelude to health and salvation (which he considers ultimately synonymous). Confession is good for the soul for it is a requisite to being a "new creation" in which "old things are passed away and all things are become new."

Confession which results in catharsis must come voluntarily from the counselee, however. When he comes to the point of faith and trust in his counselor, he will then dare to reveal himself. The overeager therapist who presses when the client seems on the verge of revealing a significant incident, will often observe a retreat back to defensiveness and a therapeutic setback, occasionally even to the point of breaking off therapy. The Christian therapist must always reckon the Holy Spirit as a "participant observer" in the therapy circle and rely upon Him to stimulate this aspect of the counseling process.

INTERVIEW TECHNIQUES

1. Dream Analysis

Our fantasies in dream life are some of the most common and least understood of our life experiences. Scientists have now entered this area, long the stronghold of poets, and are beginning to report on their results. We are told that ordinarily each of us dreams several dream periods each night; that the total time lapse is not a twinkling of an eye, but a total period of more than an hour; and that our emotional control can be seriously affected when we are inhibited from dreaming. There are several sleep laboratories where serious scientists are engaged, with the most modern apparatus and the latest chemical aids, in probing into the secrets of the dream.

However, long before this time there has been the conviction that there is an important link between's man's dreams and waking life. Dreams were held to be predictive and a means of scanning the future. They were considered the voice of God in human affairs. At the dawn of the twentieth century, Freud published his classic work, *The Interpretation of Dreams,* which established the dream as the basic tool of psychotherapy. He stated that the dream is a fulfillment of a wish. It was the protest of the unconscious as it tried to smuggle in the illicit pleasure forbidden by the censoring and censuring superego. The dream content had a link with recent historical events of the dreamer, but was to be interpreted largely in terms of desired sexual experience. The objects in dream fantasy were mostly phallic symbols, and the themes largely longings for oedipal incest. The analysis of the dream, the most ready avenue to the unconscious dimension of personality, became one of the chief weapons in the arsenal of psychoanalysis.

Jung also was extremely interested in dream analysis. It is reported that he had a file of more than 150,000 dreams which he had analyzed. He held that the dream was not merely a masked "movie" of sexual desire, but rather frequently a symbolic analogy of man's hopes and aspirations, of his fears and fancies. The emotional health of the individual is indicated by his dreams. Thus analysis became a diagnostic and prognostic device, as well as a basic method of psychotherapeutic counseling.

Dream analysis is a useful technique for a Christian psychotherapy also. Though they do not seem to present a significant element of prophetic insight, at least in my experience, in the sense of Biblical prophecy, dreams do seem to be a valuable revelation of the patient's unconscious life. Attitudes toward the therapist, progress in therapy, crisis experience, and termination fantasies are common components of dreaming. Those who refrain from utilizing dreams for therapeutic purposes on the grounds of unscientific superstition, or the supposition that dreams are no more than unintelligible reactions to what we eat, are missing a vital opportunity to observe an important function of personality and an "inside look" at the person behind the mask of everyday life. Murray believes that dream analysis is essential to a Biblically oriented counseling system. "The dream, when better comprehended, may yet prove to be not only the authentic voice of the subconscious, but a path toward a fuller knowledge of the unseen world in which our finite life is set. When thus analyzed, and not subjected to materialist axioms, or straitened by Freudian presuppositions, every fibre of the dream may be found to point to the central fact of all creation, and our dream-life may thus become an index to Eternity."[16]

My own method is to have the client record his dreams each morning after waking. This is to be done before anything else, for dreams are elusive experiences which may be vivid memories at the moment of waking and then completely gone in just a few minutes. Often a negligent client will report embarrassedly

---

[16] *An Introduction to Christian Psychotherapy*, p. 253.

that the dreams were so clear that he did not write them down, but that they now have utterly forsaken him. Those persons who "never dream" will discover that they dream regularly. With some practice, each patient will be able to report a rather full series of dreams.

With the client, I discuss the dreams and we endeavor to interpret them in the context of his life and problems. It is amazing how much insight a person gets into his own personality through dream analysis, with no special training. I always assume that the client is the best judge of his own dream meanings. Sometimes the dreams are so sketchy or commonplace that little seems to be gained, but often they reveal the attitudes to oneself, to the counselor, to therapy, to significant persons and events, to the spiritual life, and to a host of other important aspects of the therapeutic process. In the next chapter, several dreams will be recorded from my files to illustrate the significance of the dream to therapy.

Often I have a client re-experience the dream under hyponotic suggestion. This frequently recalls vivid details that were previously forgotten and also often drifts off into a fantasy which was not present in the original dream. In either case we are confronted with an immediate experience, invaluable to personality analysis.

The therapist who takes a "dream book" approach to dream analysis, and finds in every minute dream detail a major insight, is in danger of going down a dead end street in the therapeutic process, or becoming entangled in a hopeless jungle of disjointed facts. When the dream series are viewed as a subtle and significant phase of the total life of the client, and patiently examined in the full context of his world, the therapist has a valuable technique for understanding and aiding his client. The Christian therapist will be well advised to keep abreast of research in dream analysis, and to learn the language of this "voice from the deep."

2. Hypnosis

A therapeutic technique which is enjoying a contemporary revival is hypnotic suggestion. This mysterious experience has been known and used for many centuries, but only since World War II has it become a respectable scientific procedure.[17] Freud turned his back on hypnosis after a brief but enthusiastic flirtation with it early in his career, and his influence caused the developing psychotherapeutic field to ignore it also. The fact that it was the stock in trade of stage magicians and mountebanks also tended to cultivate a superstitious hesitancy to consider hypnosis as a useful process by both layman and scientist.

However, increasingly hypnosis is being used in medicine, as the circle is being completed, and lessons that Braid and Esdaile learned in the nineteenth century are being taught to the twentieth century anesthetists. Currently research in hypnosis is very active, professional societies of clinical hypnosis are large and flourishing, and hypnosis is generally accepted as a fruitful technique for the psychotherapist.

Evangelical Christians have been rather slow to embrace this long presumed demonic device, and are often quite assured that it is somehow contrary to Christian morals. Hypnosis is occasionally asserted to be a state of demonic possession, or, at a minimum, the usurpation of the prerogatives of God to try to attain control over another person. Just two years ago in Holland, during an evening of fellowship with a young university educated, wealthy Dutch business man, the conversation came around to the topic of hypnosis. He became very agitated when I confessed that I used hypnosis as a therapeutic technique and he actually tried to exorcise me! He has been informed by a well-meaning Christian friend and spiritual advisor that hypnosis was a modern type of demon possession, and that a

---

[17] Cf. F. L. Marcuse, *Hypnosis: Fact and Fiction*, Penguin, for an up-to-date discussion of the history, practice and future potential of clinical hypnosis.

means of combatting this evil was to make a challenge concerning the blood of Christ. It was for him an act of great courage, and for me, insight into a tragicomedy. At an annual conference for foreign missionaries in Europe at which I was a guest lecturer, I was informed by the director of a Bible training institution that he had just had an "expert" give a series of lectures on the "Evils of Hypnosis and Demonism." This man was widely received in Christian circles as an authority in the field of mental health.

Superstition is not confined to Christian or lay groups concerning hypnosis, however. A student of mine was warned by her brother-in-law, a student in a world famous medical school, not to participate in any hypnotic studies. He, in turn, had been advised by one of his professors concerning hypnosis that "there is nothing to it" and, in addition, "that it is very dangerous!" I heard, just a few years ago at a professional conference on psychology and psychiatry, a man who for nearly three decades was the superintendent of a neuropsychiatric hospital, give a solemn suggestion to the assembled brethren that they avoid hypnosis on professional, moral, and religious grounds. Such attitudes are, fortunately, becoming a small minority. Most of the negative reaction to hypnosis is based upon an almost absolute ignorance of it as a process and a complete lack of first hand information.

Hypnosis is, in some scientific opinion, physiologically and behaviorally identical with sleep, after which it is named from the Greek word for sleep, *hypnos*. An article in the *Scientific American* of April 1957 adduces research as evidence for this. If this be true, and there are many aspects of sleep and the hypnotic state that are similar, it is nonetheless a very different sort of sleep. It seems to me that this is somewhat like saying that black is white because they are both achromatic.

This state of heightened suggestibility is artificially induced and is dependent upon a strong rapport between the subject and the hypnotist. The subject is conscious during the hypnotic state and usually will remember the events taking place during hypnosis, unless suggestions of amnesia are made. Suggestions are more easily and intensively accepted than is possible in the normal waking, or in the normal sleeping, state.

Memories, dreams, and emotional moods are more easily and vividly recalled. This provides the therapist with information and an opportunity to observe a reasonable facsimile of the emotional reactions of prior traumatic events. These abreactions, or removal of repressed emotional complexes, which is greatly expedited by hypnotic relaxation, give dramatic cathartic results. In addition, hypnotic suggestion can enable a client to maintain an emotional control which would otherwise be a practical impossibility.

Ordinarily I use hypnotic relaxation for the analytic phase of counseling. This technique provides a therapeutic "short cut" and also permits a more controlled emotional state during the revival of painful experiences. No attempt is made to press for a specific level of hypnotic trance or persistently to try to induce a recalcitrant subject. Therapy is not directly dependent upon hypnotic success, for hypnosis is only a useful therapeutic measure. Repeated lack of success may make rapport difficult to maintain (or more likely indicate that rapport has not been effectively established), and jeopardize therapeutic progress.

Though there are a great number of novel "tricks" that can be demonstrated in the hypnotic state, the counseling office is hardly the place for them. Free association, dream analysis, mood analysis, and induced fantasy are the usual procedures. The latter, which is the suggestion of a "day dream" to the patient, is a very fruitful technique (of page 158 above). It is in many respects similar to a sleeping dream, with the added advantage that the hypnotic subject gives an "eyewitness report" of the events, and the plot can be improvised according to the interests and intentions of the therapist. Some instances of hypnotic relaxation will be cited in the next chapter as well as an account of physiological changes induced by hypnotic suggestion.

This section is not included as an introduction to hypnotic therapy, but rather to stimulate the Christian therapist to avoid the religio-superstitious reaction to hypnosis, and to take advantage of a most helpful therapeutic technique. The stock objection of placing one's will in another's power is an empty argument. We place ourselves in the power of the butcher and baker, as well as the doctor and educator, and in every phase of life. The point to remember is that one should trust carefully. Just as a man would not permit a passing tramp to administer an ether cone, so should he be cautious about serving as a hypnotic subject to someone whose competence and trustworthiness is in question. I regularly suggest hypnotically to my clients that they permit no one to hypnotize them who is not absolutely trustworthy and who has not their health and welfare as his motive. The danger of negative reactions or side effects of hypnosis is real, though greatly exaggerated in the popular, as well as the "scientific," mind. In the hands of a fool or a knave, the most harmless object may become a lethal weapon.

Though I have occasionally prayed with clients who were in a state of hypnotic relaxation, I do not believe that challenges of the "leap of faith" should be suggested. This tends to relieve personal responsibility of the emotionally crippled counselee, who must mature to free and responsible decisions in the fulness of his faculties. A discussion of religious experiences is pertinent, however, and suggestions to consider God's will are just as appropriate as are any other suggestions of decision options for the patient. Murray's comment on hypnosis closely approximates my own opinion: "Such suggestions is no implantation, as many think, of an alien and unnecessary element into the personality. Religious suggestion is as potent and as necessary to the full expression and development of that personality as any other, and has as much right to be given. Nevertheless, one stipulation, peculiar to the Christian system, must be made. Religion is built up from two influences, man's desire and God's power. We can but educate and release the first; we cannot command the second. Therefore, it is illegitimate to suggest to a man under hypnosis, "When you wake up, you will believe in Christ"; that is altogether outside our province, and in God's. What we can and ought to do, is so to open up his mind, so to give play to his religious instinct, so to clear the channels, that a new perception of God's presence may do the rest."[18] To bear witness in as psychologically positive circumstance as is possible is but to follow in the way of the Holy Spirit, the Great Psychologist. We need to remember, however, that healing decisions are to be free, clear and responsible decisions, made by the sufferer himself.

Hypnosis is a very helpful technique in a Christian psychotherapy. In the hands of the competent therapist it can be an amazing ally in the guidance of the therapeutic process. Ill considered objections, on the grounds of Christian ethics, previously have delayed the full utilization of hypnosis, but new understanding, and the increasing acceptance of it in the scientific community, augurs well for this method in the advancement of Christ's Kingdom in the field of psychotherapy.

3. *Paradoxical Intention and De-reflection*

Two therapeutic techniques that have grown out of the existential psychiatry of Viktor Frankl[19] are "paradoxical intention" and "de-reflection." These are derived from the fact of a spiritual dimension in man, though Frankl's view of the spiritual dimension does not entail a religious point of view as does mine.

Man's ability to transcend himself, to rise above his circumstances and symptoms, is challenged in paradoxical intention.

18 *An Introduction to Christian Psychotherapy*, 233.
19 I have discussed his "third Viennese school of psychiatry," Logotherapy, fully elsewhere. Cf. Tweedie, *Logotherapy and the Christian Faith*.

The primary causal factor of the neurotic symptom is the anticipatory anxiety of a recurrence of the symptom. This anxiety tends to guarantee the precipitation of the symptom rather than to prevent it. This makes the vicious cycle that is so obvious in phobias and obsessions.

The application of paradoxical intention is to cut across this anxiety-symptom cycle by encouraging a change of attitude to the symptoms. A patient of mine who had a reactive depression in conjunction with the onset of a menstrual cycle, was having little relief from the pressure of depression and was experiencing anticipatory anxiety about a possible severe reaction during the next menstrual period. After a few suggestions to the point of adopting a "devil may care" attitude to the depression (for if it came, it would come, and she might as well make the most of it), she was able to stop the anticipated dread by jokingly deciding to be the world's champion depressed person. This paradoxical intention, or a voluntary "opening up" to the threatening object, the depression, brought about an immediate change. She reported that the fog of depression seemed literally to "lift up from around my brain" for the first time in weeks, and she subsequently approached her menstrual period calmly and experienced no depressive effects.

I have found paradoxical intention effective in many cases of phobia, obsessions, impotency, and depression. It is disarmingly simple at first glance and might well be laid aside as a puerile persuasive procedure (although it is actually the reverse of persuasion). However, it is a most helpful technique in psychotherapeutic counseling and a very valuable adjunct to Christian psychotherapy.

De-reflection is not so carefully worked out by Frankl and needs further clinical evidence in his research, but it is a basic technique in Christian therapy. De-reflection is the turning of the client's attention away from his symptoms to positive goals. The bondage of the symptoms consists in the attention they receive, and thus de-reflection takes the "wind out of the sails" of the anxiety being built up. Attention to the needs of others, to vocational opportunities, and to religious realities is a diverting and healthy action on the part of the patient. The Christian therapist believes that only the Christian faith contains the potential and power for effective de-reflection. Only Christianity has the sure promise that "all things work together for good."

4. Prayer

It seems somewhat awkward, and perhaps sacrilegious to think of using prayer as a "technique"; this seems to smack of Pharisaism rather than of faith. However, prayer is an important part of the Christian therapist's life, both privately and professionally. In the brief interlude between appointments, nothing is more refreshing to the counselor's own personality, nor more helpful in "getting set" for the next client, than to ask for blessing and wisdom from on high. This gives to me a sense of assurance that God will watch over the departing patient in times of emotional crisis and will make the imminent interview to be eternally significant. The Christian counselor has need to "pray without ceasing" in order that his vocational goals of advancing Christ's Kingdom may be kept properly before him so that, in his business and busyness, he will not forget that it is really God's business.

Whether the Christian therapist will pray with his patient or not will depend upon the circumstances. His evaluation of the patient's spiritual condition and attitude toward prayer will be a significant factor. Some individuals are reassured, comforted, and strengthened when led in prayer by the counselor; others are threatened. With Christian clients, I incorporate a brief period of prayer as a regular aspect of the introductory and termination phases of counseling. At other times during a counseling program, I do so whenever I feel it to be appropriate to the therapeutic process and the needs of myself and the patient.

This is admittedly, somewhat mystical, but it is predicated upon a prior request of God to guide me, especially in the spiritual dimension of therapy. It is important that prayer be spontaneous — a communication with the Heavenly Father — and not a rigid ritual.

With clients who are non-Christian, prayer during the interview may not seem appropriate. Once again, I utilize the opportunity of prayer as I "feel led." In every case the client knows that I am praying for him, whether I do so during the interview or not. Prayer is a vital part of the counseling context which is truly Christian, but it should not be a planned portion of the program, rather the calling of a third party, the Holy Spirit, directly into a therapeutic triangle — from the role of participant observer to leader, to give strength and direction to both counselor and counselee.

The following is an interesting illustration of the use of prayer by a Christian psychiatrist. "A girl patient came to me recently whose condition had been diagnosed as a schizophrenic reaction, paranoiac type. Six years ago I would have agreed with the diagnosis, and the girl might have spent the rest of her life in a mental hospital. At our seventh session we had a prayer meeting. She unburdened her soul and yielded her heart and life to the Lord Jesus Christ. Today she is in Bible School, praying and preparing to go to the mission field."[20] The use and results of prayer in counseling are not always so dramatic, but the opportunity and potential power is in the possession of every therapist who knows Christ.

Paul Tournier has as an important aspect of his counseling, a period of "quiet communion" (*stille Sammlung*) during which both parties in the therapy session wait before God for His guidance. "The "quiet communion" is neither the recall of forgotten dreams, nor a free association of ideas, nor the constella-

---

[20] F. Milkie, "A Psychiatrist Prescribes Peace," *Decision,* February 1961.

tion of repressed thoughts from the unconscious. The communion is the process of God directed thinking."[21] Tournier believes that this technique will center the attention upon God for help and health rather than upon the therapist and will provide an opportunity for divine direction.

It is important that the Christian therapist be spiritually mature to the point that prayer with his patient is an unembarrassed and natural expression of his faith in God. Prayer will help to keep the counseling program Christ-centered and God-guided, the indispensable foundations of a Christian psychotherapy.

5. The Use of the Bible

Christian therapy, with its Biblical basis and orientation, is fundamentally involved in a reliance upon the Bible. Not only does the Christian therapist utilize the Bible for his personal rule of faith and practice, but he also applies it to the patient. It is from the Scriptures that he gets the insight into the nature of the patient, as well as the basic needs of the patient and the ultimate solution to his life's problems.

I believe that the following statement by W. Hiemstra with reference to pastoral counseling holds also for the Christian therapist who does not have a specific pastoral function: "The pastoral counselor must also acquire skill for his highly responsible work by a right use of the Bible and prayer, together with a legitimate use of psychotherapeutic techniques. In this integration, God will not be irrelevant nor will human need become inconsequential for this life or for that which is to come."[22]

Muedeking, in his interesting book, *Emotional Problems and the Bible*, points up the areas in which the use of the Bible is pertinent in therapy. "Within these six areas of our emotional configuration, then, the Bible can be of help. It promotes realism

---

[21] *Krankheit und Lebensprobleme*, p. 252.
[22] "Psychotherapy and Pastoral Care," *Christianity Today*, January 30, 1961, p. 12.

toward life. It releases the native healing powers of the soul. It keeps the mind focused on the present, on what the psychologist calls 'reality testing.' It encourages honesty. It liberates with its permissive offer of forgiveness. It is supportive. It directs toward ego-integration."[23]

I encourage a consistent program of Bible reading and, for Christian clients, a regular daily period of devotional meditation. Occasionally it can be observed that Christians are carrying on futile and confused lives because they are ignoring these common means of grace. A few years ago a college student came to see me concerning her general frustration in life and her negative attitudes. She came from a large Christian family, of which several members were ministers, and confessed that she no longer believed the Bible, nor had any goals or meaning in her life. She wanted me to refer her to some books which would "prove that the Bible is true." I listened to her for some time and observed that she had no particular intellectual difficulty with the Scriptures; that is, there was no Biblical incident that caused her faith to founder, but just a general reaction, apparently a symptom of rebellion to parental authority. The book which I suggested was the Bible. She reacted to this rather negatively, but I encouraged her to resume her neglected Bible reading for a trial period of one month, a few pages each day from selected passages. Though she "knew it wouldn't work," she agreed, as a favor to me, to do so. The incident slipped from my mind until a few weeks later when I saw her and she smilingly assured me that "things are all right now."

Recently a young lady arranged an appointment with me and told of her inferiority feelings, difficult social adjustment, and of her attempt to try to find a solution to life through a variety of churches that she had been visiting. At this point I told her how that Christ had given meaning to my life and had redeemed me

---

[23] P. 26.

from a confused pleasureless hedonism, and how the Bible gave me both direction in life as well as "daily bread." She spontaneously brought a Bible to the next interview and we spent a profitable hour in discussing God's Word. Later she informed me that this had really challenged her to a serious commitment to Biblical truth.

The Bible should be a ready reference for the Christian therapist, and a useful means for attaining his therapeutic goals. As is the case for all techniques of counseling, the counselor must use discreet judgment concerning the introduction of the Bible into the counseling program. Moving faster than the client is prepared and eager to go, the counselor endangers rapport and invariably retards the therapeutic process. The Bible in particular is a threat to the "backslidden" Christian and the non-Christian. Only after the Scriptures are seen to be a source of strength to the competent counselor, will such a person have a positive attitude to them. The therapist must "hide the Bible in his own heart," and then carefully consider whether it should enter directly, or only indirectly, into the counseling program.

6. The Power of Positive Parting

It is important that the client in therapy should leave each session in a positive mood. Frequently this is not possible for the counselor to attain, but with experience comes a sense of timing and opportunity that will help to secure a buoyant mood. One important advantage of weekly appointments is the opportunity of reflection and personal growth in the intervening time. The client who goes forth with specific tasks and aims for independent actions will tend to make gains as the whole life context becomes therapeutic. At the end of each session it is good to review the interview summarily and to stimulate the client with positive suggestions of paradoxical intention and de-reflection. The patient who leaves with hope and courage is not at that moment, at least, a patient — a suffering one, nor burdened by dis-ease. Positive moods are just as contagious as negative ones, and much healthier.

THE BASIC TECHNIQUE

The chief technique (which means, etymologically, "art" — and no technique of psychotherapy is effective unless it is artistically applied) of the Christian therapist is the coincidence of his own life and the goals which he sets for his patient. If his motives are godly, and empowered with spiritual insight and dependence upon God, then he can expect God to work in his counseling office. The honest therapist realizes that in himself there is no therapeutic power, for healing power is a gift of grace.

Murray lucidly details this "basic technique" of Christian psychotherapy, which does not attempt to substitute piety for professional competence, nor mistake sterile secular solutions for the real answers to spiritual needs. "A therapy which starts from the fact that it has behind it the healing power of Christ, which envisages every psychopath as a potential Christian, and which, over and above its processes of reconciling conscious and unconscious, never loses sight of its purpose of leading a man's soul nearer God, can never fall into either of the two errors already named. It has far too much reverence for the dignity and integrity of man, ever to descend to the level of the bungling amateur; and it has far too much sensitiveness to the voice of God, ever to let its science be earthbound."[24]

The Christian therapist should be "a man of God thoroughly furnished unto all good works" and have this as a goal for his clients. All techniques are subservient to this goal; it is the basic technique of Christian psychotherapy. When the Christian therapists seek other goals for their patients, then they become, in the words of Wendell Rooks, "guilty of corporate or profes-

---

[24] *An Introduction to Christian Psychotherapy*, pp. 173-4.

sional guilt in that we escape or deny the truth. We are, in a way, neurotic ourselves in creating an unrealistic goal and straining almost compulsively to attain it."[25]

PROFESSIONAL PROBLEMS OF THE CHRISTIAN PSYCHOTHERAPIST

Two practical problems, most often voiced to me, concerning Christian psychotherapy are those of counseling fees and professional ethics.

It is not easy for me to see the force of the supposed argument against accepting fees for a Biblically oriented counseling program. This is apparently not universally true, however. A psychiatrist, for instance, who is an evangelical Christian, told me that he could not charge twenty dollars an hour and bear witness of the Christian faith at the same time. It seemed to me that he is either not convinced that the statements of the Scriptures concerning man's need and the provision for it are true, or else he is a bit insecure with reference to the level of his fees. Another Christian, a psychologist in private practice, told me that he would not deal with a person "spiritually" until he was finished "clinically," and then he would arrange an appointment to discuss the man's spiritual need without fee! Such bifurcated attitudes would suggest that such professional persons were not sure of their calling, and did not remember that "a workman is worthy of his hire."

The range of fees and the restriction of services because of non-payment and/or economic inability to meet the fee schedule, certainly provide very real and practical ethical problems. This, however, applies to every Christian worker, whether miner or minister, paper hanger or preacher, and not just to the psychotherapist. The Christian psychotherapist must bear the high cost of professional preparation and current professional expenses of offices and equipment, and these will be reflected

---

[25] "Reactions of a Psychiatrist," *Proceedings of the Christian Association for Psychological Studies,* 1960, p. 30.

in his salary needs. He should be alert to the perpetual dialectic between his needs and his desires, however, lest he slip into the folly of living for this world only.

The second problem is considered, by many who would bring into question the concept of Christian psychotherapy, to be more basic. This refers to the fact that the Christian therapist will have motives that are devious to the hopes and aspirations of many of his clients, especially those who are unbelievers, or communicants of a non-Christian religion. This is, of course, a problem, but not necessarily an ethical one, unless he practices subterfuge and deceit concerning his philosophy of life and his therapeutic goals. If he hides the fact that he is a Christian therapist, then he is culpable.

This, more than any other factor, seems to cause the splitting of faith and professional practice in many psychotherapists professing the Christian faith. The dangers of professional non-acceptance by one's own colleagues or a limiting of clientele are not easy to face, but are more imagined than real factors. It is true that some potential clients will turn elsewhere than to a Christian therapist. This is much to be preferred, however, than to enter into a compact with an individual to whom it would be unethical to bear witness! The competent therapist will be kept busy apart from this and will have clients who will come to him in spite of the fact that he is a Christian. A Christian atmosphere should pervade the whole counseling program. "At any preliminary interview it should be stated frankly that the presuppositions of the analyst are those of the Gospel, and that his Christian psychotherapy is the only one, in contradistinction to all others, which can offer complete mental health in readjustment not only to the world but to God."[26]

Both of these frequently cited objections to Christian psychotherapy are really only facades for an underlying hesitancy regarding a basic commitment to Christian vocation.

---

[26] Murray, *Ibid.,* p. 213.

Non-Christian Therapy and the Christian

A logical inference from our discussion would be that all therapists ought to be Christian therapists. Though defensible as an ideal, it is far from being an established fact. Actually there are so few Christian psychotherapists, that pastors and other leaders in the Christian community are at a loss as to whom to make psychotherapeutic referrals. This leads to the question, or perhaps to the ethical factors involved, of making referrals to non-Christian psychiatrists and psychologists.

No problem arises if man is divided into a compartmental trichotomy. If the body and the psyche and the spirit are exclusive, then there is no more of a problem than when contemplating having a non-Christian mechanic service one's car. If, as I believe, the individual is an indivisible unity, and every counseling relationship has spiritual factors, then the referral to non-Christians is a pertinent problem.

There are some non-Christian therapists (and they are easier to locate than many suspect) who, following in Freud's footsteps, believe a religious commitment is basically unrealistic and a neurotic tendency in itself. Referring an emotionally disturbed Christian to such an one would be a dangerous decision, for such a therapist will assume that the religious commitment is a causal factor in the emotional disorder. J. S. Bonnell's advice seems to me to be sage counsel: "The wise spiritual counselor, while gladly utilizing all the constructive techniques and insights of psychiatry, will be careful never to recommend a parishioner to a consulting psychologist, psychiatrist, or psychoanalyst who is inimical to religion and unaware of the impressive resources it makes available for the building up of reliant healthy-minded personalities."[27]

In terms of the present necessity, the lack of Christian psychotherapists, there is frequently no choice but to refer a person in

---

[27] *Psychiatry for Pastors and People*, Harpers, 1948, p. 23.

an emergency emotional crisis to a therapist who is an unbe-
liever. This ought to be considered only in an emergency situation, however, if our argument is valid; and ought also to be
a stimulus for Christians to enter this needy field. I do not
mean to imply that non-Christian psychiatrists cannot help individuals who are emotionally distraught to reduce personal
tension. Many are those who have been able to find comfort
and emotional stability through the aid of psychiatrists who are
radically opposed to the Christian faith. My firm conviction is,
however, that a non-Christian therapist who is consistent with
his presuppositions often overlooks the essential causal factors
in mental illness, purposely avoids what may be the essential
needs of the patient, and ultimately falls far short of establishing
him on the road to true mental health.

PSYCHOTHERAPIST AND/OR PASTOR

There are many who believe that the splitting of the roles of
pastor and therapist has been an unnecessary and unfortunate
historical development. Mowrer is at present the most forthright
in decrying the situation. "If religious leaders had been deeply
involved in the care and redemption of seriously disturbed persons for the past century, instead of systematically 'referring'
such persons, there would have been no Freud and no necessity
for a Tillich or a Fosdick to try to legitimize him!"[28]

Bonnell also presses for an active psychotherapeutic role for
the "pastor-counselor," a role that is Biblically oriented. "The
pastor-counselor will remember that above all else he is a Christian minister. His chief reliance, therefore, is not on the principles of psychology and psychiatry but on the spiritual power
released through faith in God. His ministry to individuals will,
therefore, go beyond that of the professional therapists who limit
themselves to the sciences of the mind. What the pastor-coun-

---

28 *The Crisis in Psychiatry and Religion*, pp. 170-1.

selor offers is not merely another form of psychotherapy directed to the regulation of feelings and emotions. It is a therapy to the spirit, and because of the interrelationship which exists among these three, it exerts a powerful influence also upon the mind and body."[29]

Walters sees the minister's counseling role as being broader and less intense than the Christian therapist. "The minister's counseling may assist in making the unconscious conscious or in exposing and reorganizing unsound defense mechanisms, but these usual objectives of the professional psychotherapist are only incidental to the primary objective of the minister. His task is to set the whole life of the troubled individual in a Christian context and help him discover the healing power of divine love — agape — in human and human-divine relationships."[30] He envisions a pastor-therapist team which, working together, will most efficiently meet the total needs of the mentally ill. "Such collaboration invokes supra-empirical resources to utilize a healing force that has been attested throughout Christian history and which violates no valid scientific truth. As the psychiatrist and the minister join in such a division of labor, each can avoid the peril of superficiality that must result from inadequate grounding in the other's discipline. The patient may then find himself the beneficiary of the best that science can provide and, if he will, the redemption and life-transforming grace of God."[31]

The same sentiment seems to follow from the article by J. D. Plekker, a Christian psychiatrist, in *Christianity Today*, along with the reassurance that this teamwork need not "dilute" the pastoral function of the minister. "Objections have been raised as to the inroads which psychology has made in the study of religion, and many have expressed fears that the former discipline might displace the principal pastoral prerogatives of authority.

---

29 *Ibid.*, p. 189.
30 "The Consultation Clinic," *Pastoral Psychology,* September 1959.
31 "The Psychiatrist and the Christian Faith."

Intelligent application of psychology, however, does not minimize the stark reality of sin, nor ascribe all misconduct to 'sickness,' nor rule out the importance of personal responsibility, nor
supplant Scriptural authority. It is no substitute for the work of
the ministry, but it can be an enriching supplement to it."[32]

Mowrer, on the other hand, who is pressing the opinion that
sin is the primary, if not the exclusive, etiological factor in mental illness, is a strong proponent of pastoral therapy. He is con-
ducting research and giving postgraduate training to theological
seminary professors of pastoral psychology, in an attempt to re-
store psychotherapy to what he believes to be its proper role.
While such an attempt, if kept in a conservative evangelical
context, would correlate with the general thesis of this book, it
would, I think, expand the role of the parish minister to an impossible scope. The demands of therapeutic counseling would
necessitate neglect in other areas of the ministry. I have no
objection to the identity of the two roles in principle, but believe
it to be a practical impossibility. From the perspective of a
Christian psychotherapy, the important factor of any or all vocational roles is whether they are expression of the Word of
God and entailed in the advancement of Christ's Kingdom.

SUMMARY

In this chapter an effort has been made to delineate, not in
detail, but in theory and brief outline, the work and training of
the Christian psychotherapist. Many of the techniques which
are useful in a Biblically oriented therapy are presented, with
emphasis upon the basic "technique," the orientation of the
whole context of therapy with the presuppositions and purposes
of the Christian faith.

---

[32] "Psychology and Pastoral Care," November 9, 1959, p. 7.

CHAPTER VI

THE TRANSFORMATION OF
PERSONALITY

The goal of Christian psychotherapy is quite similar to the challenge of the Apostle Paul to the Romans: "Be not conformed to the world, but be transformed by the renewing of your mind." This transformation is a deeper (or perhaps one should say, higher) experience than is within the purview or possibility of psychoanalysis and other secular therapies. It is a personal experience which deals with the person in his unity and totality, sensitive to the various aspects of the dimensions of his personality, yet not depersonalizing him to an aggregate of compartments which can be treated in isolation. Seward Hiltner aptly observes the comprehensiveness of true personal healing: "If healing is all of a piece, all in the same field although not all equally important or central, then there can be no categorical division between secular and religious healing, between salvation for another life and for this, between healing by religious means as against those of the world, of nature, or of science."[1]

The personal transformation that is sought in Christian psy-

---

[1] *Preface to Pastoral Theology*, Abingdon Press, 1958, p. 100.

chotherapy is that which seeks, in Pauline terminology, "the reasonable service of a living sacrifice," which is a meaningful commitment to the Christian life. This is a confident turning from the self-centeredness of present doubts or past defeats to the openness of the future, a future that utilizes the past — "works all things together for good" — and gives significance and meaning to the present.

Such a personal change is, like the familiar adage, more easily said than done. In reviewing what I have written to this point, I fear that I have made Christian therapy sound too easy. In actual fact it is often a difficult, usually tiring, vocation, not always crowned with success. There are many apparent failures. Comfort may be taken in the reminder of Johannes D. Plekker, however, that meaningful goals are not necessarily destroyed in failure. "The goal of the psychiatrist must be the total welfare of the patient — a full restoration to fellowship with God as the goal. The goal is not nullified if it is not attained."[2] This transformation is, in the last analysis, not a contriving of the therapist, but a mysterious decision of the patient, grounded in the grace of God. Suddenly the fearful pushing of the past is transformed into a positive beckoning of the future, a complete reversal of direction and attitude. The therapist can only behold it and marvel. He can experience it only in his own life, though, and this gives him the foundation for empathy in the client's transformation.

Above all the therapist must bear in mind the fact that the responsibility belongs essentially to the patient. The counselee is only too glad to give it up, but the wise and wary counselor will be careful not to accept it. Recently a young man conferred with me concerning a compulsive masturbation habit, which he attempted to curb with no success and with acute guilt feelings. At the beginning of the second interview, he informed me, re-

_____

2 *Proceedings of the Christian Association for Psychological Studies,* 1961.

sponding to my inquiry, that he had masturbated several times and had made no effort to control his impulses inasmuch as now it was my problem! Doubtless I had unconsciously promised him much more than I had intended.

This incident of attempted transfer of the responsibility of the client to the counselor brings to the fore another problem which is widely discussed concerning psychotherapeutic relationships, that of transference in the Freudian sense. Freud felt that the relationship between the patient and the therapist was characterized by an emotional attachment, or in the case of negative transference, an emotional reaction. The patient had developed a certain emotional relationship to his parents, and possibly his siblings, in his early development days and these emotional attitudes were somehow involved in his pathological condition. These emotional attitudes were now brought to the surface by the spotlight of the analytic inquiry and were transferred from the parental objects to the person of the therapist. These, when positive, become attitudes of love and affection and are described as positive transference; when negative, they reveal aggression and hatred, and constitute negative transference. These raw emotions are masked somewhat by the social situation so that they often appear in the therapeutic situation as attitudes of friendliness and confidence, or questioning and mild rebuke. According to Freud, in his later writings, the "transference neurosis," a guided neurotic process contrived by the therapist and based upon the transference attitudes of the patient toward him, is the secret of successful psychotherapy.

While the concept of transference may be useful to describe the relationship between the counselor and client, it seems to me that it is an unnecessary construct which gives too much significance to the spectres of past childhood experiences and tends to reify that highly touted modern myth, the Oedipus complex. It is obviously true that persons in the family unit will have a good deal of emotional stimulus value to children

growing up in this social unit, but that there is any particular
guiding theme, such as an unconscious sexual longing for the
parent of the opposite sex and an unconscious murderous agres-
sion toward the parent of the same sex, is much better characterized as a bit of imaginative philosophic fantasy rather than
scientific fact. When one uses such Freudian terms as transference in the psychotherapeutic relationship, care must be
given so as not to confuse these sometime useful words with
their connotation in the context of psychoanalytic theory. In a
rather animated discussion following a paper which I delivered
at an annual meeting of the American Scientific Affiliation, a
psychologist asked me (apparently she was somewhat shocked
by the idea) if I really meant to say that I utilized the transference situation in therapy by directing the positive feelings
and attitudes of the patient from myself to the person of Christ.
I replied that this was precisely what I attempted to do, though
exercising care that this would be a responsible decision of the
client and not an imposition of my own ideas. "Thus we see
the whole of the New Testament to be the only answer to the
problems we have studied in this book. In it we read the
wonderful dialogues through which Jesus transforms the lives
of those whom He meets, drawing out the person buried beneath
the personage, and revealing personal contact to them. . . . Christ
is the re-establishment of contact. Through Him to make contact
again with God is to rediscover life, spontaneity, liberty and
our fellow-men."[3] "The psychotherapist . . . must strive for a new
birth in his patient. In terms of his own science this means a
radical change of the personality from Egocentricity to Object-
centricity. In religious terms it means the initial movement
from self-obsession to Christ-possession."[4]

The basic difference between psychoanalysis and Christian
psychotherapy concerns their respective presentations of the

---

[3] Tournier, *The Meaning of Persons,* pp. 172-3.
[4] McKenzie, *Psychology, Psychotherapy and Evangelicalism,* pp. 139-40.

major emotional impulse which guides the life of man and which in psychopathology has been restricted or distorted in its healthy expression through personality. For psychoanalysis it is sex. The neurotic personality is seen as one whose healthy sex expression has been curbed through the unnecessarily rigid restrictions of those social factors surrounding him which make up the super-ego. Freud said that sex was always at the base of neurotic reactions and it should be of no surprise that an encouragement to sexual freedom is a frequent admonishment of the Freudian analyst. It is true that many modern analysts theorize this freedom of expression as valid when it sublimated in and through socially acceptable activities, yet there is a majority of them who believe and act as though the patient's problems would be largely resolved through the development of a greater freedom in the area of sexual activity. "The patient, while in treatment, *may* be encouraged to "reality test" in the matter of greater expression of sex and aggression; but anything so radical as turning over a new leaf and trying to put one's moral house in order is strenuously discouraged."[5] Tournier aptly points out that this is not a fulfillment of science in the sense of Freud's ideal of science, but rather the outcome of a new theology. "The psychotherapist who suggests, naively enough, that as part of his therapeutic treatment his patient should indulge in a 'sexual adventure' outside marriage, is not at that point engaging in psychotherapy, but in soul-healing — a soul-healing inspired by his own theology, which makes a god of the instincts."[6]

The Christian therapist does not deny the great importance of sexuality in human personality development and in a proper adjustment to the social context. It is also true that in many, probably a majority, of personal problems sexuality is a component of the symptomatology. However, he believes that there

---

5 Mowrer, *The Crisis in Psychiatry and Religion,* p. 139.
6 *Ibid.,* p. 110.

is a more basic human emotion, love, of which sex is only a secondary expression insofar as personality adjustment is concerned. This love is presented in the Scriptures as the nature of God, the reason for the "Good News" of the mission of Christ, and "that which is shed abroad in our hearts by the Holy Spirit" when we come to know Christ as Savior. The proper orientation of this in man should precede the attempted adjustment in man of the sexual and aggressive problems, for it enables them to flow in their proper place in the life of a human being. "The focal fact of the divine-human encounter is likewise a focal psychological fact, that love is the universal solvent of conflict within man, between man and man. Freud came at long last to this conclusion, but in the need could not bring himself to believe in the kind of love that is central in Christianity, *agape,* — the unearned, unmerited love of God that extends to man."[7]

Lars Granberg, in an address concerning the "Self Theory" in the psychology of Carl Rogers, points out this Christian concept of love as being the real basis of non-condemnation in client-centered therapy and the means by which the therapist can accept, unconditionally, an otherwise unlovely and broken personality. "Moral relativism, however, is not the sole basis for non-condemnation. The supreme Christian virtue is *agape,* love 'in spite of,' or forgiving love, which is derived from God, who 'demonstrated his love toward us in that Christ died for us while we were still sinners' (Rom. 5:8). Non-condemnation on this basis has a different quality to it than when based on moral relativism, for although these things do matter to the Christian, the person matters more because God loves the sinner in spite of the sin and enjoins his people to be likewise. Thus the person is confronted not only horizontally with a non-condemning counselor but vertically with a loving and

---

[7] Walters, "Christian Faith in an Age of Anxiety," Radio lecture, University of Illinois, September 27, 1958.

forgiving God who invites him to 'be reconciled.' "[8] Thus the Christian therapist evaluates the transference relationship in terms of this *agape* love. He does not attempt to guide the patient in an infantile regression in order to bring about the transference neurosis, but rather uses the positive transference by the client toward the counselor, in terms of his trustworthy Christian convictions and Christian love, to that object who is alone worthy of love and who alone can resolve the ultimate problems of conflict in the human heart, Jesus Christ.

The Christian therapist should bear in mind that he in no way can effect the transformation of personality. It is the patient who must make the momentous decision of commitment that will bring this about, and this in turn is dependent upon the grace of God — "for by grace are you saved through faith, and that not of yourself, it is the gift of God." However, it is my firm conviction that an essential aspect of Christian therapy is the witness bearing of the therapist concerning the significance of Christ in his own life. Because of this, my own therapeutic practice has been one involving a majority of Christian patients. These are persons who suppose themselves to be Christians and come to see me because I am known as a Christian therapist and, they feel, will not attempt to eradicate their Christian faith. In addition, there are those who suppose themselves not to be Christians, but who come in spite of the fact that I am a Christian therapist. I use the term "suppose" in these instances for there are many who say "Lord, Lord" but who do not have any apparent insight into the essentials of the Christian commitment of faith; while others who do not confess Christ as Savior, seem to have attitudes that bring them very "near to the Kingdom." It is impossible for the therapist to judge with any precision the spiritual condition of the counselee, and, of course, it is not within his province so to do. It is true, how-

---

[8] *Proceedings of the Christian Association for Psychological Studies,* 1958, p. 30.

ever, that some indication of the spiritual condition of the troubled client will be of help in administering the psychotherapeutic relationship. Ernest White gives an interesting comment with reference to the indications of Christian life. "We have, then, three cardinal signs of the new life within, a desire to pray, a desire to bring others to Christ, and the urge to join other Christians in worship. These are all signs of spiritual health and the absence of one or other, or all of them, is evidence of spiritual sickness, perhaps of spiritual death."[9] The following selection of brief psychotherapeutic case studies will give information concerning the practice of psychotherapy, the variety of problems encountered, and some of the various outcomes of therapeutic contact. These were the deciding factors in the selection of them, rather than whether or not they were trophies of successful psychotherapy.

CHRISTIAN THERAPY WITH A NON-CHRISTIAN

An attractive young coed came to my office one day complaining of her inability to stay at school. Whenever she was in a classroom she would get feelings of anxiety and after a few minutes would be forced to leave the room in a state of panic. This occurred also in the student dining hall and at social gatherings on campus, and this made her campus life intolerable. She was failing in her studies and was not feeling physically strong enough for school life due to the fact that she had been eating, for several days, only candy cars and small snacks from the college coffee shop. She mentioned to me that she was Jewish, that she had no boy friend, and that she would very much like to leave school but that her parents did not want her to do so. She thought that I might be able to help her. I arranged a second interview with her and suggested that she should come with her mother, with whom she said she had a

_____

[9] *Christian Life and the Unconscious*, p. 39.

good relationship, and who had encouraged her to get some psychotherapeutic help. I informed them both of my Christian convictions and mentioned that I would be willing to see the girl for a few interviews, providing that they understood that my own philosophy of life might have a bearing on the psychotherapeutic relationship. The mother felt that this was not a serious obstacle but suggested that any correspondence should be between myself and her and not with the father, who "might not understand."

In the next couple of sessions, the client was not particularly communicative. She related several instances at religious feasts, experiences in a movie theater, and other events in which she had felt the same claustrophobic reaction, but felt that she could not remember many significant things in her life. I thought it rather strange that she had not had better social contacts with fellows inasmuch as she was an attractive girl and seemed to be quite poised, and not lacking in social grace.

During the next interview she was induced into a deep hypnotic trance, in which she related the following "dream-fantasy": "I am watching a ship sail out of Boston Harbor. It seems to be a Navy ship and there are several people on the deck, but they're so far away that I can't make out who any of them are. (Get closer to the ship if you can, so that you will be able to see the faces clearly.) There are two persons by the rail, a boy I knew in high school, and...the other is——Joe! Now they're sailing out of the harbor. Hah! Hah! Now it is coming right into North Station. Joe is getting off and going into the station to a phone booth. He's calling somebody. (Watch his fingers on the dial and see what number he calls.) Why, he's dailing my number! (Where are you?) I'm sitting on the floor in the living room, reading a book..[smile]..a psychology book. Now the phone is ringing and my sister gets to it before I can. She says it's for me. I'm talking to Joe and he wants to come see me. I say no, because I have to read this book, and then I hang up and go back to the book. That's all there seems to be to it, except I'm still reading the book. (Look closely at the book. Tell me the page number and read a paragraph to me.) I can't see the words, it's just a book, a psychology book. (Look closely.) It's page 169, but I can't read it .. [sudden heavy perspiration] .. It says 'When two people of different faiths become romantically involved, the social problems are very intense and conflicting."

The client started to sob at this point and spontaneously came out of the hypnotic trance. She confessed that she had been having a romantic affair with a Gentile boy named Joe and had been terrified that her father, an orthodox Jew, would discover this. At the next interview she said that she had had no difficulty with her past fears and feelings, and felt a great deal of freedom and relief about attending classes. However, she still wanted to leave school and did not feel that she could break off with Joe. Thus in this case, guilt feelings about her parental deception were manifested in a crippling series of phobic defenses. She had experiences like this earlier in her development, but the present symptoms seemed to be correlated with her romantic alliance. She did not return for her next appointment, or thereafter.

MARRIAGE COUNSELING

A prominent Christian business man and his wife came to see me one day and confessed that they were seriously considering breaking up their marriage, which had started about twenty years prior, but which for the last ten years had been held together only by common concern for the welfare of their children and the testimony of the evangelical church which they attended. There was a great deal of hostility and aggression manifest between them during the interview, and in the case of the wife, this was also directed toward me when I suggested that I would like to see her for some counseling sessions. The husband complained that she was cold, a poor housekeeper, and hard to get along with. She retorted that he was oversexed, acted like a little boy, and made a fool of himself in public. There seemed to be no question of a third party, comprising a marital triangle, and they both confessed that their courtship and early marriage was a time of mutual happiness and contentment.

The reason that I singled her out for individual therapy was due to the fact that she seemed to be less willing of the two to try to make a go of the marriage and that her hostility toward her husband (to whom she ascribed the entire blame for the domestic problem) was very much more intense and open. I felt that any attempt to reconcile the two would depend upon a radical change of her attitude. In the following interviews she mentioned to me her initial anger for my "laying the blame all on her" and letting her husband go "scot free." However, effective rapport was quickly established in the counseling relationship and she revealed to me a history of psychosexual maladjustment. She had gained the attitude from her mother that the sexual responsibility was a burden in marriage "and the only thing that men wanted." She had been taught "the facts of life" by a young couple in the neighborhood for whom she often baby sat and also had received some flirtatious advances from the husband. A covert homosexual experience had been quite traumatic in her early adolescence. This had been brought about by the actions of an older girl in a brief voyeuristic episode, and had caused her acute guilt feelings. She was very embarrassed, yet very relieved, when she related this incident. She grew up believing that sex was wrong, and "dirty," but a necessary part of the married life. She was a virgin at the time she was married in her late teens. The marriage adjustment had, initially, been quite satisfactory until they moved to a large city. She had there inadvertently witnessed a brutal attack upon a young girl and subsequently she became frigid sexually, afraid to stay in her apartment alone, and developed a rather acute anxiety state. She was referred to a psychiatrist and after a few apparently ineffective interviews, tolerated the situation until they moved to a rural area. Her fears and anxieties seemed to subside, but she was left with a frigid attitude toward sex. This seemed to increase the sexual desire of her husband and this conflicting relationship lasted for several years to the point at which they contacted me.

During these first few interviews she evinced an increasing desire to do what she could to save the marriage and mentioned that this attitude seemed to bring about a change in the attitude of her husband. We then discussed the physiology, psychology, and theology of sex and it became obvious to her that she had had a very wrong attitude toward the conjugal relationship. She felt that she could adjust if her husband would not be so "childish" in his sexual demands and if he could be more responsible in the economic affairs of the family. They had also renewed a daily period of prayer and meditation together which seemed to strengthen their determination to salvage the marriage. I saw the husband once individually, with the consent of my client, and he also reported progress in their relationship as well as a desire to benefit from their past difficulties in order to make their home a real Christian home.

She seemed to make a transition with reference to her sexual attitudes from the point where she saw the fulfillment of her conjugal responsibilities as the will of God, gained a desire to fulfill these responsibilities as a means of pleasing her husband, and finally herself derived a positive enjoyment of the marriage bed. Her positive attitude also seemed to have the effect of restricting the sexual desires of her husband, for he now seemed much more considerate of her needs, as well as to bring about an increase of her own desire.

At the last interview, at which both were present, they spoke about the great progress that they had made, and mentioned that they had discarded the thought of dissolving their marriage. They seemed now able to evaluate their whole marriage relationship as an aspect of the will of God, and could see the concept of the "unity of the flesh" extending from their physical contacts even to their acts of prayer and worship.

I relate this marriage problem because it is so commonly encountered among Christian couples. The Christian psychotherapist will be instrumental in many successful marriage counseling experiences if he is careful to relate his counsel to the will of God as it is revealed in the Scripture. Persons who had an initial mutual attraction to the extent of voluntarily committing themselves to the marriage bond, have all the necessary potential for the re-establishment of a harmonious and happy marriage.

PSYCHOSOMATIC PROBLEMS

A perpetual difficulty in psychology and philosophy is that concerning the relationship of the body and the mind. A dramatic aspect of modern psychotherapy, however, is not to theorize as to the distinction between psychological and physical, but rather to deal with the inter-relationships. The following case is an interesting account of how attitudes may affect physiological functioning:

Arthur C, 25-years of age, came for the initial counseling interview due to his anxieties concerninig his inability to retain food. He could not "keep anything down" and recently had lost a good deal of weight. This had affected his job and his home life to the extent that he was in deep despair. He stated that this was also the reason that he had dropped out of college some time before. He had intended entering the Christian ministry after college.

While in the military service he had developed an ulcer and was discharged for this condition. Later he underwent surgery (sub-total gastrectomy) in a Veterans' Administration hospital.

His recovery had been slow and he was left with a "dumping syndrome," a constant feeling of nausea when he ate, usually followed by regurgitation, or occasionally, if the food was retained, by acute diarrhea. Dairy products were especially difficult for him to digest. He had been an outpatient in the psychotherapeutic clinic of an neuropsychiatric Veterans' Administration hospital for some years, both in individual and group therapy, but had received no symptom relief. He was referred to me for hypnotherapy.

I discussed with him his dietary problems and how they affected his life, as well as tried, unsuccessfully, to induce a satisfactory hypnotic relaxation. By the fourth interview he had revealed a good deal about his personality development and also attained a very good trance level for suggestion of physiological change. I suggested that thereafter he would experience no difficulty in eating and retaining any foods that he desired, and that he should experiment with those foods, that very day, which had been especially difficult for him to eat.

He reported at the next, and last, interview that, with amazement and no subsequent distress, he had eaten chocolate cake and ice cream frappés as well as regular meals at home. I suggested that he might well profit in terms of personality development by a further series of interviews, and he decided to do so under the cost-free auspices of the Veterans' Administration. A subsequent report indicated that he had no further digestion reaction symptoms and that his personality took on a new measure of freedom and responsibility under therapy.

Masturbation

A counseling problem with which I am frequently confronted is that of masturbation. Those who are troubled by such a compulsive habit, and who seek psychotherapeutic counseling for it, are usually late adolescent Christians. This does not mean that others do not have such a problem, but at least persons within this group are frequently disturbed by intensive guilt feelings and feel driven to seeking for help.

There is no evidence that masturbation is physiologically harmful, but there is plenty of evidence that it is so psychologically. I have never met a person in a counseling relationship, whether Christian or non-Christian, who did not feel guilty and self-depreciating after an act of masturbation. This is also true of persons in a normal range of mental health, who do not seek professional help.

In addition, there is some basis for the belief that masturbation is theologically negative; in terms of the biological and natural end of sex, and not a spurious exegesis of the account of Onan in the Old Testament. In any case, masturbators feel sinful and it is a dubious psychotherapeutic goal to assist individuals to neutralize or "analyze away" their guilt feelings in this matter. This seems to be the trend among some of the more "emancipated" Christian counselors.

Direct resistance to masturbation brings almost certain failure. It is followed by a period of rationalization and then a succumbing to the impulse. Thus a "willpower" approach is self defeating. De-reflection and an encouragement to a higher degree of socialization seems to me to be most effective. The most chronic cases will often find speedy recovery through such a program. Though the analysis phase of counseling helps one to understand the dynamics of the masturbatory impulse, the act of masturbation tends to develop a functional autonomy (in the sense of Allport's use of the term), as do many symptoms, and thus one may introduce the synthetic phase at an early point. I often use hypnotic relaxation to reinforce de-reflection, and suggestions of socializing activities.

The following is a dream reported by a client during the fifth and final session. It is interesting in the light of his counseling experience. He had a chronic masturbation habit and had no success in attempts to modify or change it. During the coun-

seling period of four weeks, he "slipped" only once — the morning of the second interview (when clients are "fighting" masturbation during therapy, this is usually the time of failure —
just before they are scheduled to see the therapist). For the last
three weeks of counseling, he reported no significant impulse
to masturbate, no masturbatory activity, and an increased ability
to concentrate on his studies.

"I moved to a house I used to live in (from age 1-6) and was
very angry at how rundown the steps to an outside door had
become. The steps were made of stone and were on the outside
of the house. I think I placed the blame for the condition of the
house on my father.

"Inside the house an older woman was living. I think it was
her house and that we were going to visit her. The living room
had green wallpaper (lime green). There was a dead cat in the
room that had died several weeks before and had shrunk and
become quite stiff. The cat began to come back to life while I
was there and I began to beat it on the head to keep it dead. I
think I was scared of it. I continued to hit it and jump on it
but to no avail. Finally I gave up and decided to suffer the
consequences, and instead of attacking me after the terrible
treatment I had just finished giving it, it didn't attack me but
was very friendly towards me."

THE HYPNOANALYSIS OF A MINISTER

A seeming occupational hazard of the ministry is a "nervous
breakdown." Some presume that this is due to the tension inherent in this vocation, the long hours involved, the variety and
intensity of the interpersonal problems encountered, and such
other factors as the vague boundaries of one's parish. Often the
victims of this experience are hard working successful young
men whose churches are flourishing. Upon investigation, the
reason for the neurotic defense is often discovered not to be
due to the minister's "burning out for the Lord" but rather from

trying to escape from self-confrontation. A work regimen which does not allow a proper time for rest and relaxation is more likely the symptom of a neurotic tendency rather than the cause of it.

The following case indicates something of the hypothesis mentioned above, as well as something of the drama involved in the "unfolding" of personality development:

Tom M. came to see me a few weeks after he had been forced to resign his church due to his inability to preach and to carry on his ministerial duties. The acute cramps and severe chest pains which he had experienced when he tried to speak before the congregation were diagnosed by several physicians as having no physiological basis. He could not keep from sobbing in the pulpit and after a rest period of several months, he returned to his parish only to have the symptoms recur. He left the church and shortly thereafter "broke" to the point where, for several weeks, he was confined to bed and where his periods of sobbing could only be brought under control through the use of medication. He recovered to the point where he accepted the advice of his physician that he would have to find a vocation other than the ministry and he decided to attend a graduate school in order to prepare for a teaching position. He wanted me to evaluate his intellectual ability to do graduate work in a "secular field" and, perhaps, to help him with his emotional problems.

Inasmuch as Tom had difficulty in emotional control when he related some of the difficult experiences in the ministry and, prior to this, during his boyhood, we decided to use hypnotherapy. He was an excellent subject and the analytic phase produced many traumas, and some tragedy, which had influenced his personality development. An early hypnotic suggestion of relaxation tended to give him relief from a habit of clenching his fists when he was anxious. When he became aware that he was doing this, he said that he felt just like his arms were "turning to stone."

The usual procedure was to direct his attention, after the induction of a state of deep hypnotic relaxation, to a recent dream, or a particularly disturbing mood, and have him "free associate" in a daydream fantasy. Sometimes the results would be an interpretation of a dream, a painful memory, or a fantasy narrative with no apparent time references. Occasionally Tom would be directed to open his eyes and project the fantasy as a "moving picture" on the ceiling. This fascinated him and often brought forth interesting and significant material. In every case Tom seemed to feel improved for a few days after any particularly moving abreaction. Of special interest was the negative effect of "grade skipping" in his early school days and sibling tensions both at school and at play. A death in the immediate family was a disturbing developmental factor. He had also been the "runt" of his gang and had fared poorly in athletic activity in the neighborhood.

The analytic crisis took place without any apparent warning although Tom later mentioned that he had slept poorly the night before. He had a fantasy of working on a construction job during which he suddenly fell down an elevator shaft. He curled up as though to cushion the fall and then started to shriek and writhe on the couch. After a brief period, he relaxed and said that he was in a strange room and very much afraid. He mentioned that this was the identical format of a nightmare that he had experienced many times while growing up. He would remember having had it previously during the dream but could never recall it upon waking. The reaction always was to be tired, to clench his fists more than usual, and to be vaguely aware of having had a "horrible nightmare." This had happened to him perhaps a dozen times.

Tom reported that he was, in the fantasy, in a cage in the strange room and that the walls kept closing in on him as though they would crush him and then they would withdraw. In addition, a bushy bearded man was threatening him from a hole in the wall and peered at him with a great "searchlight" eye. His whole body seemed to be stiffening and turning to stone. After he had obtained some emotional control, we analyzed each aspect of the dream fantasy. The room seemed to him to be an actual memory but he could not place it in his experience. He suddenly recognized it as his bedroom in a home from which the family had moved when he was only two and one half years old! He was in a baby's bed with slatted sides and was fondling his penis. His mother entered and shouted at him, "Stop that! If you do that again, you'll turn to stone!"

The bushy bearded man was the janitor of the church which Tom's parents attended, who frequently picked Tom up and paid him attention. This terrified Tom and he would make every effort to avoid the man. The latter understood this to be a playful game and this only increased his attentiveness. The bright light, the "searchlight eye" seemed to refer to an experience at church also, when he saw his first motion picture projection. He was standing in the pew beside his mother one evening when the lights suddenly went out and the projector started up. He turned just in time to see a gleaming beam of light bearing down from the balcony. He was so frightened and caused such a commotion that his mother had to take him from the church.

These three experiences had somehow blended into a composite nightmare which had distressed him greatly. The analysis of this nightmare gave him a very marked relief and this seemed to be a turning point in therapy. He gained in confidence daily thereafter and began to entertain thoughts of returning to the ministry. Up to this point he had resigned himself to another vocation. We were now becoming involved in the synthetic phase.

Sometime later Tom had another disturbing hypnotic fantasy which was a crisis in the synthetic phase of the psychotherapeutic process. He imagined himself to be the principal character, a baseball pitcher, in a television program which he had recently seen. This pitcher was always "in a hole" and faced with a "three and two" pitch. Tom saw himself as playing such a role in the ministry. He sobbingly related that his pastoral zeal had not been so much motivated by an earnest desire to serve the Lord (which he wanted very much to do) but rather by the haunting fear of failure and the fear of what people thought of his decisions. This self-confrontation was a remarkable step in the therapy program. Tom seemed to grow in personal strength by leaps and bounds. His whole personality seemed to take on a unity of purpose and confidence.

Therapy sessions were held less frequently during the last month and, after a total relationship period of ten months, they were terminated. Tom returned to the pastoral ministry and, several years later, recently reported feeling well and confidently pursuing his vocational tasks.

Hypnotherapy with a Homosexual

Robert was referred to me by a minister who had been contacted by Robert's friend, Don. Both the minister and Don had phoned me for an appointment for Robert. The minister mentioned that it concerned a homosexual problem and he seemed concerned that Robert might subvert some of the young people in his church.

When Robert come to my office he was very anxious, averted any eye contact, and seemed to be in a state of confusion. He was rather hostile when he first started speaking but then relaxed somewhat as he hesitantly told me something of his background. He certainly had been raised in a negative social setting! His two older sisters were conceived out of wedlock, and although his parents were married before he was conceived, they were divorced before he was born. He had a very poor relationship with his mother, siblings, and especially with two subsequent stepfathers. He started to leave without further discussion, but suddenly turned pale, paused, and blurted out that he was a homosexual and that was the real reason that he had come to see me. This had been a continuing pattern of development from the time of puberty. He mentioned briefly some of the background experiences, saying that he was first stimulated by seeing his sisters' underwear and then by wearing it himself. He had an intense attraction to female underclothing. After he had experienced pubertal changes, he noticed that he was unusually stimulated sexually by seeing some young fellows in a car with their shirts off. He believed that he was homosexual in nature and that this was for him a normal state of adjustment. He had, for some years, been attached to Don in a homosexual relationship.

Both of them had subsequently made a profession of faith in Christ and Don was eager to break off the relationship. Robert stated that he had heard that a homosexual could, through psychotherapy, learn to sublimate his desires and live an apparently normal life. He said that he desired to do the Lord's will and felt that it would be a better Christian testimony if he were able to contain his homosexual impulses. He confessed, however, that he would not enter into a psychotherapeutic relationship except for his love for Don, who had insisted upon it as a condition for a continuing friendship. Robert was convinced that homosexual adjustments would be perfectly normal for certain people and expressed doubt that he could ever change. I told him that I could see him only on the basis that a homosexual personality pattern was psychopathological, contrary to the Christian faith, and that he "really meant business."

Robert mentioned that he had one or two dates with girls but only as a facade to cover his homosexual attitudes. He spoke of extreme repugnance at even the thought of heterosexual interests. He had no personal information as to what it would be like on "the other side" but said that he would be willing to change for the sake of Don. He had been in love with Don for several years and life would have no meaning without him. Due to the fact that there must be a high level of motivation for homosexuals to overcome their personality defects, I did not encourage Robert to enter therapy, but rather pointed out the difficulties financially, in terms of the travel distance, and in terms of the poor record of homosexuals in carrying through a psychotherapy program. He left without making a further appointment. I presumed that I would not see him again.

Robert called twice about two weeks later in order to confirm an appointment. He spoke of being very anxious to start therapy. He arrived a half hour late for the appointment and I discovered some time later that he had hitch-hiked the thirty mile distance (this was his mode of transportation for the next few sessions, which accounted for his occasional tardiness and also indicated his level of motivation).

In a later interview, he seemed rather discouraged. He had talked with the minister, whom he discovered knew about his homosexual problem. He said that he still thought going through with the therapy was God's will. It was very difficult, however, and he found that raking up old memories had been very unpleasant. Although he "wasn't going to mention it," he proceeded to tell me that he had lost his job. He had asked for a raise in order to get his car fixed and to pay the counseling fees, and had been fired instead.

We agreed upon the use of hypnotic therapy and after a very rapid induction, Robert related the following two memory-fantasies. They were very traumatic experiences and the abreaction was rather intense:

"I am at my grandmother's house. I spent several summers there. (How old are you?) Fourteen years. I'm in the bedroom, grandmother's in the kitchen. Grandmother goes outside and now I'm playing with myself. It is before my puberty change. She comes in and scolds me severely. She is telling me that it is a terrible sin. I feel terrible. She says that in the Old Testament law it says that it is better that "men cast seed into the belly of a woman than upon the ground." I remember something my mother told me that she read in a book that you could go blind from masturbation. (Did this frighten you?) Yes, I had headaches. I thought maybe there was some connection. Grandmother is still here. I deny that I did it. She makes me get dressed. We have scrambled eggs for breakfast. I feel better, she fed me. (Did she forgive you?) No, she's going to write to mother. She's praying—grace, and then for me. I feel like quite a sinner. It is Sunday morning. Now the scene is fading, now it's gone.

"I'm thinking of something else now for some reason. Mother met a younger woman during the war and they became good friends. I'm young and don't know how to use toilet paper yet. I call for help. The woman — Auntie Ruth — comes in. She wipes me. I stand up and she pats me. I'm so ashamed that I run to my alcove and hide in bed under the covers. I'd forgotten all about this. I have on a brown corduroy suit and a T shirt which is red and white. I'm about three years old, I guess. They're calling to me. They want to give me some applesauce. They're laughing about it. I decide that I've got to learn to use toilet paper. They all — my sisters, my mother, and Aunt Ruth — they're all laughing at me. It's no joke. (Are all women against you?) Yes. The girl from next door, she's there too — I haven't thought of her for a long time. Grandmother likes her. I'm outside now but I'm all tied up inside and they're still laughing. It didn't happen this way, Doctor, this laughing, laughing, laughing. I'm under the picnic table now, but it's in the kitchen. More and more people are coming in, they're all women. They're laughing. The table doesn't really belong in the kitchen — it didn't happen this way. The house is full now, and they tell each other the joke and it passes all through the crowd. They're supposed to be Christians but they're saying mean things."

Robert missed his next appointment but later I received a letter saying that he had tried to call me twice. He now had a new job and was free to come see me only early in the mornings. "I am certain that the Lord has led me in this direction and pray that we will be able to arrange morning meetings."

It was nearly a month before I saw Robert again. After each session I felt that perhaps he would not return again, but he persisted in his determination to carry on. Immediately after the hypnotic induction, his lips repeatedly formed a word, but he did not say anything. The word seemed to be "Mama." Shortly thereafter he reported the following fantasies:

He burst out painfully with the words: "MY PURPLE TRUNKS! We used to go to the beach all the time and I had a pair of purple trunks. They were too tight and they bulged in the wrong way. I didn't like them. I always went with my sisters and their friends. I didn't like it. I can feel straw-straw-straw-straw seatcovers. It is a 1941 car. Mother is in a blue bathing suit. I don't like bathing suits. I'm ten years old. I'm in back, in the corner. I always have to go with all the girls; my sisters and two other girls are in the car. They always tease me. I don't like to go to the beach with all those girls. I wish I could get dressed first and dress before going home. I don't like those purple trunks, they're too tight.

"Now I'm in a 1949 Buick and the seat covers are leather. I still have the purple trunks on and I'm twelve years old. They're the same ones. My grandmother is there. I ask for a new pair. My mother says they're cute. I don't like them at all [sobbing]. *I almost want to hit her!* (Do you almost hate her now?) *Yes!* Those crazy purple trunks are terrible. They're utterly ridiculous. I can't stand them. Besides they're too tight. Besides I don't want to go to the beach. I just get burnt. I don't like going outside. I don't like them. I like leather cushions; they're nice. I just don't like going outside. I just can't compete with people, whether with older ones or younger ones.

"Now I'm at the beach. I'm sixteen or seventeen years old. I'm trying to play volleyball. I just can't compete. Stan keeps making remarks. He's not so good himself — though a better student and a better athlete. Now I have on pink trunks and they aren't too tight. I never get a tan though. I just burn. *I wish there was a way to sandpaper these freckles off.*

"Now I'm seventeen again. I'm at the Pine Camp. I've forgotten her name. What's her name. It's supposed to be a religious conference. What's her name? I don't like her, she's fat. What's her name? She's fat. I've never kissed a girl. She wants me to! It's terrible. I want to go inside. She's awfully fat. Terrible. I'd rather kiss Andrew and he's skinny. She makes me put my arms around her. I feel sick. What's your name? *Marianne!* Andrew teases her. He's gone in and left me with her. I wish Don would come. [Robert begins to sob.] I'm sad because Don isn't here. I only came because I thought he would be here. I just dislike her. I wish I could fall in the lake and take a bath. I feel funny."

In a later interview, Robert brought, at my request, a lengthy autobiography. In it he detailed the difficulties that he had with his stepfathers and how that he had grown up with an increasingly intense feeling of inferiority. After the ninth grade he avoided any contact with girls. Don was the first person whom he met that really seemed to like him and accept him. "He accepted me so readily; my life for the first time no longer seemed difficult."

At the beginning of the next interview, he related a nightmare that he had had the night before. In the dream he was being swallowed up by an amoeba. Immediately after the trance induction, the dream was recalled. "I'm lying down in the sun in the park. There is green grass everywhere. A pond is near me. Out of the pond a jelly-like mass is beginning to ooze. It is not round, it's a jagged edge mass of protoplasm. It has a center. I don't pay attention to it and its getting closer and closer. I don't try to get up and its oozing all over me. It's

not as soft as jelly, it's harder, like skin. Just like being wrapped
up as he comes over you. There's a funny brown thing in the
center, an eye, I guess. It's springtime; the sky is blue and
everything is perfect except for the amoeba. It just came all
over me. It's absorbing me. I don't try to get up. I feel myself
breaking through the protoplasm inside. It's like little suction
cups all over me. Like being inside a bowl of jello. (How do
you feel?) Not repulsed, I don't like it but it's not too bad.
You just lie there and he does it all. (What does the dream
mean?) The first thing that comes to mind is that mother used
to come home at night. She worked from eleven to seven in
the hospital. She's always getting in my bed, she wanted to
snuggle up. *I don't like that!* That's the only thing I can think
of. I was in the eighth to the tenth grade. I'm passive but I still
don't like it! She knew it. I used to get up and get out sometimes.
It made her mad, but I don't like it."

In this interview, Robert also mentioned an incestuous relationship between his sisters and his stepfather. The grandmother was "thrown out" of the home when she rebuked the
stepfather for this. Robert started to cry and said, "I wish Don
was here. My mother used to do the same thing with my little
brother. *I hated it!* She didn't mean anything by it. Just wanted
to cuddle. Not like my stepfather. She didn't have a very fulfilling life." He then mentioned some intimate experiences with
Don and as he was leaving, he turned and said, "I didn't think
I could talk to anyone about Don."

I did not see Robert again for a week and a half. He had
called to cancel the appointment and then called a little later
to see if I could still see him. He was late and appeared to be
rather distressed. He said that he had eaten something that
had made him sick to his stomach.

"I'm not well emotionally, either. Well, I might as well tell
you. The pastor gave Don the book by Bergler. He's decided
that it would be best to part our ways. This was Saturday night.

At first I didn't believe him. It depressed me. I wasn't angry, just extremely depressed. It wasn't like I'd hoped it would be. I had hoped things woud gradually change and we would still have friendship. I probably depended upon it too much. [Robert's eyes began to fill up with tears.] It seems final. I don't know whether I want to change my personality now or not. My motivation isn't so high now."

I then induced hypnotic relaxation and the following significant fantasy ensued:

"I'm falling in a hole. I'm not falling, I'm really suspended. Don is at the top. I keep slipping down. I'm stuck in the tunnel. It's greased. No, not really, I guess it's like gunk. I'm still stuck. (How do you feel?) I don't know, I'm scared. I don't know what to do. Don's putting the manhole down — Oh! Oh! It's completely dark in here now [sobbing]. I've reached the bottom of the tunnel. Water's running underneath. I'm falling into the water. The water's clear though, clean and clear. It's carrying me away. Down and — oops! there's a bump — there's a big castle! I'm floating into a moat and the water stops. I'm climbing up on the bank and walking toward the drawbridge. There are no guards, nothing but fields and trees. There are no signs of civilization at all. Inside every footstep echoes and there's armor alongside the walks. I go through the entrance and see that everything is bricks and moss and damp on the walls. The sun is coming down in the middle and there is a stairway to some rooms. I'm going up. I circle around the court below. The stairway seems to circle up to the sky. There are many towers. There's nobody around. I'm going up the next flight now — and the next — and the next. I'm running. I'm looking for the hole where the sun shines through to the bottom. Now I don't want to go on; if I do, I'll jump or fall. I'm backing away from the edge and I hit some armor which is standing next to the wall. It's just standing there. I push against the wall and a door opens up into a bedroom. There's a girl in bed. She's very pretty. (How do you feel?) I feel very vicious, I want to hurt her."

Robert then related an attempt to make a brutal sexual assault on the girl, but her friendliness, tenderness, and responsiveness took him aback. He became embarrassed and said that he "didn't know what to do."

"(I thought you were going to be mean and vicious.) She's changed my mind, but I don't know what to do. (Do you still want to do something bad?) No, I'm afraid. (Wouldn't you like to establish a warm relationship, if you weren't afraid? If it were natural? If the Lord gave you a wife?)." Robert began to sob vigorously and this brought him out of the hypnotic trance.

We discussed the possibility of moving away from Don toward the establishment of happy, heterosexual relationships. Robert seemed to think that this was, for the first time, a real possibility. "At first I thought that the water was going to be dirty, like a sewer, but it wasn't. (Why did you cry?) When you mentioned the Lord giving me a girl, it seemed so hard to believe. It's hard to believe for, like when I was at boarding school, everybody disliked me. The entire school gave me the silent treatment. I was considered an oddball. Word got to the girls and I turned my back on the girls and never tried to get a date. I had homosexual feelings before this however.... *I hate to break up with Don!* (Do you feel that you could establish happy homosexual relations after this experience?) No, I guess I really couldn't. Do I have a couple of minutes left? Saturday night we had a long discussion and I went back to his room with him. I think we could have been reconciled then, but I just couldn't have performed sexually. I just couldn't do it! It seemed so different, and then as I was walking home, I thought about girls and sexual intercourse. I just couldn't do it with Don."

Robert was very enthusiastic when he left, but he broke his next appointment and I did not see him thereafter. He writes me occasionally and reports that everything is going well, although he avoids any reference to his psychosexual attitudes.

COUNSELING A FAILING STUDENT

Kim first contacted me by telephone. He sounded depressed and appeared to be about to cry. He said that he had been referred to me by a young minister whom he had turned to for counseling assistance. When he came to my office, Kim was very depressed, a slow talking, slow walking, sad faced oriental boy. He reported that he had been unable to study during the semester and was in danger of being dropped from the university, where he was a junior, because of failing grades. He also had difficulties in social relationships and was extremely upset by his intense inferiority feelings.

Kim was from a wealthy, broken home and alternated between living with one parent and then the other. He had wanted to study in the humanities area but had been persuaded by the father to take a science major so as to follow in the father's footsteps. He was evaluated as being very superior in diagnostic psychological tests and his academic difficulty was presumed to be due to his emotional conflicts rather than to an attempt to accomplish a task beyond his ability.

During his freshman year in college, he had gone to the university counseling service for several weekly visits in order to alleviate difficult tensions arising early in his collegiate experience. He had been converted through the Campus Crusade for Christ and the Inter-Varsity Christian Fellowship that same year and shortly thereafter stopped going for counseling sessions. He hoped that his new faith would strengthen him emotionally. Early in the sophomore year he again utilized the university counseling services and felt "let down" in his Christian faith. When he contacted me, his faith was somewhat tenuous and he wondered if he had really become a Christian at all, or whether his conversion had merely been a reaction to his emotional problems. He was no longer active in campus religious activities, went to church infrequently, and had no joy in his Christian experiences. He felt that I could, perhaps, help him to make a better synthesis of his life, and also to help him to determine whether his religious experiences had been genuine or not.

Because of the distance which he would have to travel, I recommended to him two psychotherapists who were Christians and living much nearer to him. One of these therapists wrote me a few days later: "Thanks a lot for referring to me this Chinese boy. I played 'psycho-drama' with him for an hour (acting as the father) but decided to discourage him from returning. I have had two Chinese boys this past year, both Christians, and these were the toughest, hardest, most refractory material I have met for some time. With this in mind I felt that I could not do much for this boy." A few days later, Kim called again and was rather importunate about getting some help, so we arranged some appointments.

We decided to use hypnotherapeutic techniques and this seemed novel and intriguing to Kim. He produced several dreams each night and his fantasy narratives were short and multitudinous. The analysis brought out a very disturbing family setting, ambivalence in psychosexual development, poor study habits, and feelings of non-acceptance from the peer group. The one stabilizing factor from Kim's point of view had been a series of two or three girl friends in high school. These seemed to understand him. He said of the first romance: "This was the first time that I had contact with the outside world. With her everything was peaceful, no emptiness."

One obstacle in the counseling program was Kim's tendency to give a Freudian interpretation to all of his experiences and to try to employ a psychological jargon in our sessions. He was devoting a good deal of time to reading psychological literature and had decided that he would be a psychologist. I recommended to him a couple of Tournier's books in order to reorient his psychological thinking. He was very interested in these and they seemed to bring us into the synthetic phase of the program.

I told Kim about my own conversion experience and we discussed the great freedom and responsibility of the Christian faith. Kim came to the next interview cheerfully and announced that he had made an "existential decision" on Monday morning. He woke up and didn't want to get up, but suddenly he thought of my suggestion "to face the world" and determined to follow it through. The week had been a very pleasant experience. He had gone to church the day before and the sermon had given him the idea that God gives us drives and motives and that it is up to us to direct them. "I guess I just have to yield to the energies of God." The following is a "free association" under hypnotic relaxation during this interview:

"[smiling] I'm thinking of work (He had been forced to drop out of school earlier and now had gotten a job. This had been a major decision for him and up to this point he was frequently late for work and had decided to quit several times. His boss considered him a good worker, but Kim felt that he could not do the job.) It's strange for me to be planning what to do tomorrow. There is a new girl at the lab about twenty-eight years old. She just started working and I've been giving her things to do. I was thinking about what to do; it's so different, making decisions for others! Today I felt as though I could handle it. I made some pretty good decisions. I feel pretty good about work. I can do a good job. I talked to people at work, I feel more confident and am more sure of myself.

"I can't see much yet [referring to the dream fantasy]. I was afraid I would fall asleep. Now I see a wheel. It's like a pie plate. Now it has an axle on it and the axle is up in the air. Like a sex symbol, though I saw a wheel first. It's weird. I'll leave that for a while. Now there's a handle to a drawer, a piece of equipment at work, perhaps a handle to pull. Maybe I'm being pulled to a goal. Now it's attached to a briefcase and I'm walking along all dressed up. Like a professional man and not a technician. This morning I thought of going back to the university to finish up. Now that would be a problem of competition with my brother. I could help him though. He has more needs than I do. I'm still walking down the street. I seem to be going some place at last. The thought of escaping just came to me and I saw someone running backwards the other way.

"[smiling] Now I'm skiing down a slope.

"I'm thinking of work and how I could do a good job. Aside from my record and the money I make. I think about working hard and getting things done and being a man. [Laughing] A very, very new attitude for me and a good one. Seems like this is how God must have intended people to be. Anne, also, [a Christian girl he had met], she feels so good when she's helping people. When she does things wrong, she prays. She really believes that all things are going to turn out for good. It's seeping into me, too.

"[Smiling] I'm thinking of Dad and Mom and my brother and sisters. Dad has a serious emotional problem. I'm sure God is going to direct me.

"I'm going back to the wheel now. It still has an axle on it but it's going down the track without the other wheel [he later interpreted this as a termination fantasy]. Now I'm not going along like I originally was, all up in the air, but rather now I'm directed, I'm being *guided along the track!*"

Kim seemed to improve rapidly during the next few days. His dream themes reflected personal courage and confidence. Things were going very well at work and he had definitely decided to return to school. He mentioned that he had a "pretty good relationship with God. I haven't had this for a long time, if ever. I'm consistent now, I can meditate." We decided to terminate after the next interview.

Kim was late for his last appointment, but came in beaming

broadly and said that he felt excellent. He had been on a week-end religious retreat and had reaffirmed his faith, or accepted Christ for the first time. He was not sure which, but felt that it made no difference for it was a genuine commitment. He seemed full of the anticipation of the future. We discussed termination and were mutually agreed upon it.

Several weeks later I received a letter from which the following are excerpts: "It has been a long time. God has blessed more abundantly than I ever could have imagined. I am now a supernormal young man, rapidly maturing in the Christian faith....I have lost myself in God and so found my identity. It has been quite a miracle. It is as Paul wrote 'old things are passed away, behold all things are become new'....Thanks for the work we did together. God used it."

SUMMARY

The Christian psychotherapist will have the opportunity to utilize many different techniques and methods in his attempt to bring about the transformation of personality from illness to health. It will be important for him to realize that his Christian philosophy of life makes him neither omnipotent nor omniscient. It does, however, give him the goal, the potential, and the direction for essential and effective psychotherapy. The foregoing excerpts from case studies were depicted in an attempt to afford some insight into the difficulty and disappointment along with the success and satisfaction of a Christian psychotherapeutic practice.

CHAPTER VII

CONCLUDING COMMENTS

There is a growing conviction within the ranks of evangelical Christianity that the gospel lays a claim upon man in every aspect of his life. It challenges him in his state of sin, offers the means to transform him to a state of grace, and infuses meaning into his vocation. It is within this conviction that a truly Christian psychotherapy will either flourish or die.

There are many, however, both Christian and non-Christian, who would welcome an early demise of such a therapeutic approach. The intentional developing theme of this volume is that this would be catastrophic in terms of both Christian responsibility, and the theoretical and practical potential of a Biblically oriented psychotherapeutic system.

We live in an age alerted to, and perhaps oversensitive to, a distressing problem of mental health, as well as an era replete with diagnostic tools, psychopathological titles, and psychotherapeutic techniques. Persons involved in this area professionally, however, cannot help but observe the general confusion and lack of normative standards that stultify progress. The distressing tensions in mental health research seem to be clustered around the lack of an adequate anthropology, an objective axiology, or value system, a distinct therapeutic direction, and a governing goal. Psychotherapists in general can be, without great distortion, characterized as "blind leaders of the blind" and men "swayed by every wind of doctrine." The Christian world and life view provides stability in each of the above problem areas and affords the Christian psychotherapist a base of great theoretical and practical advantage. A fond hope undergirding this present literary task is that a large number of Christians will latch on to this advantage and thus bring succor to a needy society.

The preceding chapters are intended to be neither definitive nor exhaustive in the establishment of a Christian psychotherapy, but rather suggestive and stimulating to this end. The unique potential of the total person perspective in Biblical Christianity will support a wide and effective ministry in the field of mental health if Christians will respond to their responsibility. This does not mean that all Christians should, or could, be psychotherapists, but rather that Christians who are psychotherapists should carefully consider their commitments and convictions, and that young Christians seeking God's vocation might consider the opportunities for ministering in the mental health field. It goes without saying that Christians distressed by emotional disorders might also be alerted to the potential for health inherent in the gospel of Christ.

I should not lay down my pen without expressing my gratitude and indebtedness to Viktor Frankl of the University of Vienna. Although the content of this work, apart from the copious quotations, is largely of my own formulation and experience, there is, nonetheless, a large obligation to the founder of Logotherapy. Especially in the areas of anthropology and the existential aspect of psychotherapy did his books give new insights and new assurances. The opportunity to spend a year at his clinic in Vienna provided a manifold of experience, as well as the stimulus for this project, which is a sequel to my *Logo-*

therapy and the Christian Faith.

In the investigation of Frankl's "school of psychiatry," I found this well established clinical movement to be more cordial, both theoretically and practically, to a Christian approach to psychotherapy than is any other contemporary psychiatric development. The intriguing name, "Logotherapy," also seemed to offer rich associations for the Christian therapist. However, Frankl's reasons for coining this particular name (to emphasize the "spiritual" dimension of man, to stress the meaningfulness of "meaning" in human motivation, and to avoid further confusion of his existential analysis *[Existenzanalyse]* with the existential analysis *[Daseinsanalyse]* of Binswanger) seemed to lack the comprehensiveness, or, from another angle, the specificity, entailed in a Biblically oriented Christian perspective. Another reason that might be put forth, and which Frankl would no doubt share, is the common meaning of the Greek word *logos.* This is its reference to "word," and the wonder of verbal communication which makes possible the context of mutual understanding and fellowship which are necessities in the psychotherapeutic relationship.

The deeper significance of "Logotherapy" for the Christian, however, is provided in the use of *logos* in the Gospel of John to depict the God-man, Jesus Christ, who is the beginning and the end of any Christian theory and practice, the Word of God incarnate — "and the Word became flesh and dwelt among us." In addition, the *logos* of God enscripturated, the Biblical revelation, is the standard, and the great resource material, for a Christian psychotherapy. For these reasons the theme of this volume seems to me appropriately expressed as an introduction to Christian Logotherapy.

BUT...

The last few months and years have afforded the opportunity not only to observe Christian Logotherapy in practice, but also to confront a variety of audiences with it. I have frequently

lectured before student groups, church congregations, and professional gatherings concerning the Christian and the couch, as
well as presented these themes in the context of academic
courses relating to counseling and psychotherapy. The reaction
has been, in general, quite favorable, though dissension is almost invariably voiced. These dissensions are not particularly
threatening, for they represent the kind of questions that I keep
asking myself.

*But isn't this a rather dogmatic and even arrogant approach?
After all, aren't there many different psychotherapeutic approaches and many different religious viewpoints? Can you
prove that Christianity and Christian psychotherapy are the
only true ones?*

It surely is dogmatic (as is every opinion presented as fact),
but hopefully it is not arrogant. One of the most difficult tasks
of the Christian is to stand firm in the rather intolerant and
exclusive system of truth revealed in the Scriptures. Complete
theoretical tolerance, as a friend of mine sagaciously, though
saltily, observed, is the mark of an empty head. The Bible forthrightly presents certain principles and precepts, and to aver that
they are true, and that other, contrary, ideas are also true, is
more fitting for the social context behind the looking glass than
in the real world. Alice and Kierkegaard may have struggled to
swallow absurdities before breakfast, but I could hardly recommend it for the evangelical Christian, or for anybody else. At
the same time the Christian therapist must exercise every care to
be personally tolerant. He must learn to love his neighbor as
himself even though his neighbor hold radically differing, non-
Christian views. Theoretical intolerance does in no way obviate
personal tolerance, and for the Christian this latter can only be
defined in and through love.

There are a multitude of different religions but Christ asserted
that He fulfilled *the* religion which alone could *religere,* could

bind again, could reconcile men to God. The Christian accepts this as true and the Christian psychotherapist recognizes that this entails a view of man and his problems, together with the solution of his problems, which excludes most psychotherapeutic theories.

The rejoinder that this Christian truth cannot be proved is, for me, a fact, though not a very troubling fact. Actually no world view or philosophy of life that touches upon our experiences and relates to the historical scene can be proved. Life is deeper than logic. Logic must guard the heart, however, and it does so for the Christian. The Christian faith may not be subject to an irresistible mathematical demonstration, but it is, in my opinion, that theory which best accounts for all the facts of life and is attended by the fewest difficulties.

But isn't this definition of Christianity very narrow? What's the difference between your viewpoint and bibliolatry?

These questions were presented to me recently by a theological professor during the discussion period of a theological forum at which I had presented a talk on "Mental Health and the Christian." I confessed to the first query that it did seem to present Christianity as a rather narrow viewpoint. However, Christ set the clear pattern of the narrowness of Christianity in the sermon on the mount. Truth is not particularly characterized by "elbow room."

Concerning bibliolatry, the professor was so hard pressed (to the great amusement of his students) to explain exactly what the term meant that I did not have to reply. In any case, the Bible seems to me to be much more a fruitful instrument than an idol.

But aren't you imposing a value system upon your patients? Isn't this unethical and "untherapeutic"?

This is really a question put to every therapist. Each one

brings to the psychotherapy relationship a rather fixed system of values and an impelling idea of what a whole or healed person is. A majority of therapists hold this implicitly rather than explicitly and it seems to me that they are the ones who are treading upon thin ice; more so than the Christian therapist. Being blind to one's values and prejudices is a much more precarious position than forthrightly regarding them.

In any event, the imposition of values upon a counselee is neither desirable nor possible. This is the point at which rapport dissolves and therapy founders. A human being must make his own free decisions. However, the Christian therapist believes that confrontation with Christian love and Christian truth, rather than attempted imposition, may provide the value option that will enable the patient (the suffering one) to emerge from darkness into light, from fearfulness to joy. In every therapeutic program the therapist, whether he will or not, bears witness. The Christian therapist has the opportunity to bear witness of the Truth.

Unethical aspects in the witness bearing of values for living only enter when there is subterfuge. The very nature of the appeal for psychotherapeutic help contains the request for assistance in a commitment to values that are worthy goals for life and death. The patient must make the leap but the Christian therapist may point the direction in confidently declaring that such values inhere in Jesus Christ. The person identified initially to his clientele as a Christian psychotherapist does in no way deceive them.

But do you really mean that the non-Christian psychotherapist cannot really help people who are emotionally disturbed?

It is difficult to measure the full inflective force of these "really's," but the essential answer of the Christian therapist seems to me to be "yes." The Grace of God is not an item controlled and dispensed by men, whether Christian psychothera-

pists, ministers, or any other vocational category under the sun.
It may energize and heal a human when we least expect. This
does not exclude a human being who is the patient of a non-
Christian psychotherapist. However, the healing of the patient
in the significant sense would be in spite of the therapist rather
than because of him. The counselee may honestly confront himself and encounter God, even to the distress of the non-Christian therapist who would seek to "cure his soul" by some secular
solution. The only acceptable goal for Christian psychotherapy
is "a man of God thoroughly furnished unto all good works."

Another problem that follows from these considerations, and
may appear to be more threatening, is that the non-Christian
therapist himself is in dire need of a radical psychotherapy. He
is, in this sense, one of the more sick, for he is presumably unaware of his need. Perhaps one should at this point distinguish
between psychopathology in the sense of neurotic, psychotic,
and sociopathic symptoms, on the one hand, and this deep
psychopathy or "soul sickness" of the "well-adjusted" non-Christian, on the other. However, if the Christian therapist is to be
true to his premise, the reality of the inevitable grim symptoms
of terrifying isolation and personal destruction in eternal punishment should impel him to a careful and proper diagnosis of his
colleagues outside the faith, in the face of social and professional
pressure.

This was a very existential consideration for me recently when
I lectured to a group of about two dozen non-Christian psychotherapists (by their own admission — it is important that one
does not attempt to categorize others) on this theme. This is a
challenge of their existence and an implied negative criticism of their entire professional impact. Nonetheless, it is my
firm conviction that they ought to be challenged from a Christian perspective on both theoretical and practical grounds. Moreover, I experience that a careful presentation in an attitude of
love (an intolerant precept in the setting of personal love and

tolerance) gains respect, if not acceptance, and, who knows, may perhaps stimulate to consciousness a personal need which shall eventuate in the advancement of Christ's Kingdom. In a paraphrase of Mordecai, who knows but that the Christian psychotherapist was brought to the Kingdom for such a time as this!

But aren't you confusing the well man and the good man? Isn't there a difference between being healthy and being right-eous?

It seems to me that in the area of mental health, the confusion is rather on the side of secularism. In the total person perspective of the Christian faith, the two are basically identified. This does not mean that a Christian could not be ill in a physiological or psychological perspective, nor, conversely, that the non-Christian could not be well adjusted in such areas. It does imply, however, that true health, personal wholeness, must have a radical beginning — in the *radix,* the root, in the heart, in the pneumatic dimension — and that psychotherapeutic treatment with any other premise is purely palliative. It may ease the "disease," but it does not cure it. The therapist must often give immediate and careful attention to a particular dimension of personality, but he should exercise care to retain a whole person perspective and to remember the primacy of the spiritual dimension.

But, do you really mean to say that all emotional problems are spiritual problems?

This seems to be precisely the point, and an analysis of the instances of personal distress provides abundant evidence for this thesis. A problem is not constituted by a condition of the physical or social environments, nor even in the somatic, psychic, or noetic dimension. Personal problems, cropping out of the critical context of anxiety and/or guilt, result from one's attitude to a complex of the above conditions. Personal problems are spiritual matters.

HOWEVER...

Lest these proliferating dissensions cause the courage of the potential Christian logotherapist to falter, it should also be emphatically reiterated that a Christian psychotherapy can stand unapologetically (in the shame-faced sense) and apologetically (in the I Peter 3:15 sense) in the twentieth century. It is a Christian psychotherapy alone which can utilize the results of modern mental health research and can fill those lacunae, or gaps, in the gaping spectrum of contemporary psychology: an adequate anthropology, an objective axiology, a distinct direction for psychotherapy, and a governing goal for personal fulfillment.

There will be pressures perpetually present which will make the establishment and maintenance of a Christocentric psychotherapeutic "movement" a vigorous and laborious task, but the theoretical and practical advantages, coupled with the reality of the divine commission, make it a pleasant prospect.

I draw this work to a close with the hope that the reader will become existentially engaged with the great potential of its basic thesis; and that the Christian in the field of mental health may, perhaps, be caught up in the author's confidence that the future of Christian Logotherapy is as "bright as the promises of God."

GLOSSARY

acute: Attended with symptoms of some severity, coming speedily to a crisis; as opposed to chronic.

affective: Pertaining to a person's emotional feeling tone; emotional.

agape: Divine love; that which is "shed abroad" in the heart of the Christian by the Holy Spirit in regeneration and sanctification.

ambivalence: The coexistence of two opposing drives, desires, feelings, or emotions toward the same person, object, or goal.

analytic: Pertaining to the resolving or breaking down of a problem into its constituent parts; often may refer to the diagnosis and treatment method of psychoanalysis.

anthropology: The scientific study of man.

anxiety: Apprehension, tension or uneasiness which stems from the anticipation of danger, the source of which is largely unknown or unrecognized. Anxiety may be regarded as pathologic when it is present to such an extent as to interfere with effectiveness in living, the achievement of desired realistic goals or satisfactions, or reasonable emotional comfort.

apperceptive: Referring to perception characterized by clearness and by the relating of what is now presented to previously acquired knowledge.

archetype: The original pattern of which all things of the same species are representations or copies; in Jung's theory, a representation in the unconscious of an experience of the human race, an inherited idea or idea-feeling.

ataraxia: A state of untroubled calmness; the absence of anxiety.

atonement: The redeeming effect of Christ's incarnation, sufferings, and death; reconciliation between God and men, especially through Christ.

autistic: Concerning the tendency in one's thinking or perceiving to be regulated unduly by personal desires and needs, at the expense of regulation by objective reality; fantasy thinking.

axiology: The scientific study of values.

behavior: The way in which an organism acts, especially in response to a stimulus. This is a central concept for most psychologists and the way in which it is defined or delimited will characterize a psychological theory.

229

behaviorism: A body of psychologic theory, first developed by John B. Watson, concerned chiefly with objectively observable, tangible, and measurable data, rather than with so-called subjective phenomena such as ideas and emotions.

catharsis: The healthful release of ideas through a "talking out" of conscious material accompanied by the appropriate emotional reaction; or, the release into awareness to some extent of repressed (i.e., "forgotten") material or experiences from the unconscious.

character: An integrated system of traits and behavior tendencies that enable one to act, despite obstacles, in a relatively consistent way in relation to moral issues; formerly this term was used as a general synonym for personality.

chemotherapy: A form of therapy which is based upon the chemical action of certain drugs and medicines.

chronic: Pertaining to disease conditions which persist for a long time.

client: A person who comes for counseling or psychotherapy.

clinical: Characterizing the study of the individual as a unique whole. Specific behaviors are observed and specific traits are inferred, but the goal is that of understanding and helping the particular individual.

concept: A general meaning, idea, or property which refers to one or more individual items or "things."

connotation: The meaning of a term when defined by the essential characteristics of the group of objects designated by the term; as opposed to denotation which designates the objects referred to. For example a connotative definition of "skyscraper" would necessarily include size of the building, especially height; a denotative definition would be The Empire State Building, Chrysler Building, etc.

conscience: The morally self-critical part of oneself whereby standards of behavior, performance, and value judgments arise. In theological perspective this is usually seen as innate or divinely implanted, as opposed to the superego of psychoanalysis which has a similar function but which is gained exclusively through social contact.

conscious: Being aware.

construct: A concept, formally proposed, with definition and limits clearly related to empirical data.

counselee: A person who receives counseling.

counseling: A relationship in which one person endeavors to help another to understand and to solve his adjustment problems.

counselor: A professionally trained person who does counseling.

defense mechanisms: Any enduring structure of the person's psychological make-up which enables him to avoid awareness of the unpleasant or anxiety-arousing; also known as mental mechanisms or mental dynamisms.

demythologizing: Pertaining to the currently popular theological method of R. Bultmann whereby the "mythical" data of the Scriptures are discovered and sloughed off in order to understand the "true" gospel; a non-evangelical theological perspective.

depression: A morbid sadness, dejection, or melancholy; differentiated from grief which is realistic and proportionate to what has been lost.

de-reflection: A technical term in the psychiatric theory of Viktor Frankl which refers to the diverting of a person's attention away fom his symptoms.

diagnosis: The identification of a disease or abnormality from symptoms and/or test responses, and from a study of its origin and course.

diagnostic tests: Tests which are designed to identify, or locate the particular source of difficulty of a disease, abnormality, or personal maladjustment.

dialectic: Reasoning about matters of opinion in the attempt to discriminate truth from error.

dichotomy: Literally, to cut in two; the division of a group into two classes on the basis of the presence or absence of a certain characteristic.

didactic: Pertaining to teaching; sometimes as contrasted to learning by direct observation or study.

dimension: Any characteristic by which an object or event can be positioned in a quantitative series. The term referred originally to length, breadth, or thickness but is now extended. For scientific description, dimensions should be independent and should collectively describe all of a coherent group of facts.

directive counseling: The procedure when a counselor endeavors to control, directly or indirectly, the topics about which the counselee speaks, describes the choices which face him, and/or advises him what to do.

dispensationalism: A theological perspective which, among other emphases, posits a trichotomy of the nature of man into body, soul, and spirit; a theological point of view expressed in the Scofield Bible Notes.

dynamic: Pertaining, in psychology, to the causes of behavior and motivation.

eclectic: Choosing, as doctrines or methods, from various sources, systems, etc.

ego: The "I," self, person, or individual as distinguished from others; that which is postulated as the "center" to which all a person's psychological activities and qualities are referred.

emotional disorder: A condition in which emotional reactions to reality situations are disproportionate, either too intense or the reverse.

empathy: An objective and insightful awareness of the feelings, emotions, and behavior of another person, and their meaning and significance. To be distinguished from sympathy, which is non-objective and usually non-critically emotional.

empirical: Pertaining to, or founded upon, experiment or experience.

endogenous: Refers to that which originates within a structure or system; especially originating within the body.

etiology: The scientific study of causes; especially the investigation of the causes of any disease.

etymology: The origin or derivation of a word as shown by its analysis into elements, by pointing out the root or primitive upon which it is based, or by referring it to an earlier form in its parent language.

euphoric: Pertaining to an exaggerated feeling of physical and emotional well being.

evangelical: Designating the point of view which holds that the essence of the gospel consists mainly in its doctrines of man's sinful condition and need of salvation, the revelation of God's grace in Christ, the necessity of spiritual renovation, and participation in the experience of redemption through faith.

existential: Pertaining to an intense awareness of one's contingency and freedom; usually referring to a theory which stresses the individual's responsibility for making himself what he is.

explicit: Distinctly stated; having no disguised meaning.

fantasy: A product of the imagination; it is usually pleasant and represents a sort of wish fulfillment.

functional autonomy: A concept in the psychological theory of Gordon Allport; a mode of behavior may be initiated to fulfill specific needs and then later be carried out to fulfill other needs; i.e., a person may begin to smoke in order to attain status and later the need shifts to that of physiological-emotional craving.

functional disorder: A condition in which one or more of the normal activities of the organism cannot be properly performed, though there is no known pathological change in organic structure which can be related to the disorder.

genetic: Pertaining to the origin, history, and development of an organism.

gestalt: A form, configuration, or unified whole which has properties which cannot be derived from the sum of its parts; Gestalt psychology is a "school" which holds that psychological phenomena are organized, undivided, articulated wholes, or "gestalts."

grace: Divine mercy or forgiveness; divine assistance given to man for his regeneration or sanctification; unmerited favor.

guilt: The fact that one has violated ethical moral or religious principles, together with a regretful feeling of lessened personal worth on that account.

holistic: Pertaining to the doctrine that a living being has properties which refer to the whole rather than to its constituent parts, and that the dynamics of a living whole cannot be explained as resulting from independent elements.

homeostasis: A relatively stable state of equilibrium, or a tendency toward such a state, between the different but interdependent elements and subsystems of an organism of any kind.

humanistic: Pertaining to a mode or attitude of thought or action centering upon distinctively human interests or ideals.

hypnoanalysis: A method of analytic psychotherapy carried on while the patient is under hypnosis.

hypnosis: An artificially induced state characterized by greatly heightened suggestibility to the hypnotist.

hypomanic: A mild state of mania. There is excitement, energy, impatience, and flightiness; yet, in an otherwise normal person, the condition may be productive.

hypothesis: A tentative theory or supposition provisionally adopted to explain certain facts and to guide in the investigation of others.

hysteria: An illness resulting from emotional conflict and generally characterized by immaturity, impulsiveness, attention-seeking, dependency, and the use of defense mechanisms of conversion and dissociation; classically manifested by dramatic physical symptoms involving the voluntary muscles or the organs of special senses.

id: In Freudian theory, that part of the personality structure which harbors the unconscious instinctive desires and strivings of the individual.

implicit: Not directly stated, but understandable or deductible from what is stated.

inferiority complex: In the theory of Adler, feelings of inferiority stemming from real or imagined physical or social inadequacies which may cause anxiety or other adverse reactions.

instinct: An inborn drive.

introverted: Preoccupied with oneself, with accompanying reduction of interest in the outside world.

libido: The psychic drive or energy usually associated with the sexual instinct; also used broadly to connote the psychic energy associated with instincts in general.

logotherapy: A psychotherapeutic theory formulated by Viktor Frankl of Vienna which emphasizes the spiritual nature of man, and the significance of meaningfulness in the life of an individual.

manic: Pertaining to a mental illness, mania, which is marked by heightened excitability, acceleration of thought, speech, and bodily motion, and by elation or grandiosity of mood.

masochistic: Refers to a state in which pleasure is derived from suffering physical or psychological pain.

materialism: Any theory which considers the facts of the universe to be sufficiently explained by the existence and nature of matter.

mental hygiene: The science and art of preserving and maximizing mental health.

mental illness: A disorder of behavior; a breakdown of adjustment so severe that professional psychotherapy is indicated.

metabolism: The sum of the processes concerned in building up and breaking down of living cells and tissue.

metaphysics: That branch of philosophy which is concerned with the ultimate nature of existence.

micro-organism: Any organism so small as to require a microscope in order to observe it.

neurosis: An emotional maladaptation due to unresolved personal and/or unconscious conflict. Usually less severe than a psychosis, with a minimal loss of contact with reality.

noetic: Pertaining to the psychological data concerned with cognition, or knowing, and memory. In Frankl's theory, this term refers to the dimension of personality which enables existential behavior.

non-directive therapy: A therapy, usually related to Carl Rogers, based on the doctrine that psychotherapy consists in helping the client to mobilize his own latent psychic resources in the solution of his own problems. The therapist seeks to understand the client on his own terms, and encourages, but does not guide, the client's exploration of his troublesome attitudes and feelings.

noologism: The point of view which would reduce all psychological data to the noetic dimension.

obsession: An idea which is persistent and unwanted; usually associated with anxiety or dread.

organism: A living being capable of maintaining itself as a system, and composed of parts capable of performing certain coordinated functions.

organismic: Pertaining to an organism; in a psychological context, the term usually refers to that behavior which depends upon the organism as a whole, rather than upon particular parts.

palliative: Easing or reducing pain or discomfort without removing the cause.

panacea: A remedy for all diseases; a cure-all.

paradoxical intention: A specific psychotherapeutic technique in the Logotherapy of Viktor Frankl in which the patient is encouraged to intend the object or situation which is feared.

patient: A suffering person who is under professional care or treatment.

perception: An act of cognition, or awareness, stimulated by sensory excitation; the interpretation of sensation.

personality: The sum total of the individual's internal and external patterns of adjustment to life; or, the expression of the person, or individual.

philosophy: The search for a coherent understanding of reality.

phobia: An obsessive, persistent, unrealistic fear of an object or situation such as heights, closed spaces, dirt, and animals.

phylogenetic: Pertaining to the origin and development of any biological group.

physiogenic: Designating that which originates in the functioning of the body or of some organ or tissue.

physiology: The study of certain functions, such as digestion, circulation, and respiration, of a living organism.

physiologism: The point of view which would reduce all psychological data to physiological factors.

placebo: A preparation containing no medicine which is administered to the patient in such a way that he believes himself to be receiving treatment.

pneumatic: Derived from the Greek word **pneuma**, spirit, and used in a special sense in this volume to refer to the spiritual dimension of man, the "core" charactertistics of the individual.

prognosis: The prediction of the duration, course, and outcome of a certain process or activity, especially of a disease.

projection: The defense mechanism whereby one ascribes to others one's own unacknowledged desires or faults. This is presumed to be unconscious defense against a sense of guilt or anxiety.

psyche: The mind; mental life; in psychoanalysis it is often used to indicate the performer of psychological functions or acts.

psychiatry: A medical specialty dealing with the prevention, diagnosis, treatment, and care of mental illness.

psychoanalysis: A body of doctrine set forth by Freud. The primary assumption is that psychotherapeutic analysis is based upon the theory that abnormal mental reactions are due to repression of desires which are consciously rejected but subconsciously persistent.

psychogenic: Refers to that which has a psychological origin, or originates in experience.

psychologism: The point of view which reduces all psychological or behavioral data to the emotional or psychic dimension of man.

psychology: The scientific study of behavior, especially of human acts and mental processes, and with the mind, self, or person who acts or has the mental processes.

psychoneurosis: Generally used as a synonym for neurosis.

psychopathic: Refers to behavior which is predominantly immoral or anti-social and characterized by impulsive, irresponsible actions satisfying only immediate selfish interests. There is often no concern for obvious and implicit social consequences and there is a minimal outward evidence of anxiety and guilt.

psychopathology: The scientific study of morbid, or abnormal, mental conditions.

psychosomatic: Referring to illnesses in which the manifestations are primarily physical with a psychological, or emotional, etiology.

psychosurgery: Treatment of serious psychiatric disorders by brain surgery.

rapport: A comfortable and unconstrained relationship of mutual confidence between two or more persons, especially between counselor and client.

rapprochement: A coming together; the establishment or state of cordial relations.

reality principle: In psychoanalysis, the awareness of the demands of the environment and adjustment of behavior to these demands in such a way that the individual ultimately secures satisfaction of instinctual needs.

reductionism: A general point of view which holds that complex phenomena are to be understood and explained by analyzing them into ever simpler, and ultimately into strictly elemental, components (more likely used by the opponents than the advocates of a particular theory).

reflex arc: The theoretical unit of function of the nervous system. At its simplest, it consists in a receptor, or afferent, nerve which, excited by a sensory stimulus, transmits this excitation to an effector, or efferent, nerve.

regeneration: The act or state of spiritual rebirth in a theological context.

relativism: Opposed to absolutism; the attitude or belief that the truth about anything is always dependent upon the context, that standards of conduct are not absolute but relative to time, place, culture, and historical circumstances.

Rorschach inkblots: A psychological test developed by the Swiss psychiatrist, Hermann Roschach, which seeks to disclose conscious and unconscious personality traits and emotional conflicts through eliciting the patient's associations to a standard set of inkblots.

salvation: The saving of man from the spiritual consequences of sin, especially deliverance from sin and eternal damnation through Christ; redemption.

schizophrenia: A severe emotional disorder of psychotic depth characteristically marked by a retreat from reality with delusion formations, hallucinations, emotional disharmony, and regressive behavior. Formerly called dementia praecox.

secular: Pertaining to the worldly or temporal as opposed to the spiritual or eternal; any point of view which is expressed apart from any reference, either explicit or implicit, to God.

self-conscious: The special state of being explicitly aware of what one is doing; also refers to an emotional condition of heightened attention to the impression one is making on others.

self-transcendent: The ability to regard oneself as an object of thought; also pertains to the ability to exercise freedom of choice of an alternative apart from, or in opposition to, one's biological, psychological, and social motivations.

shock therapies: Psychiatric therapies in which electric current, insulin, carbon dioxide, or metrazol are administered to the patient and result in a convulsive or comatose reaction intended to alter the course of the illness favorably.

sin: An act of disobedience to God, either by commission or omission.

sociopathic: Sometimes used synonymously with the term psychopathic; pertains to disorders in one's relationship with society and with the cultural milieu, including antisocial and dyssocial reactions such as sexual deviations and anomalies.

somatic: Pertaining to the body, the physical dimension of personality.

stimulus: A physical event, or a change in physical energy, that causes physiological activity in a sense organ.

sublimation: A defense mechanism through which consciously unacceptable instinctual drives are diverted into personally and socially acceptable channels.

superego: In psychoanalysis, a system within the total psyche developed by incorporating the parental standards as perceived by the ego; popularly equated with the conscience, cf. **conscience** above.

symptom: A specific manifestation of an illness.

symptomatology: The scientific study of symptoms.

synthesis: The composition or combination of parts so as to form a whole; or the whole thus formed.

therapy: Treatment intended to cure or alleviate a disordered condition, so that normal functioning is brought about.

transference: The unconscious attachment to others of feelings and attitudes which were originally associated with important figures such as parents or siblings in one's early life. In the patient-therapist relationship the transference may be negative (hostile) or positive (affectionate).

transformation: A thorough change of form, structure, or composition; may refer to conversion, or a change in disposition, heart or nature.

trichotomy: Division into three parts; specifically, the division of the nature of man into body, soul, and spirit.

unconscious: A collective name for unconscious psychic activities; a part or region of the psyche or person defined by the character of the activities ascribed to it. The activities are not open to conscious scrutiny but have dynamic effects on conscious process and behavior.

Weltanschauung: A German word meaning a view of the universe; one's total outlook on life, society, and its institutions.

world view: As above; any comprehensive explanation of reality and of one's relation to it.

Author Index

Adler, A. — 49
Adler, M. — 40
Adolph, P. — 24, 113
Alexander, F. — 67
Allers, R. — 93
Allport, G. — 48, 125

Bakan, D. — 118
Barbour, C. — 32, 48
Bauma, J. — 65, 131
Bijkerk, R. — 107
Blanshard, B. — 52
Boisen, A. — 105, 106, 146
Bonnell, J. — 183, 184

Carnell, E. — 127
Clark, G. — 127
Cleckley, H. — 89, 91
Curran, C. — 47

Daling, J. — 55
Darwin, C. — 39
Delitzsch, F. — 27, 59

Edwards, D. — 117
Ellis, A. — 105, 130

Feifel, H. — 129
Finch, J. — 57
Fosdick, H. — 184
Frankl, V. — 39, 49, 60, 94, 95,
    173, 221, 222
Freud, S. — 12, 16, 21, 31, 58ff.,
    67, 75, 101, 118, 119, 125,
    146, 166, 184, 189, 191

Goodykoontz, H. — 25, 26
Goulooze, W. — 115
Granberg, L. — 140, 192
Grounds, V. — 22

Hall, A. — 24
Heerema, E. — 26, 43, 94, 135
Heidegger, M. — 98
Hiemstra, W. — 177
Hiltner, S. — 187
Howitt, J. — 132
Hulme, C. — 100, 103, 108, 131

Jaarsma, C. — 46
Jaarsma, R. — 149
Jansma, T. — 33, 115, 126
Jung, C. — 12, 49, 125, 166

Kierkegaard, S. — 98
Kingma, J. — 107
Kunkel, F. — 138

Laidlaw, J. — 43, 44
Lindquist, S. — 32, 74
Little, G. — 23, 24
Lockyer, H. — 132
London, P. — 116, 129
Lynn, D. — 129

Mairet, P. — 29, 32, 62
Marcuse, D. — 169
Marquart, P. — 44, 98, 112, 113
Maslow, A. — 49
May, R. — 98

239